AREA HANDBOOK
for
FINLAND

Coauthors

Theodore L. Stoddard

William K. Carr
Shaheen Dil
John Johnson
Carlo La Porta
Nils Ørvik
Douglas K. Ramsey
Kirk H. Stone
Carla Lofberg Valenta
Jiri Valenta

Prepared for

The American University

by the

Institute for Cross-Cultural Research

Research completed February 1973

First Edition

Published 1974

DA Pam 550–167

Library of Congress Cataloging in Publication Data

Stoddard, Theodore Lothrop, 1926–
  Area handbook for Finland.

  Supt of Docs no.: D 101.23:550-167
  "DA Pam 550-167."
  "One of a series of handbooks prepared under the auspices
of Foreign Area Studies (FAS) of the American University."
  Bibliography: pp. 221-244
  1. Finland. I. Institute for Cross-Cultural Research. II. American University,
Washington, D.C. Foreign Area Studies. III. Title.

DK449.S83   914.71'03'3   73–600338

For sale by the Superintendent of Documents, U.S. Government Printing Office
Washington, D.C. 20402—Price $5.10

FOREWORD

This volume is one of a series of handbooks prepared under the auspices of Foreign Area Studies (FAS) of The American University, designed to be useful to military and other personnel who need a convenient compilation of basic facts about the social, economic, political and military institutions and practices of various countries. The emphasis is on objective description of the nation's present society and the kinds of possible or probable changes that might be expected in the future. The handbook seeks to present as full and as balanced an integrated exposition as limitations on space and research time permit. It was compiled from information available in openly published material. An extensive bibliography is provided to permit recourse to other published sources for more detailed information. There has been no attempt to express any specific point of view or to make policy recommendations. The contents of the handbook represent the work of the authors and FAS and do not represent the official view of the United States Government.

An effort has been made to make the handbook as comprehensive as possible. It can be expected, however, that the material, interpretations, and conclusions are subject to modification in the light of new information and developments. Such corrections, additions, and suggestions for factual, interpretive, or other change as readers may have will be welcomed for use in future revisions. Comments may be addressed to:

The Director
Foreign Area Studies
The American University
5010 Wisconsin Avenue, N.W.
Washington, D.C. 20016

PREFACE

After surviving centuries of Swedish or Russian domination, the Finns established their independence as a republic in December 1917. Since World War II they have rapidly industrialized their economy and have successfully followed a foreign policy of active neutrality, serving as a buffer and as an occasional interlocutor between Eastern and Western powers.

This handbook attempts to provide a comprehensive view of the dominant factors affecting the social, political, and economic life of the country. The approach is interdisciplinary, but the results are not exhaustive. The authors are indebted to numerous United States government officials and members of the Finnish communities in Washington, D.C., and New York for their generous and thoughtful guidance to the wealth of official and scholarly information available. Nevertheless, there appears to be a serious lack of definitive information on the Finnish social system.

Many terms appearing in this handbook have Swedish alternates, but only the Finnish spelling is used. Unless otherwise stated, tons used in production and commodity figures are metric tons. An index has been compiled for the benefit of the reader.

COUNTRY SUMMARY

1. COUNTRY: Republic of Finland, an independent country since December 1917, is the northernmost nation on the European continent.

2. GOVERNMENT: A democracy with legislative power invested by the Constitution of 1919 in a unicameral Parliament and president. Executive power is vested in the president and the State Council (cabinet), appointed by the president and responsible to Parliament. The Constitution of 1919 has been supplemented by fundamental laws including the Parliament Act of 1928, governing legislation; the Impeachment Act of 1922, creating a High Court of Impeachment; and the Ahvenanmaa Islands Act of 1951, granting them internal autonomy.

3. POPULATION: 4,683,000 people in December 1970, declining from a peak of 4,704,321 people the preceding January. The decline is attributed primarily to emigration (mainly to Sweden), which peaked in 1970 at 45,565 people.

4. GEOGRAPHICAL DESCRIPTION: *Topography.* The land slopes gradually from low northern mountains toward narrow coastal plains on the south and west. A massive lake district occupies the southeastern part of the country. Soils are thin and poorly developed but they support a dense boreal forest covering 70 percent of the land surface and providing the country's major natural resource. Area including lakes is 130,126 square miles; greatest length, 724 miles north to south; greatest width, 337 miles east to west. Borders Sweden on the west for 335 miles, Norway on the north for 453 miles, the Soviet Union on the east for 788 miles. About 690 miles of coast extends along the western (Gulf of Bothnia) and southern (Gulf of Finland) shores. *Climate.* Ameliorating effects from the gulf stream keep temperatures higher than the Arctic situation suggests. The February mean ranges from 26°F in the south to minus 7°F in the north; the July mean ranges from 63°F in the south to 55°F in the north. Precipitation ranges from twenty-seven inches per year in the southwest to sixteen inches in the northwest.

5. LANGUAGES: Finnish is spoken by 93 percent of the population and Swedish, by about 6.5 percent; both are official languages.

6. RELIGION: Freedom of religious belief and association is guaranteed by law. The Evangelical Lutheran Church of Finland is the state church, and its membership claims about 93 percent of the population. The Finnish Orthodox Church claims about 1.6 percent, and the remainder belongs to smaller religious groups or is not affiliated with

any organized religion.

7. EDUCATION: Compulsory and free for first eight years. Private and public secondary schools provide either vocational or liberal arts curriculum. Seven universities and eight other institutions of higher learning located in seven cities. Adult education in folk high schools is free. Literacy is virtually 100 percent.

8. HEALTH: Medical care and facilities thoroughly socialized. Facilities provided one hospital bed for each seventy-two persons in the late 1960s. One physician per 1,081 persons. Diseases of the circulatory system accounted for the highest death rate (372 per 100,000 persons in the 1960s). Malignant tumors and tuberculosis also major health problems.

9. JUSTICE: Administered by independent courts, including courts of justice, circuit courts, town courts, courts of appeal, and the Supreme Court. Law is codified and some derives from the eighteenth century.

10. ADMINISTRATIVE DIVISIONS: Twelve provinces, each with a governor appointed by the president. Local government units are communes, which undertake such functions as local planning, providing local services, schools, and welfare. There were 515 communes in 1971 of which 78 were urban, 437 were rural.

11. ECONOMY: Basically industrial. Public utilities, transports, and services are the largest industries in terms of production and employment. Private enterprise predominates in an essentially free market.

12. EXPORTS: Primarily wood and wood products, especially paper; also machinery and metal products. Primarily to the United Kingdom, the Soviet Union, and Sweden.

13. IMPORTS: Raw materials, especially fuels, minerals, and chemicals. Primarily from the Federal Republic of Germany (West Germany), the United Kingdom, and Sweden.

14. FINANCE: The Bank of Finland, a bank of issue supervised by Parliament, controls the monetary system. The markka, or Finnmark (Fmk), is the monetary unit. The currency is convertible, and the rate of exchange established with the International Monetary Fund in 1967 is Fmk4.2 equal US$1.

15. COMMUNICATIONS: At the close of 1969 there were 4,754 post offices, 827 telegraph offices, 1,089,700 telephones, 1,744,039 radio licenses, and 1,014,523 television licenses. These services are government owned.

16. RAILROADS: In 1969 there were 3,553 miles of railroad lines, of which all but twenty-four miles were owned by the government. The five-foot-gauge tracks carried trains with 25.6 million passengers and 22.4 million metric tons of freight during that year.

17. RIVERS: In addition to 4,100 miles of navigable rivers in 1969 there were 25,770 miles of floatable logways. The Saimaa Canal and adjacent deepwater channels in Lake Saimaa in southeastern Finland provided

another 323 miles of navigable waterway.

18. ROADS: In 1970 there were 24,760 miles of main roads and 19,940 miles of local roads. By the end of the year there were 643,057 cars, 45,210 trucks, 51,825 vans, and 7,861 buses.

19. AIR TRANSPORT: Finnair and many international airlines bring passengers in and out of the country. In 1969 domestic airplanes flew 10.5 million miles and carried 1,035,280 passengers over a network connecting seventeen airports. During the same year 13,970 tons of freight and mail also were carried by air.

20. MERCHANT MARINE: In 1969 there were 508 vessels aggregating 1,242,300 gross tons serving twenty-three ports.

21. INTERNATIONAL AGREEMENTS, MEMBERSHIPS AND TREATIES: Agreement of Friendship, Cooperation, and Mutual Assistance signed with the Soviet Union in 1948 and reaffirmed in 1955 and 1970 obliges Finland to forestall an attack on the Soviet Union through Finland. Member of the council of ministers of defense of Nordic countries; United Nations and its agencies; the Nordic Council; the Social Security Convention; the General Agreement on Tariffs and Trade (GATT); the Organization for Economic Cooperation and Development (OECD); the European Free Trade Association (EFTA). Receives most-favored-nation treatment from the Soviet Union; maintains commercial missions with both the German Democratic Republic (East Germany) and West Germany, and cultural exchange programs with the United States.

22. ARMED FORCES: Military service is compulsory. The defense forces are limited by the 1947 peace treaty. In 1972 the total armed forces included about 39,500 men on active duty—34,000 in the army; 2,500 in the navy; and 3,000 in the air force. Reserves totaled about 685,000.

FINLAND

TABLE OF CONTENTS

LIST OF ILLUSTRATIONS

LIST OF TABLES

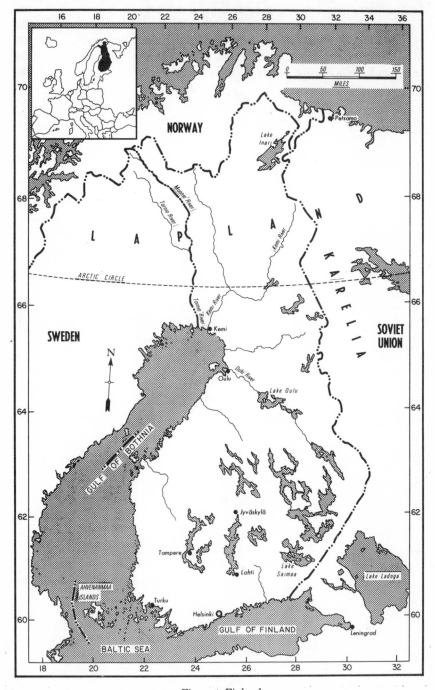

Figure 1. Finland

SECTION I. SOCIAL

CHAPTER 1

GENERAL CHARACTER OF THE SOCIETY

Finland (in Finnish, Suomi) was one of a spate of nation-states born of the principle of self-determination that characterized the post-World War I era. After a half century of nationalist agitation in reaction to growing Russian oppression, Finland took advantage of Russia's internal disorder during the Bolshevik Revolution of November 1917 to declare its independence the following month. The Finns as a people, however, existed centuries before the birth of the Finnish nation-state. Semiautonomous subordination for 700 years to Sweden and then for more than a century to tsarist Russia gave the Finns a degree of cohesiveness that served them well in forming and building their republic. The factor of geographic location—Finland's high northern latitude and its position between powerful neighbors—has also played a demonstrable role in the cultural, social, and economic development of the Finns as a people; it continues to play a critical role in the course and alternatives of foreign policy open to the modern Finnish state.

As a small state Finland maintains its viability as a member of the international system by practicing a strict policy of neutrality. Such a policy is understandable in light of Finland's proximity to the Soviet Union. At the same time Finland promotes Nordic cooperation and will probably do so more actively as international politics evolve from a bipolar to a multipolar framework with regional arrangements gaining greater leverage. It was through Soviet sponsorship that Finland was admitted to the United Nations (UN) in 1955. It has largely been within the framework of the UN that official Finnish neutrality since the 1960s has shifted from a passive to an active stance. In contributing military forces to UN peacekeeping operations and in hosting East-West conferences, Finnish statesmen have acquired a new expertise in foreign affairs and have steadied the precarious balance with the Soviet Union. Finland's interaction with the Soviet Union gave rise in the early 1970s to the term *finlandization*, which describes the circumspection with which a small state acts vis-a-vis a powerful neighbor.

Isolation is a term repeatedly applied to Finland. Geographic situation and linguistic uniqueness combine to give the impression to outsiders as well as to the Finns themselves that Finland is, and yet is not, Scandinavian, Western European, or Eastern European. Finland's

1

official policy of neutrality is in itself an isolating factor. Consequently, the Finns throughout their history have frequently found themselves in impossible circumstances in which they can rely only on themselves and a saving sense of humor.

Scholars conjecture that the ancestors of the Finns came from central Russia. Ethnically the Finns remain relatively homogeneous and are distinct from the people of Sweden, Norway, and Denmark. Unlike most other major European languages, Finnish is of Finno-Ugrian and not of Indo-European origin. The Finns have a rich folk heritage of songs, customs, and handcrafts that was maintained and cultivated along with the oral language during the Swedish period. Swedish, however, was the language of culture, education, and official activities not only during the Swedish period but well into the Russian period. The promotion of the Finnish language was a principal element in the nationalist movement in the second half of the nineteenth century. The Language Decree of 1863 declared Finnish on equal footing with Swedish.

During the Swedish period the Finns were allowed to conduct their own administrative and financial affairs. Swedish legal statutes established then became the backbone of contemporary Finnish law. The legislative investigator, the ombudsman, originally a Swedish institution, has been retained by the Finnish republic. The transfer of Finland from Swedish to Russian rule was one of the results of the Napoleonic Wars, marking the demise of Sweden as a great European power. Certain important elements of continuity were retained, however, because of the tsar's intention to keep Finnish allegiance. The legislative, administrative, and judicial systems established during the Swedish period continued intact, and the governor general and senate members were replaced by Russian appointees. The Finns continued to enjoy the right of petition, freedom of movement, and equality before the law. Freedom of the press and of assembly, along with control over foreign policy, however, came only with independence in 1917.

An event that sparked first thoughts of a Finnish nationalist movement was the appearance in 1835 of the first Finnish-language publication, the so-called national epic, the *Kalevala*. This legend, which recounts the adventures of ancient Finns, provided the people with a sense of national purposefulness. The tales and characterizations portrayed in the *Kalevala* furnish the Finns with a means of seeing themselves as a people over a historical continuum. The influence of the *Kalevala* continues as a reference point to which Finns have strong negative or positive reactions. Elements of nationalism and *Kalevala* folklorism persist today and are increasingly confronted with an emergent internationalism that has come with expanding foreign trade, Finland's role in the UN, and the growing exchange between Finland and the world in arts and crafts and in science.

Ninety-three percent of the population speaks Finnish as a first language; all but a small minority of the remainder are Swedish speaking. Most Swede-Finns are in fact bilingual, but most Finns learn Swedish only to gain admission to the universities. The historic debate, at times heated, between Swedish-language and Finnish-language proponents for priority of their respective languages subsided when Tsar Nicholas II promulgated russification of the Grand Duchy of Finland in 1900. In protest against Russian oppression at that time and in response to subsequent conflict with the Soviet Union in two world wars, many Swede-Finns adopted the Finnish equivalents of their names and joined Finnish military units.

The language problem flared periodically in the twentieth century, but strict application of antidiscrimination laws in the post-World War II period has largely defused the issue, and Finnish and Swedish are held in equal status in law and in fact. Street signs and advertisements are printed in both languages; there are Swedish schools, theaters, a press and a literature; administrative districts are bilingual where the Swede-Finns constitute more than 10 percent of the district's population. Intermarriage is frequent. The Swedish People's Party has a primarily cultural rather than political objective, that of preserving the Swedish heritage. In short, the Swede-Finns are politically if not fully culturally assimilated into the Finnish state.

Another nonnative group, the Lapps, attracts attention out of proportion to its numbers. Nine-tenths of the Lapp population live in Norway and Sweden, and one-tenth—fewer than 2,000 Lapps—live in the northern areas of Finland. The Lapps speak their own Finno-Ugrian language and have their own economy based on reindeer herding. The razing of large tracts of forest in Lapland to supply raw materials for industry in the south of Finland has reinforced the Lapps' longstanding sense of detachment from the Finns, although it was the Finns who brought literacy to the Lapp settlements.

The achievement of virtually 100 percent literacy derives from the emphasis placed on learning by the Evangelical Lutheran Church of Finland since its establishment in the sixteenth century and from quality education developed in the twentieth century. Adults are heavy readers of the free press and books. Television and radio broadcasting services are largely owned and supervised by the state. Like the Russians, the Finns are lovers of poetry, and Finnish poetry has drawn international critical notice. Artists and intellectuals enjoy high social prestige and continual coverage in the media. Finnish designers, craftsmen, and architects have gained world attention with their functionalist, or modern, work.

Although the churchgoing public is small, almost all Finns are confirmed members of the state church, the Evangelical Lutheran Church of Finland. The relevance and advisability of the church's close ties with the state is a prime topic of public debate. The closeness of those ties is demonstrated in the facts that blasphemy is still punishable by law and that religious boards censor films and books on moral grounds.

Perhaps the most widely discussed and reviewed subject is the Civil War of 1918, which is less and less frequently referred to as the War of Independence. The Civil War, which pitted bourgeois against socialist, resulted in 20,000 deaths and a continuing schism in the political and social consciousness.

Sovereign power lies with the people, who are represented by their elected delegates in the Parliament or Eduskunta. The judicial system is completely independent of the executive and legislative branches. Although the republican constitution adopted in 1919 specified the primary role of Parliament in the system of government, the inability of the contending parties to sustain a majority accounts for considerable instability of the political process. The State Council, or cabinet, was intended by the constitution to act as a counterbalance to the executive, but its vulnerability to votes of no-confidence has made it another factor for discontinuity as votes from one or more parties repeatedly bring down the government.

The necessity for quick action in emergency situations and the growing importance of foreign policy have contributed to the primacy of the presidency and thus provides some stability to the system as a whole. Furthermore, the president, while serving a six-year term, is expected to be an impartial executive and is not expected to act as leader of his party. Theoretically, then, the president is considered to be above party interests and above public criticism. In the 1960s and early 1970s there was growing public discussion over the wisdom of investing so much power in the presidency and over the use of an electoral college to choose the president.

The principal means of political participation have been the political parties and economic interest groups, which can be classified generally as leftist, conservative, and center. The majority party, the Finnish Social Democratic Party (Suomen Sosialidemokraattinen Puolue—SDP) has built a broad popular base, receiving support from the working class as well as the urban lower middle and professional classes. The Finnish Communist Party (Suomen Kommunistinen Puolue—SKP) is represented in Parliament by the Finnish People's Democratic League (Suomen Kansan Demokraattinen Liitto—SKDL), which includes noncommunist leftists among its members. In the first postwar election (March 1945) the SKDL won forty out of 200 Parliament seats.

Finland's military organization is shaped by the terms of the Finno-Russian Treaty of Paris of 1947, which restricts the size of each branch of the armed services and prohibits their use abroad. Accordingly, Finland's contribution to the United Nations Emergency Force is composed chiefly of nonprofessionals. The function of the military is to provide for internal security and to guard the borders. The objective is to establish conditions of stability and preparedness such that the Soviet Union will never perceive a defensive weakness in Finland and thus feel justified to send in troops in response to provisions agreed to in the Agreement of Friendship, Cooperation, and Mutual Assistance signed in 1948. The military establishment remains mindful of an old Finnish military axiom "Stand in Your Own Strength and Wait Not for Foreign Aid."

In the early 1970s Finland had a population of 4.6 million, which had achieved a per capita income figure that was fourteenth in the world. Realistic demographic projections anticipate a decline in the rate of population growth, with no more than 5.5 million inhabitants expected by 1980. Seventy percent of the population and of industry is to be found in the south in the inland cities of Lahti and Tampere and in the coastal cities of Helsinki, Hanko, Turku, Pori, and Vaasa. One-tenth of the population resides in Helsinki. In the immediate post-World War II period almost 1 million Finns, or about one-quarter of the total population, shifted their place of residence. This phenomenon, called the new nomadism, was owed either to resettlement (Finland was obliged to cede 12 percent of its prewar territory and 10 percent of its productive capacity to the Soviet Union) or to industrialization and urbanization. Finland strikes the visitor as a country of the young, a reminder that Finland lost 7 percent of its population in World War II.

Although Helsinki is the cultural and commercial as well as the national capital, it does not wield the centrifugal force exerted by the capitals of many small countries. Responsibilities of decentralized government devolve on the twelve provincial centers and the hundreds of communes. Cultural activity is widespread.

So accustomed are the Finns to traditions of close, hard work in the field that most Finns, at least in theory, do not consider themselves naturally disposed to urban living. The dream of many city dwellers is to earn enough money to purchase land and build a summer cottage having a Finnish bath called a sauna. A common denominator of the Finns is their love of the sauna, of which there is one for every seven inhabitants. The sauna is a relaxing social occasion enjoyed with members of the same family or sex.

The egalitarian character of contemporary Finnish society is owed in part to the absence in both the Swedish and Russian periods of an elaborate feudal system such as was found in other European countries. The peasants were freeholders, living in villages and pooling the land and forest. Such communal arrangements persist today. Political equality of the sexes was conferred in 1906 when Finland became the second nation after New Zealand to give women the vote. Like the other Nordic countries, Finland has a greater proportion of women who have achieved high economic and professional status than most other developed nations. In the 1960s in Finland women accounted for over 90 percent of all pharmacists and over 75 percent of all dentists, and women were well represented among architects, physicians, and economists. In the early 1970s women constituted 17 percent of the members of Parliament and more than 30 percent of Helsinki's municipal council members. Finland abounds in maternity and day care centers, because over one-half of the married female population is employed full time.

Before World War II Finland was still largely rural in both residence and occupation. Not until 1970 was a majority of the population living in urban areas. In the postwar period industrial productivity has outstripped agricultural productivity and accounts for over 40 percent of the gross national product (GNP). This phenomenon is in large part a response to the Soviet reparations demands stipulated at the conclusion of World War II, forcing the development of entirely new industries, such as metallurgy and engineering. Another industry—prefabricated housing—developed to meet the demands of resettlement and reconstruction. By 1952 Finland had completed its payments and goods shipments to the Soviet Union, a transfer valued at 1952 prices at approximately US$570 million.

Most industrial enterprises in Finland's capitalist economy remain privately owned except for those deemed essential to national security, such as transportation and communications. Unemployment is generally low, but there are regional disparities. About one-third of the labor force is unionized. Strikes are relatively rare because workers' interest groups are effective in lobbying in Parliament and in the ministries.

The leading sectors of industry are those related to timber processing: wood pulp, paper processing, plywood, and newsprint. In order to meet the needs of these sectors, Finland is a net importer of timber, even though timberland covers 70 percent of its land surface. For purposes of efficiency, several wood-processing activities are located at one site; thus, the mill town is a common feature of the countryside. Finland imports some of its investment capital and most of its fuel. To alleviate the latter need, a number of atomic energy plants are under construction.

Finland exhibits characteristics of a mature economy: a growing service sector, inflation, a growing dependence on export industries—and pollution. In turn, Finland presents an increasingly attractive market for foreign investors. Exports play an important and growing role in the economy, with wood products, cotton textiles, icebreakers, glassware, and ceramics among the significant items. Most of Finland's foreign trade is transacted with Western Europe, the world's fastest growing export market. Thus it is becoming increasingly important for Finland to conclude a commercial treaty with the European Economic Community (EEC—often called the Common Market) in the 1970s.

Finland is largely self-sufficient in foodstuffs and produces a surplus in dairy products, a major achievement considering the dearth of arable land, the immaturity of the soil, the short growing season, and the sub-Arctic climate. Successes in agriculture have ameliorated the hunger problem, or as one expression has it, the "tradition of hunger."

6

Major famines have occurred in the twentieth century. The unique problems of high-latitude agriculture have been overcome by mechanized farming which, in turn, has thrown a large number of farm laborers out of work. Thus a pattern has emerged: slums have appeared in rural areas but not in cities. The best farmland is in the southwest; farms in central and northern areas are abandoned with greater frequency, the surplus labor either emigrating (usually to Sweden) or entering retraining programs for jobs in the industrial south.

The structural changes in Finland's economy and, consequently, to its society have contributed to a distinct north-south dichotomy in economic opportunity, quality of education, and social welfare services—all of which are causing antagonism between the two areas. The Ministry of Labor has established manpower policies and investment incentives to counter the unequal development of the north and the south. Most citizens, in the north and south alike, agree that the economy of the northern areas must be underwritten. Dispute arises over the amount and form of subsidization.

In the 1970s the regional issue and others relating to national priorities will receive sustained attention and long-term treatment in part because Finland no longer expends so much of its energies for physical and national survival. Economic prosperity and the policy of active neutrality provide Finland with greater room for maneuver. In contrast to the older generations Finnish youth and the intelligentsia in the early 1970s feel less constricted by geography and appear more receptive to international influences, be they Western or Eastern.

CHAPTER 2

HISTORICAL SETTING

Finland's history as a nation relates the passage from Swedish to Russian domination, then from Russian domination to independence. That history has been significantly shaped by Finland's geopolitical position with regard to Scandinavia, Imperial Russia, and the Soviet Union. Modern Finland has arrived at a political accommodation with the Soviet Union and has managed to safeguard a Western cultural heritage that makes it Nordic in customs and institutions.

During this evolution, however, the economy and society of the Finns were shaped more by the rough land of forest and water than by the neighboring powers' centuries-long struggle for influence in the area. These natural barriers to communication isolated the Finns and made them dependent upon their own skills and ingenuity for survival. Then, as contact with the outer world increased from the eighteenth century on, the resources provided by the land became the raw material for industrial development and a medium of exchange and contact. Both the political and the economic development of Finland have been marked by an East-West orientation, so that despite the need to consider East European interests and relationships, the country has been able to maintain and extend close relations with the West European and Scandinavian countries.

SWEDISH UNION (1154–1809)

Finnish recorded history only begins with development of Swedish-Russian rivalry over the area that includes modern Finland, from about the twelfth century. The country's earliest historical records are archaeological ones. The scarcity of even these records precludes any definite knowledge of the origins of the Finnish people, which has been a much debated topic. Anthropological evidence suggests that their Finno-Ugrian ancestors migrated from an area south of the Gulf of Finland between 200 B.C. and A.D. 400. These migrants, whose ancestors had in turn come from the Volga River area of Russia, absorbed indigenous peoples believed to have been in the territory comprising modern Finland as early as 8000 B.C. The earliest Finns lived in relative isolation until Viking raiders and traders initiated more contacts after A.D. 800. Communication over the Baltic Sea was easier than through the dense forest and swamp barrier to the east so that Finland

9

was more open to Scandinavian influence than to influence from Imperial Russia and Roman Europe.

In the eleventh century the Swedes sought to revive trade with Novgorod, the ancient Russian city-republic situated on the shores of Lake Il'men, but at the same time the Swedes were concerned about increased Russian forays and influence in the area of modern Finland. To make the trade route across Finland safe, the Swedes conducted a series of crusades that lasted over a 200-year period. Also, in this episode of Swedish contact with Russia lay the origins of Finnish recorded history.

According to popular legend, the crusade most critical in establishing Swedish rule over Finland was that led by King Eric and the Roman Catholic Bishop Henry of Uppsala. This crusade is thought to have occurred in 1154 or 1157. Eric's successors continued the conquest, and by the mid-thirteenth century, a trail of forts secured the Swedish position. The Roman Catholic Church was closely allied with the Swedish crown in the colonizing process and established a diocese in Finland in 1216. Christianity, like Swedish rule, however, did not appear after only one crusade, for a rough and inaccessible hinterland and the tenacity of indigenous beliefs delayed the process (see ch. 6).

Administration

At the time Swedish domination began, the only Finnish political structure was clan based. In the clan an assembly called the *ting* regulated kin affairs, and a *lagman*, or lawman, made rules. Consequently, the Swedes were relatively free to set up their own administration, and Finland was ruled by a provincial governor appointed by the king. The governor wielded considerable autonomous power, especially when troubles in Sweden itself meant little attention could be given to outlying provinces. Once the Swedish administration was in place, the *pitäjä* (local parish) was its most significant element. Although it was actually a judicial district meant to administer the law, the local parish officials often were responsible for daily government action. The traditional *ting* council was retained at the local parish level to provide a meeting ground for the local inhabitants and allow participation in the governmental process. The *ting* participated in the taxation process, for which a local crown appointee, the bailiff, was responsible.

Middle Ages—Society and Economy

After the thirteenth century, four distinct social classes (referred to as estates) developed: nobles, clerics, burghers, and peasants. No native Finn nobility really existed at the beginning of Swedish rule so, as a governing class of Finnish nobles grew, it became closely tied to Sweden and spoke Swedish. Most nobles lived on rent from large estates. Later the class increased in size as prominent soldiers, diplomats, and civil servants were included. Their privileged status provided them freedom from crown taxes and allowed them to dominate the political institutions in Stockholm.

The predominant position of the noble class led to a number of political conflicts between it and the crown. From the 1400s the Swedish kings gradually transformed the monarchy from an elected to a hereditary one and steadily centralized their governing power. The nobles resisted this process because of the loss of their power, and as late as the 1780s the struggle continued.

The predominantly Finnish clergy in Finland was affected by these power struggles as well. The Roman Catholic Church was fully established in Finland by the fourteenth century, and after 1385 the head bishops, located at Turku, the administrative capital of Finland, were Finns. The church was wealthy, holding a great deal of property and land, and influential because of its role in education and its voice in politics. However, as the crown sought to increase its own power, the Swedish kings encroached upon the church, especially for financial reasons.

Finally, the 1527 Västeras Edict of King Gustavas Vasa (1496–1560) transferred church property to the crown, severed relations with Rome, and made the king head of the church. The church lost its independent wealth and influence and was no longer able to affect state politics as it had in the past. Moreover, the crown control and restrictions on religious activity and ceremony opened the door for new ideas and change so that the Protestant Reformation began in Sweden-Finland about 1540. King John III's Church Ordinance of 1571 led to official acceptance of Lutheranism in 1593.

Outstanding Finnish clerics who brought their country into the mainstream of the Reformation were Pietari Särkilahti, Paavali Juusten, and Mikael Agricola. The Lutheran Church continued to grow and became an important force in the social arena. Its efforts to teach were responsible for the large degree of literacy of the population, and when Turku University was founded in 1640, the church had an important part in it. The church also helped bring some organization to the frontier settlements through its administration of the interior parishes, provided employment for artisans, and promoted trade and communications with its religious holidays, fairs, and festivals. Moreover, the church conducted its affairs in Finland in Finnish, not Swedish, giving the language a strong base and preserving a degree of Finnish separateness from Sweden.

Throughout history, peasants composed the largest social group in Finland but, unlike those in Russia and Europe, the majority were freemen. The freemen in the peasant class owned 96 percent of agricultural and forest land; the remainder were tenants on land belonging to nobles or to the crown. All owed the kingdom some form of taxes, labor, or military service. Freemen generally lived in villages and pooled their surrounding land in common ownership and management.

The forest was important in this scheme because hunting and fishing were crucial to the economy. Cattle were the most important farm animals; oats, wheat, and barley were the most important grains; turnips and potatoes were staples of the Finn's diet.

The peasantry was not bound in a feudal relationship to the nobility; consequently, when the crown tried to free itself from domination by the nobility, the peasantry developed a spirit of independence from the noble and cleric classes and a subsequent desire to be represented in political affairs. The wild frontier further reinforced an independent pioneer spirit that emphasized man's lonely independent struggle with nature. Often, when burdens of war and taxes became excessive, farmers gave up their settlements and moved to the interior.

The peasant class provided the trade goods, furs, and naval stores that supported the towns. Despite this trade and the fact that peasants could only sell agricultural produce to the burgher-class merchants in the towns, there were but eighteen such settlements as late as the eighteenth century. Nor were towns politically important, as they were not the centers of political control. In addition, foreign merchants controlled much of the trade, siphoning off its income, and not until the eighteenth century did Finnish merchants challenge them. All these factors, in addition to weakness in numbers, made the town burgher class the least powerful in the kingdom.

The Parliamentary Riksdag

Sweden's early status as an association of provinces with an elective monarchy had an inherent instability that was settled only as royal rulers established a hereditary and absolutist monarchy. Constitutional institutions, however, also grew alongside to check regal power, and a parliamentary body, the Riksdag, began to take shape in the fourteenth century. For a long period it had no more weight than that of its most influential members, the nobility. Then in 1617 it became a national body with clear parliamentary procedure, representing the four major social classes: nobles, clerics, burghers, and peasants. In the eighteenth century the executive Council of State and the Riksdag were the important seats of power, with the Riksdag legislating and controlling the executive. Moderation and common sense prevailed in this parliamentary system, which lasted until 1772 when a swing back to royal absolutism occurred.

Finland was poorly represented in the Riksdag because the distance made attendance a burden, especially for those in the poor areas. Moreover, Finland's farmer class interests suffered because Riksdag affairs were controlled by a secret committee that barred the peasant estate. There was also the language problem (see Between the World Wars, this ch.). Besides this, Finnish representatives generally spoke as members of their estate, not as Finns about Finnish problems.

12

Sweden-Finland—Great Power

Sweden steadily grew stronger in the Middle Ages. Gustavas Vasa made a final break from the Danish-controlled Kalmar Union of Scandinavian countries (1397–1523) and established an independent hereditary monarchy. Finland, somewhat freed from Sweden by many Kalmar Union wars, was returned to close control by the Swedish monarchy and was ultimately named a grand duchy in 1581. King Gustavas Adolphus (1594–1632) brought further change and progress to Finland, installing a more efficient administration, formalized in the 1634 Form of Government Act.

Sweden's participation in the Thirty Years War (1618–48) marked Sweden as a great power, but that status did not come cheaply. Although Finnish troops in the Swedish armies distinguished themselves in battle during this particular conflict and during another fifty years of war, the toll in men and taxes was heavy.

The Great Northern War (1700–21) was even more costly in human terms. Russia, allied with Denmark, invaded Finland in 1710, occupying it all by 1713. War and plague decreased the population during the war from 400,000 to less than 300,000. The land was ravaged, cities and towns were burned. The Peace of Uusikaupumki (1721) that ended the war marked Sweden's decline for, although the Russians departed, Sweden's Baltic empire was finished, and Finland's eastern border was pared. Worse, however, the peace was not final. Conflict recurred until all Finland was ceded to Russia in 1809.

The wars were costly to Finland, but some aftereffects were beneficial. A Finnish literary movement began, and great intellectual and administrative advances were made. European interest in Finland increased, and ties between Finland and Sweden were strengthened.

Finland's legacy from 700 years of Swedish rule is great. There was never a marked clash between the two "nations," and their culture and politics grew to be similar. Yet, the Finns retained an independent spirit so that, although Finland became a Scandinavian country in many ways, it retained differences. Swedish law as applied in Finland had a Finnish element; the Swedish Lutheran church in Finland was Finnish in language and custom. Folk history, song, and customs remained Finnish. A growing awareness of these differences formed the basis of Finnish nationalism, which after 100 years of Russian hegemony was to triumph in independence.

RUSSIAN GRAND DUCHY (1809–1917)

In 1809 Finland became a Russian grand duchy under the personal rule of the tsar. This ended centuries of conflict that resulted from the inevitable Russian reaction to Sweden-Finland's attainment of great power status. By the early seventeenth century, Swedish expansion had provided Finland with a territorial buffer along its eastern

13

border, but Peter the Great's ascendant Russia checked Swedish expansion and, after Sweden's defeat in the cataclysmic Great Northern War, its influence in this area diminished. The Napoleonic Wars ultimately gave Russia the opportunity to wrest Finland from Sweden.

A Russo-Swedish war began in February 1808, when Sweden was attacked for not cooperating with the Franco-Russian blockade against England. Russian troops overran Finland, and an armistice was signed in November, 1808. Swedish resistance continued, however, and the war was not completely over until the Hanuna Peace, September 27, 1809, by which Finland and the Ahvenanmaa Islands were ceded to Russia. The French general, Jean Bernadotte, elected to the Swedish throne and crowned King Charles XIV in July 1810, conceded the transfer. Finland was formally recognized as part of Russia by Swedish-Russian accords in April 1812.

To placate the Swedes and Finns, Russian advisers persuaded the tsar, Alexander I (1777-1825), that a conciliatory policy toward Finland should be followed. Consequently, although Alexander declared himself grand duke of Finland in December 1808, he officially confirmed in March 1809 that Finnish institutions would be upheld; that Swedish constitutional law, along with ancient rights and customs, would continue to govern the country; and that the tie with Russia was based only on the tsar's position as grand duke. Continued Finnish resistance forced Alexander to convene the Estates-General (formerly the Riksdag) and convinced him of the strength of popular sentiment for Finnish autonomy. It was not a policy popular with all the Russian court, but endured until Pan-Slavism swept Russia in the late nineteenth century.

Government and Administration

The legal framework for Finland's administration under the tsar was Sweden's 1772 Constitution, as amended by the Act of Association and Security of 1789. The tsar preferred it because its autocratic structure favored the royal executive over a parliament. The existing provincial and local government was retained, so that only higher echelons were changed. It was clear that the tsar would make final decisions regardless of the Finnish Estates-General, and such a regular parliament was not guaranteed until the 1860s.

The governing body was the Senate, whose twenty members were appointed by the Russian tsar for three-year terms. Ten senators formed the Supreme Court; the other ten headed the administrative departments. All civil administrators had to be Finnish, and Finnish nationality separate from Russian was maintained by law. This government, however, was limited in its powers so that its position was mostly an advisory one, although its recommendations were usually accepted. Still, the Senate was at the top of the pyramid and was viewed by the Finns as a real national government, particularly after

14

Russian concessions in the 1860s enabled the Estates-General as a parliament to gather power and make the Senate its executive.

The tsar's personal representative was the governor general; except for one instance, only Russians were appointed. The governor general was the titular head of the Senate but, because the Russians could rarely speak Swedish, a Finn usually presided at its sessions. Until the reign of Tsar Nicholas II, the governor general was no more than the tsar's observer and commander of the few isolated garrisons of Russian troops.

More important than the governor general in the actual direction of Finland's administration was the minister-secretary of state for Finnish affairs. This official was appointed by the tsar and worked with a small staff in Saint Petersburg, the Russian capital. Because Finland had special status as a grand duchy under the tsar's personal rule, the minister-secretary did not come under the Russian Council of Ministers but dealt directly with the tsar.

Personal rights of the Finns were greater than those of the Russians because they were guarded by the Swedish Law of 1734, an impressive codification that covered civil, criminal, and administrative justice. In contrast to the Russian serfs, Finland's citizens were equal before the law, could petition, and were allowed free movement. In addition, a procurator oversaw the operations of justice and administration in order to protect the common citizen from abuses of power. The same liberality, however, did not apply to political rights; freedom of the press, freedom of assembly, and other rights were curtailed.

Estates-General Reconvened, 1863

The first fifty years of Russian hegemony were relatively uneventful. Despite the tsar's oppressive policy, there was a strong undercurrent of Finnish nationalism. Demands included a request that the Finnish Estates-General be permitted to assemble because the tax base needed revision; there were complaints about restrictive policies such as press censorship. Finland's response to Tsar Nicholas I's death in 1855 was very calm compared to the open revolt that followed in Poland. Finland was rewarded in June 1863 when Nicholas' successor, reformer Tsar Alexander II, granted the request for a parliament.

Alexander II addressed the Estates-General in September 1863, saying that he would consult it on fiscal matters, that it could pass tax laws, but that the Swedish constitutional form would be retained. All laws would be passed to the tsar before going to the Senate for enactment. Alexander also reminded Finland that it was still part of the Russian Empire. This meant that the Estates-General could not liberalize itself beyond some minor reforms, and only slowly did it become an effective barometer of public opinion.

The Estates-General saw as its first task maintenance of Finland's autonomous status, either by insisting on the rights inherited from the past or by strengthening newer institutions. Actually, the executive Senate was more successful in this respect than the Estates-General; one reason was that until 1883 the Estates-General could consider only what was placed before it by the administration. The Senate, however, was little disposed to rapid change. Nominated by the governor general, the senators had become used to their status as a ruling class and were particularly slow to realize that their own interests and those of the nation were not always the same. Thus, conservatism delayed democratic change until the first decade of the twentieth century when, in the aftermath of Russian oppression, the parliaments of the 1900s enacted reforms that made Finland a much more democratic state.

Even before the Estates-General made itself into a representative parliament from 1905 to 1907, there already were political groups that would later develop into Finland's political parties. The nascent political formation existed from the middle nineteenth century and was closely related to issues involving the church, education, and institutional reform. Another most important issue concerned adoption of Finnish as an official language. Swedish was the language of the upper classes and educated people as well as the official medium of government, and only by speaking Swedish could one advance in society. That 85 percent of the population spoke Finnish could not be ignored, however.

Thus, because of the language issue, embryonic political groups in the Estates-General formed the basis of a triangular conflict among: Swekomen (favoring Swedish), Fennomen (favoring Finnish), and the Liberals, who were in favor of Finnish but were primarily interested in strengthening Finland's autonomy. Also the Fennomen were divided into Old Finns, or moderates, and the more extremist Young Finns. Although these language-related political groups were relatively new from the 1860s on, Finnish language use had had earlier proponents and was not really a new issue.

Among the earliest proponents of the use of Finnish as an official language was Adolf Ivar Arwidsson. Citing fear that Finland might be swallowed by the Russian Empire, he urged that Finnish be officiallly accepted and formally taught. A significant contribution to this cause was made by Elias Lönnrot (1802–84), whose monumental compilation of oral legends in Finnish, the *Kalevala*, roused nationalistic spirit (see ch. 8). His use of the language brought it recognition as a viable literary tool. In the 1850s Finnish-language newspapers and periodicals appeared, and the work of Finland's most famous nineteenth-century nationalist, Johan Snellman, did much to push acceptance of Finnish.

Finally, Tsar Alexander II, in the same spirit that led him to grant the Finnish request for a session of the Estates-General, proclaimed that from August 1, 1863, Finnish would be an official language of the Russian grand duchy of Finland. Law called for its use in administration and justice and that it be taught in the schools. This only began a new struggle, as there was still strong resistance to the measure. Many

16

nobles and upper bourgeois insisted on keeping Swedish the official language to protect Finland's autonomy and their own status, for they feared that the masses would take over direction of Finland's affairs and would be more susceptible to Russian pressures. It took nearly twenty years for equal status of the languages to be accepted and much longer for practical aspects to work themselves out.

Russification and Difficult Times

Despite its strength as an issue, the language problem was almost eclipsed in the 1890s and later when the Imperial Russian Government began a series of steps designed to end Finland's autonomous status. Tsar Nicholas II (1868–1918) conceded to pressure from Russian adherents of pan-slavism, who felt that Finland should not be administered differently from the rest of the Russian Empire. Russian businessmen were also concerned about special customs status Finland enjoyed. The measures taken to end Finland's autonomy were termed *russification* and began with modification of the customs laws and postal system in 1890 to make them uniform. In 1899 the Finnish minister-secretary of state in Saint Petersburg was replaced by a Russian; Finland's army was abolished; and the Estates-General was reduced to considering only laws of local interest. In addition, the Russian language was introduced into use; a series of Russian institutions were established; Russian law was given precedence; and Russians entered the Finnish Civil Service.

The countrywide Finnish reaction was shock and outrage. Despite the unity of the population in protest, the choice between accommodation and resistance was difficult to make; resistance might incur still more repressive policies. A massive petition was presented to the tsar but was not accepted; a delegation of prominent Europeans also tried to intervene but was ignored. The Finns realized that open revolt was out of the question, so passive resistance to the military law became the major battle strategy.

The year 1903 was critical. Disturbances and mass court resignations led the governor general to assume special powers, remove officials, and harden censorship. It appeared that conciliation was impossible and that passive resistance might also fail. Finnish activist groups allied themselves with Russion revolutionaries and began to smuggle arms into Finland so that terrorism escalated. General Nikolai Ivanovich Bobrikov, the governor general, was assassinated in June 1904 by Eugene Schauman, who then committed suicide. He became a nationalist hero once his views, set forth in a letter to the tsar, were known. Shortly thereafter, the Russian minister for Finnish affairs was also murdered in Saint Petersburg.

When a new governor general arrived in September, it was clear the Russians had decided to soften their campaign, but they did not give up the basic goal. Conciliatory acts included parliamentary elections, amnesty for purged officials and exiles, and less censorship. A Finn was named minister-secretary of state for Finnish affairs, and he tried to reach an understanding with the Finnish militants. Still many of the russification measures remained, and Finnish-Russian relations continued to be unstable until World War I.

These troubles showed that the population at large was committed to preserving Finland's autonomy. Yet there were elements in the population—particularly a poor, landless rural proletariat—that were primarily interested in reform, whether Russian or Finnish. For example, the 1904 Estates-General still represented but 5 to 6 percent of the population, and it voted by estate, that is, by class. Spurred by socialist demonstrations and feeling the need for national unity in face of the Russian pressure, the Estates-General made itself into a national representative body and enfranchised the population, including women. Finland was the first European country to do so. These and other liberalizing reforms confirmed Finland's acceptance of democratic institutional guidelines and helped make Finland ready for independence.

Social and Economic Progress

During the years that Finland was a Russian grand duchy, there were important social and economic developments. Reform in education was a major accomplishment. The church administered the lower level educational system until 1869, when reform established school boards, government supervision, and additional provisions for Finnish-language education as well as Swedish. Language equality in the schools, however, was not systematically established until 1900. University education was transferred from Turku to Helsinki in 1828. With increased resources, the university became a vibrant intellectual center, particularly important for nationalism after the 1830s. Academia was influenced largely by Danish and German intellectualism, separate from what occurred in Russia.

The Evangelical Lutheran Church of Finland (Church of Finland) was governed by Swedish statutes until the 1867 Estates-General passed a law that created a central lay and clerical council to govern church and parish. This provided more self-regulation and more democratic representation of the parish members. Traditionally, the church's most political function was communication of government business and regulations to the population. During the russification campaign, this did not change, for the archbishop refused to allow the church to do more than pass on information without comment. The decision was not popular, but those ministers who refused to abide by it were disciplined, and the church's separation from politics continued.

At the end of the nineteenth century, Finland still had a sparse population settled in a large area devoid of many natural resources, except abundant forest. The infrastructure, which would provide a base for economic development, had been growing, however. In the 1870s the

Finn currency, the markka, was completely disjoined from the Russian ruble. As the economy further developed in the 1880s, national banks and savings systems appeared, and insurance companies began operating. Postal and telegraph services were extended, and the school system began to provide technical training to a portion of the population.

Progress was impeded by poor communications overland, especially in the interior. The first solution was to develop water communication routes, then the railroad. The railroad line from Helsinki to Saint Petersburg was opened in 1868, and increased export demand later supported a railroad line to Hanko on the southwestern (Baltic Sea) coast, a year-round port. This helped keep the economy from coming to a winter standstill, especially after steamships were introduced and icebreakers could keep bays and river routes open.

Despite these advances the agricultural sector, which lagged behind Europe technologically, was the dominant economic factor and was a serious brake on development. Years of shortages, and outright famine in the 1860s forced many people off the land, forming a proletariat in the towns. Then government efforts to improve land communications and import new technology, in addition to growing demand for forest and dairy products, ameliorated conditions. Eventually, the small but growing industrial sector and emigration siphoned off surplus labor and eased tensions.

Industrialization began in the 1860s when English and Western European entrepreneurs opened factories, most of them paper mills. Then steel production began and benefited from European demand. Most of these enterprises were oriented to forest products, and diversification took a long time. Eventually, Finland was forced to turn more to Western Europe as a trade outlet when Russia decided on an autarkic economic policy as part of pan-Slavism.

Although labor resources were plentiful, only 10 percent of the working population was employed in these infant industries. At first workers were gradually organized into loose local labor groups to fight a lack of legal protection for them, then into more formal larger organizations. A meeting in Turku in 1899 laid the groundwork for a coherent political program, based largely on the social democracy of Germany, that is, state socialism. In 1903 a workers council for a political party was formed, and a newspaper, *The Worker*, was begun. The Social Democratic Party, which was begun in 1901, adopted a Marxist line but remained moderate in conception and procedure. It was modeled on Western labor parties and refused to join the Communist Third International. Its members were suspicious of leaders who were not of working class origin, so that it remained purely a worker movement that was attracted by socialist militancy.

INDEPENDENCE

World War I was a catalyst for Finland's independence. Russia wanted to protect its important communication route over Finland to its Western allies and, instead of reconciling the Finns, it chose to end separate citizenship and other remaining Finnish rights, including all political activity. This oppression caused many Finns to feel that the war was their country's salvation because, if Russia were defeated, Finland might achieve its former autonomy or even independence. Activists who were planning a revolt were prone to regard Germany as an ally. Others, however, preferred the Allied powers, particularly after the idea of self-determination became more prominent; but it was soon apparent that, to keep Russia in the war, the Allied powers were being cautious regarding Finland.

The events surrounding the 1917 February Revolution in Russia, which ended the tsarist empire, made the situation in Finland complex. Russia was thrown into a state of turmoil, and the status of the tsarist territories was in doubt. In Finland political life was suddenly reborn when the Russian Provisional Government reestablished on March 20, 1917, rights and autonomy that had been previously stripped away by the russification program and the controls added during the war. In this rebirth of politics, however, lay future tragedy; the Finnish political map had been divided, and nationwide unity for independence was shattered by domestic conflict.

This was manifested by a conflict in July 1917 between Finland's socialist and bourgeois political groups—that is, the Left against the Center and the Right. The two groups had long been at odds over the means to social reform to benefit Finland's worker and peasant classes and, as the economic situation worsened, passion increased. The Social Democratic Party had strongly advocated a program designed to deal with development problems exacerbated by World War I, and they were bitter about the inaction of their political opponents. Bitterness helped a militant faction of the party to force the movement toward revolution—economic, political, and social.

In July, division arose over the bourgeois parties' desire to allow the Russian Provisional Government, which survived an abortive communist coup that month, a chance to prove itself. The Social Democrats however, pushed through legislation assigning to the Finnish Parliament all the powers of the Russian grand duchy period, save for military and foreign affairs. This caused Alexander Kerensky, head of the Russian Provisional Government, to object and send troops. A new governor general ordered dissolution of Parliament. The Social Democrats were outraged and became more radical, demanding to be free from what they now interpreted as a two-front confrontation against the Finnish bourgeoisie and the Russians.

The bourgeois parties subsequently seized the opportunity provided by the Russian acts to control the Finnish government and place their members in positions of power. Ultimately, they established the paramilitary Protective Corps to maintain domestic order. The Finnish bourgeoisie had been no less for independence than the Socialist Democrats, but the conservatives became increasingly fearful of their political opponents, some to the point that they sought outside assistance from Germany. Germany, still at war with Russia, was interested in what would distract Russia and, consequently, furnished arms for the Protective Corps. The Social Democrats sought arms elsewhere for their own military force, the Red Guard, and thus two distinct camps were forming in Finland.

The divisive political climate was apparent in the newly elected Parliament that met on November 1, 1917, to begin what would be a critical month. The first two weeks coincided with the Bolshevik coup in Saint Petersburg (renamed Petrograd in 1914; changed to Leningrad in 1924), which caused disorientation and confusion in Helsinki. During the next week the Red Guard nearly gained complete control of Finland, by way of a general strike called because of dissatisfaction with the loss of a majority in Parliament and with the conservative Regency Commission, under Pehr Evind Svinhufvud, which refused to enact socialist programs. The ensuing paralysis caused the regency to fall and Parliament to concede and declare itself fully responsible for the Russian grand duchy powers. The general strike was ended, but Social Democratic hesitation to choose between its parliamentary faction and the more extremist Red Guard allowed initiative to pass to the conservatives. Svinhufvud formed a new Senate without any Socialist Democrats on November 27, 1917.

The 1917 November Revolution in Petrograd and the resulting chaos were the final catalysts that led to a declaration of independence. Using the Bolshevik coup as an excuse for the final break with Russia, Svinhufvud addressed Parliament on December 4, 1917, and presented a statement of independence. Parliament replied affirmatively on December 6, although eighty-eight Social Democrats had voted "no" because the ruling Bolshevik Sovnarkom in Russia had not been consulted.

Concerned about the reaction of the Social Democrats and the large numbers of Russian troops still in Finland, the Senate of now-independent Finland prepared a national military force to counterbalance the Red Guard and hoped international recognition of Finland's independence would force the Russian troops to leave. With the help of German pressure—Germany and Russia were negotiating peace—the Senate persuaded the Bolshevik leaders to agree to Finnish independence on December 31, 1917. On January 3, 1918, the Russian Central Executive Committee ratified independence, and Germany formally recognized Finland. Other states proceeded to do the same. The United States and the United Kingdom, however, waited in hope that a democratic government would reappear in Russia.

Civil War

The Russian Soviet leaders apparently hoped the Red Guard could still establish the revolution in Finland and create a sister socialist republic they could recognize. The Red Guard had broken with the parliamentary socialist group and established its own arsenal and treasury. By the end of January 1918 it numbered about 30,000 men and had clashed with the Protective Corps. On January 26, with firm backing from Soviet leaders, the Red Guard seized the Helsinki railroad station, declared insurrection, and the next night began to take over the capital and country. The Protective Corps immediately disarmed Russians in Pohjanmaa Province and established its control over five-sixths of the land and one-half of the population. The Red Guard controlled the more urban and industrial south, where they set up the Socialist Workers Republic. Thus, the battlelines for a civil war were drawn with the opposing sides designated Red and White.

The White Army, led by General Carl Gustaf von Mannerheim, was largely made up of peasants but was commanded by bourgeois and upper class officers, often former tsarist army personnel. There was a Swedish corps of volunteers and an able cadre of Jägers (Finnish soldiers and officers from a special battalion trained in Germany), which had seen action in Latvia. These men filtered back to Finland, and Mannerheim used them to help train and lead his army. The Jäger contribution was significant and well remembered, leaving a germanophile imprint on the Finnish regular army after the civil war.

In addition to the Jägers and their arms, there was also an important German contribution of regular combat units—an intervention motivated by interest in strengthening Germany's position vis-à-vis Russia. This intervention was not without controversy, for it was opposed by Mannerheim. A message reputed to have come from Senate officials hiding in Helsinki led the Finnish minister in Berlin to seek active German help, despite a promise to Mannerheim by Svinhufvud, head of the government, that this would not occur. Senate officials placated Mannerheim, claiming the intervention would end Red rule sooner and save much destruction, which it did. The Germans were careful not to upset Mannerheim, but he resigned his position after the war, ostensibly because of their influential position in the country, an issue that would not be settled until he became the regent later in the year.

Mannerheim launched an all-out offensive in March 1918 to capture the Red Guard stronghold at Tampere, which fell after hard fighting. At the same time his army was able to hold the east frontier and German units that had landed in south Finland pressed the Red Guard, relieving Helsinki in April. Mannerheim's strategy prevented most of the Red Guard forces from escaping to Russia, and the war was concluded on May 15, 1918.

By the end of the war, the Red Guard numbered from 60,000 to 70,000 effectives, but it had had to resort to conscription as its core of able and willing worker recruits dwindled. Its officer corps was untrained, and the guard in many cases had to rely on Russians for staff work. The

Russian troops that remained in Finland were not completely effective as an ally for the Red Guard because many officers sympathized with the Whites, and the enlisted ranks were not enthusiastic about fighting for political ideals. These troops were later withdrawn to defend Petrograd against the Germans, and finally the 1918 Brest-Litovsk Treaty, which ended the Russian fighting in World War I, required that Russian forces be withdrawn from Finland. A volunteer force of 1,000 remained with a Russian general who became deputy commander of the Red Guard, but it was of little help.

Evidence indicates as much as 20 percent of the more than 50,000 Red Guard soldiers imprisoned in camps after the fighting died of starvation and disease in the hard times that followed the war. None were released until all were tried; thousands were sentenced to prison; and thirty of 403 death sentences were carried out before several amnesties reduced sentences. In April 1919 approximately 6,485 prisoners were still held, although by 1927 the few remaining were pardoned. The amnesties helped heal scars left from the war, yet the conflict between left and right did not end there. Whether interpreted as a civil war or a war of independence against Russia, this Finnish war of 1918 split society and left wounds two generations would be required to heal.

Svinhufvud was head of a government reestablished in Helsinki in 1918, but with a rump parliament, as all but ten of the Social Democrats were missing. He favored German aid and wanted Finland to become a constitutional monarchy, a position held in common with the National Coalition Party (formerly, Old Finn Party) and the Swedish People's Party. The Agrarian Party and National Progressive Party (liberal, Young Finn Party) were the two other major groups until the Social Democrats could reform the Left. The Social Democrat Party was rebuilt under leadership of Väinö Tanner, its most radical elements joining the Communist Party formed in 1918. The Social Democratic Party won eighty of the 200 parliamentary seats in the 1919 election. They had first opposed the monarchists in 1918, then continued fighting for legislation to make the working population share in development of republican Finland.

The Karelia Problem

Finland required peace before it could begin constructing political and social order and solve its own foreign relations problems. The latter problems involved acquiring Western recognition, made difficult because the Finns had cooperated with the Germans and were making peace with Soviet Russia, delayed as long as White Russian counterrevolutionary armies existed. From 1917 to 1922 difficulties focused on Karelia, the sparsely populated easternmost region of Finland (see ch. 3).

East and West Karelia had been a source of conflict from early times, and it became more controversial as Finnish nationalism grew; a faction claimed what had been for centuries Russian East Karelia because of its Finn-related population. All of West Karelia was already under Finnish administration. Karelia became involved in World War I when Germany asked Finland to help cut Russian supply lines and prevent the Allied Expeditionary Force from operating there. Then counter-revolutionary White Russian forces seeking to overthrow the Bolshevik regime in Moscow entered the picture, already complicated by Red and White Finns.

Relief from the complex Karelia situation, which was leading to a Finnish-Soviet Russia confrontation, began with Mannerheim's appointment as regent of Finland. The monarchist pro-German adherents lost their influence, and Mannerheim secured Western good will by helping the anti-Soviet cause in Estonia; as a result, in May 1919 the Paris Peace Conference recognized Finland's independence. The Finns then managed to divorce themselves from the embroglio involving White Russian forces in East Karelia, especially after Mannerheim was defeated in the July 1919 presidential elections, and the new president, Kaarlo Juho Ståhlberg, was supported by a more moderate bloc that would not advocate annexation of East Karelia.

In September 1919 the Soviets began offering peace proposals, so that when the Allied Expeditionary Force left East Karelia and the White Russian government had collapsed in 1920, a treaty was negotiated. Signed at Tartu (Dorpat, Estonia) on December 11, 1920, it stipulated that a state of war was ended, delineated borders and Gulf of Finland boundaries. Petsamo, an Arctic port, was ceded to Finland; Russia received additional territory, in addition to neutrality guarantees required for Petrograd defense considerations. Other articles settled debts, property and population movement, and trade provisions.

The problem was not yet resolved, for treaty and subsequent assurances that Karelia would be an autonomous entity in the Soviet Union were violated. Repressive Soviet acts in 1921 led to an open revolt by partisan troops that received backing from private individuals and organizations in Finland but not from the Finnish government. The partisan offensive gained control over much of the territory but withered under Soviet counterattacks. The fighting ended in February 1922.

Finland's foreign minister, Rudolf Holsti, managed to keep the Soviets from blaming the Finnish government for what happened, and the status quo was accepted. Thus, relations with the Soviets were settled, and Finland was able to build a viable nation over the next two decades. In 1923 the Soviets created the Autonomous Soviet Socialist Republic of Karelia, where Finnish language and institutions coexisted with Russian ones, but this lasted only until population influx russianized the region in the 1930s. In 1939 the Karelia problem rose again to haunt the Finns.

Ahvenanmaa Island Controversy

Another early foreign affairs issue concerned Swedish claims to the overwhelmingly Swedish-speaking Ahvenanmaa Islands in the Gulf of Bothnia. The islands had been ceded to Russia in 1809 and continued to be administered by Finland. When troubles began in 1917 a plebiscite voted by large majority for union with Sweden, but occupation of the islands by Red Finns followed by Germans and White Finns stopped any action. The Finnish Constitution of July 1919 granted the islands cultural autonomy and a measure of political autonomy, but the islanders petitioned the Paris Peace Conference powers to help them. A delegation that had visited the Swedish king was arrested for trea- son; Finnish troops occupied the islands; and tension with Sweden grew from this incident. The League of Nations ultimately affirmed Finland's rights to the islands and arranged an international guaran- tee of constitutional autonomy and a multinational demilitarization treaty. Thus the matter rested until World War II caused questions to be raised about their status, but the islands remained Finnish.

BETWEEN THE WORLD WARS

In the two decades that preceded World War II, Finland had to con- struct a viable political and economic system. The legacy of the past, Scandinavian and Russian influence, civil war, and the post-World War I European situation shaped the course of Finnish efforts in this task. Then a fight for survival drew the people together and forged the state.

Establishing the State

The burdens left by the independence wars and by social conditions were tackled by political leaders dedicated to reconciliation. They be- longed to a generation committed to continuing the parliamentary sys- tem that was born in the struggle against russification. This was an easier task because there was no need for major reorganization of the governing apparatus and no territorial adjustments except those con- nected with the Tartu (Dorpat) Treaty with the Soviet Union. The new constitution provided for a parliamentary system with the government formed by whatever faction or coalition could gain the necessary votes. In addition, there was a president who was the state's chief executive.

Parliament was clearly the center of political life, but parliamentary instability owing to the lack of any single-party majority weakened the government's ability to plan and carry out legislation. Unstable coali- tion cabinets were the rule. To counteract this situation, Ståhlberg, Finland's first president and author of the Constitution of 1919, made the presidency stronger in practice than had been originally foreseen. This liberal National Progressive Party leader dedicated himself to strengthening parliamentary democracy and the rule of law and, above all, to peace during his term. Ståhlberg's successor in 1925, Lauri

Kristian Relander, was a compromise candidate and a much weaker executive. Consequently, government authority was somewhat shaky until the 1930s when more stable and lasting governments evolved.

In the parliamentary framework the political parties, grouped with six major affiliations and well founded in democratic principles, played a crucial role. The largest party was the Social Democratic Party. It was led by Tanner to seek compromise and a rehabilitated role in government in order that the work of the Left could continue despite the disaster of 1918. Although Tanner was known as an arch-Communist, the conservatives did not trust the Social Democrats and tended to lump them with the Communists, who also were represented in Parliament and were in close contact with their ideological partners in the Soviet Union.

The conservatives were grouped in the National Coalition Party (also called the National Union Party), which elected about thirty members. The liberals formed the National Progressive Party, which lost representation steadily but maintained a large degree of influence by providing many leaders and heads of government. The Agrarian Party captured fifty to sixty seats throughout this period and increasingly provided more key leaders. The Swedish People's Party represented the interests of its minority constituents, and although generally conservative, the varied makeup of the party meant that its social and political goals fell under no comprehensive program. Its representation remained a constant based on population figures but began to decline about 1940. The Communists represented the extreme Left in the political spectrum. Representation of these party formations was such that cabinet coalitions of the 1920s were largely bourgeois, except for a one-year Social Democratic minority government in 1926. In the 1930s the Agrarian Party and the Social Democratic Party members increased their cooperation, and more stable governments resulted as they both worked to further the democratic process.

Social and Economic Matters

The first problem faced by the Mannerheim regency in 1918 was how to supply food to the population and restart the economy. The Allied powers were very helpful, and General Mannerheim was able to get grain shipped to Finland. Imports continued to be necessary for many months, and there were severe shortages. It was in this period that Finland contracted foreign debts, including a United States loan that has been faithfully repaid, an accomplishment that raises much Finnish pride.

Agriculture, in which nearly 66 percent of the population was engaged in 1918, posed the most critical economic problems for Finland because it was the basic industry. Before production could be improved after the war, major legislation was necessary to solve land distribution inequalities and alleviate the harsh living conditions of an agricultural proletariat. By this time the landholding pattern had changed since medieval times, during which a large percentage of the rural population owned their own property. Lean years and the poorness of the land in some areas caused many peasants to slip into tenant status; in 1901 approximately 43 percent did not own land, and nearly 20 percent had no home they could call their own.

Political and social pressure prompted Parliament to enact a law in October 1918 to provide for purchase of land by former tenants with the help of state financing. Additional laws in 1921 and 1922 eased the situation of those still renting land by providing for redemption of properties on parish and state property and also provided small holders with an opportunity to increase their landholdings to more efficient dimensions. Over 100,000 new independent holdings were created by these laws between 1919 and 1935, and the reforms were far reaching in that they helped solve social problems in addition to rejuvenating agricultural production. With technological progress spread by government programs and cooperatives, Finland reached an 85-percent level of self-sufficiency by 1940 and laid the base for its industrial development.

The manufacturing sector of the economy required stability above all to get restarted. The New Economic Policy in the Soviet Union denied Finland 30 percent of its prewar trade, making readjustment necessary. A restabilized markka, the basic Finnish monetary unit, and use of foreign long-term credits helped achieve prewar production levels and export surpluses by 1925. Industry, however, was dependent on a narrow resource base; paper pulp and timber were the backbone of industrial advance. Diversification was required. Production rose from 1921 to 1939 by 170 percent, and the industrial work force increased nearly 70 percent. Expansion also brought much needed improvement in communications and transportation.

Along with economic expansion there was a notable increase in population mobility and improvement of the quality of life. The agricultural reform and an increase in real wages combined with a drop in the cost of living improved living conditions. There also were advances in medicine and social legislation that revealed the state's active social service orientation. The cooperative movement begun in the late 1880s took hold, easing the economic conditions of the population at large, as retail and wholesale organizations with a nationwide network reduced prices and spread information and technology. By 1935 cooperatives accounted for nearly one-third of Finland's retail trade. Progress was not continuous, however; when the worldwide depression hit nations dependent upon agriculture, Finland was no exception.

Artistic and cultural growth paralleled economic progress, and a strong literary movement continued through this period (see ch. 8). Finland became widely known for its art and architecture, in which innovations in the functionalist style were significant, and for its crafts.

Finnish glass and ceramic work was greatly admired. The Finnish composer, Jean Sibelius, enjoyed worldwide fame, in addition to being a celebrated national figure. Finnish athletes gained a reputation for excellence in world competition. In contrast with these positive manifestations of economic, cultural, and social progress, however, Finns were divided by a number of issues.

One divisive issue was the prohibition of alcoholic beverages, which pitted supporters of prohibition and the government against significant numbers of the population. The Finnish Friends of Temperance had achieved complete prohibition in 1919, but the legislation and legal apparatus were unable to cope with the smuggling and illegal manufacture of alcohol. Pressure of the depression after 1929 coupled with general dissatisfaction with the flouting of laws prompted a national plebiscite that decided to end prohibition. In January 1932 Parliament repealed the 1919 law and created a more satisfactory State Alcohol Corporation to control liquor trade and consumption.

Another divisive factor was the political and social conflict resulting from the language situation. The conflict that developed during the Russian grand duchy period had been submerged by the trials of russification, and Swedish-speaking Finns even adopted Finnish family names as a patriotic gesture. With independence, however, this group (composing 11 percent of the population) demanded constitutional protection, which was granted in 1919. The Swedish-speaking minority feared domination by the majority and nationalistic discrimination through language. Legislation in 1921 and 1922 made administrative districts bilingual unless the minority population was less than 10 percent and guaranteed official use of the language of any citizen dealing with the state. Lower courts were required to use Swedish if necessary. All secondary schools had to be bilingual, and higher education required proficiency in both languages. Most civil service positions also required that applicants be bilingual.

Enactment and administration of these provisions were a major source of conflict. Ultranationalist Finnish speakers complained, sometimes using extremist rhetoric—to which the Swedes responded in a similar vein—that Swedish-speaking Finns were getting more rights than their numbers entitled them to, that they occupied a disproportionate number of administrative posts and had more influential and wealthy families. The battleground was often the university; an attempt to make Helsinki University unilingual was a great issue. Compromise in 1937, however, preserved its status and a certain number of Swedish chairs were retained. By 1972 the number of Swedish-speaking Finns had diminished to about 7 percent of the population, and there was less controversy on matters of language. Fair application of the law ended discrimination, and the allegiance and patriotism of the Swedish-speaking Finns was obvious after the wars with Russia and Germany.

Communism and the Lapua Movement

The most disruptive interwar events were related to the activities of the Finnish Communists. Many Red Guard Finns had fled to Russian Karelia after the civil war, and the Finnish Communist Party was founded in Moscow. Then, some of them filtered back into Finland and enlisted members who were bitter about their defeat in the civil war. Under various banners this proletarian party won 14.8 percent of the vote in 1922 and still had 13.5 percent in 1929, its last legal participation until 1944. Its activity in Parliament was matched by its efforts outside to establish control of the labor unions and prepare for revolution. The matter came to a head in 1929 and 1930 when communist activism provoked a rightist reaction, the Lapua Movement.

The Lapua Movement took the name of the town where a strong reaction to communist youth demonstrations occurred in November 1929. This united effort against Communism transpired when economic conditions from the depression were bad, the president was relatively weak, and minority party cabinets continued to compromise and prevent strong government action. The Lapua support came largely from the extreme rightist elements in Finland who viewed the civil war as a victory over the Bolshevik Soviet Union as well as a defeat of the Left in Finland. They never accepted the 1920 Tartu Treaty with the Soviet Union; they believed in an expanded Finland—that is, Finland enlarged by accession of East Karelia—and wished to see Finland become a powerful northern country. This view included the basic interpretation of Finland's historic role as that of a barrier against Russia. The revanchist Academic Karelian Society expressed these views for the Right and rejected as well the parliamentarianism then in effect in Finland.

As rightist agitation intensified, Parliament in November 1930 voted legislation making the Communist Party of Finland illegal. After President Svinhufvud thwarted an attempted revolt at the town of Mäntsälä in 1932, the Lapua Movement itself was outlawed. The government reasserted itself, but rightist philosophy lingered in the Patriotic People's Movement, which elected fourteen members to Parliament in 1933 and eight in 1939. Basically, the population would not go along with extreme conservatism and fascist orientation of the party.

FINLAND AND WORLD WAR II

Despite the Finnish government's established neutrality, Finland could not help but be drawn into the clash between Germany and the Soviet Union. The Finnish minister to Moscow, Juho Kusti Paasikivi, was told by Soviet Premier Josef Stalin, in answer to his protestations about Soviet acts, that strict Finnish neutrality was not possible because of Finland's position in relation to the great powers.

Winter War

Because Finland's border was close to Leningrad (formerly, Petrograd and earlier Saint Petersburg), and because Finland possessed islands that could guard water approaches to that city, the Soviets wanted to strengthen their position before war broke out in Europe. The Finns, however, insisted that no Finnish territory, even with compensation, could be ceded nor would they enter into any guarantee agreement with the Soviet Union about use of Finland by other countries to attack the Soviet Union. In early November 1939, after war had broken out in Europe and after a final refusal on the part of Helsinki's representatives, negotiations were suspended. On November 26 a "hostile incident" took place at Mainilia, a Finnish border town. The Soviet Union renounced its nonaggression pact with Finland, and the Soviet army began attacks on November 30, 1939.

The Finns were not surprised. Marshal Mannerheim had been reappointed commander in chief of the armed forces after having served as chief of the Defense Planning Council since 1932. Reserve callups, partial mobilization, and defense works that he had pushed for the frontier areas prevented the Soviets from winning by surprise alone. The crucial fighting took place in the Karelian Isthmus, where the Finns assembled six divisions to face twelve to fourteen Soviet divisions. The remaining Finnish forces were stretched over the isolated territory to the north. The isthmus was ideal for defense; lakes and bogs channeled the movement of attacking forces, and Soviet confusion along with poor tactics allowed the Finns to withstand large-scale assaults while displaying tenacity and courage that gained worldwide sympathy and admiration.

During the fighting in December and January, the Finnish army consolidated its defense and kept the Soviets at bay. Then the Soviets changed command and, learning from previous mistakes, launched major offensives in February that forced the Finnish lines to ordered retreat. Continued assaults in March finally exhausted the defenders, who without reserves would have been steadily worn down further had not a peace treaty been signed in Moscow on March 12, 1940. The Finnish decision for peace was delayed by consideration of possible help arriving from the United Kingdom and France, but Sweden and Norway would not permit passage of troops over their territory, and Finland chose to proceed with peace negotiations.

The terms were hard. Finland had to cede the province of Viipuri, in addition to two other towns, islands in the Gulf of Finland, and large areas in the north. The peninsula of Hanko, in eastern Finland, was leased to the Soviet Union for thirty years. In all, land and resource losses were estimated at 11 percent of Finland's economic output and 10 percent of its territory.

The readjustment to economic and political realities was more difficult because Germany's 1940 offensive in Europe increased tension.

Additional Soviet demands beyond the treaty were onerous and prevented Finland from establishing security ties with Scandinavia or Western Europe. Then in July 1940 the Baltic states were annexed by the Soviet Union, and many felt Finland would be next, as it was cut off from Soviet trade in early 1941. The agricultural land lost, and a poor harvest as a consequence of war and of bad weather, presented Finland with a food crisis as well as a political one.

A solution to these problems that became increasingly evident was aid from Germany. Rightist elements in Finland had been sympathetic to Germany's "progress," and German intellectual and cultural influence had always been present in Finland, as elsewhere in Scandinavia. More political ties were established, along with economic aid, until an agreement was reached allowing German troops transit across Finland to Norway.

Continuation War

This agreement, largely the independent work of Finnish military authorities, together with the multiplying expressions of friendliness toward Germany, made the Soviet Union again view Finland as a threat to safety. When Germany attacked the Soviet Union in June 1941, Soviet reaction included attacks against Finland. The Finnish government tried to remain neutral but had to resort to arms again in what has come to be called the Continuation War—this time with a strong ally and material aid.

By December 1941 Mannerheim felt Finland's war efforts had gained a viable defensive position, and he was loath to go further. Despite German pressures, he would not commit his army to the Leningrad siege or a large offensive against the Archangel supply route. Mannerheim was intent on proving that independent Finland was no grave threat to the Soviet Union; his eye was on future peace terms. East Karelia annexation fever cooled as Germany staggered in 1943. Reality hit hard; the Soviet Union would remain Finland's powerful neighbor.

Through 1943 and the winter of 1944, a peace faction grew in Finland, and various contacts were made with the Soviet government. Two delegates went to Moscow in March 1944, but the Soviet terms were considered too harsh. Meanwhile, Germany criticized the Finnish initiatives and began cutting aid. This had serious implications when a massive Soviet offensive began in June 1944; Finland, hard pressed, sought renewed aid from Germany, for which President Ryti made a personal commitment not to seek a separate peace. After retreats, the Finnish front was stabilized and serious breaches repaired, but the cost had been high.

On August 1, 1944, President Ryti resigned, and Parliament conferred his position on Mannerheim. Ryti's pledge to Germany was considered broken, and Mannerheim sought peace. The Soviets were unconciliatory, and the Finns could do nothing but accept an armistice on September 5, 1944, and send representatives to Moscow. Faced with an ultimatum and not negotiation proposals, the Finns signed armistice terms on September 18.

Difficult Peace

An immediate problem was the 200,000 German troops in northern Finland that the Soviets insisted be interned. This was impossible, for the Finnish army had to demobilize. New conflict broke out as the Germans retreated to Norway, leaving complete destruction in their wake. Thirty-six percent of the buildings and practically every bridge in the area were destroyed. It was not until April 1945 that the very last enclave in the northwest was retaken.

The armistice terms were difficult and were included in the final peace treaty signed February 10, 1947. Finland was required to return to the border delineated in the 1940 Peace of Moscow. Finland also lost Petsamo, her only Arctic port. Hanko was traded by the Soviets for a base in Porkkala, twelve miles from Helsinki; transportation rights across Finland were included in the agreement. Abandoned German property was to go to the Soviet Union, along with a war indemnity of US$300 million.

The cost of war in human misery was immense—53,750 killed, another 59,450 wounded; many were orphaned or made wards of the state. Finland had to finance relief and welfare programs. Nearly half a million people had to be resettled. Thirty thousand new farmsteads were appropriated or cut out of forest, and new urban communities were set up, but the state was not always able to use the most economic measures. These accomplishments added to the cost and raised dissatisfied complaints in some quarters.

The process of rehabilitation was made worse by the staggering burden of the Soviet reparations payments. The US$300 million was assessed at 1938 prices, and Finland ended by sending to the Soviet Union exports worth US$570 million. Forestry products were only allotted 28 percent of the total, so that Finland had to establish metallurgical and mechanical industries to supply the remainder. This forced development virtually built an industrial society shaped by public capital investment. There was doubt that what had been built would survive after the last shipment to the Soviet Union in September 1952, but in the intervening years Finland had rebuilt trade with Western Europe and had also established trade with the Soviet Union above that sent as reparations (see ch. 14).

Politics of the Ordeal

Readjustment to the postwar world required a new outlook to replace the hostile anti-Soviet Union view that had been dominant since independence. The clearest expression of this new orientation came from Paasikivi, Mannerheim's Prime minister and the moving force behind his government and later president from 1946 to 1956. A long-time politician, Paasikivi had disagreed violently with the intransigence that led to the Winter War and still more vehemently opposed the Continuation War. He held a historian's view that Finland, although culturally Nordic, was politically linked with Eastern Europe. This led him to believe that Finland and the Soviet Union could coexist if Finland were able to persuade the Soviets that no future attack on the Soviet Union would be launched through Finland. Preserving Finland's independence was his first task, but he was willing to concede any minor issues that would help relieve strained relations with the Soviet Union, and so protect Finland's democratic system. It is somewhat ironic that two conservatives would lay the foundation for reconciliation with the Soviet government, but Paasikivi's convictions and Mannerheim's autocratic view made them suited for the task.

The political formations survived the war years largely intact, except for the demise of the Patriotic People's Movement Party and the addition of the Communist Party as part of the peace terms. The latter party formed a Finnish People's Democratic Association to coordinate communist activities, and this became its national political arm. The reappearance of the Communists caused the Social Democrats to lose their position as the largest parliamentary party, so the postwar governing coalition included the Social Democrats, Agrarians, and Communists, with each group holding cabinet posts. Fear of a coup rose in 1948, and particular dislike for communist Minister of the Interior Yrjö Leino caused the Communists to be eased out of cabinet participation until 1966.

Parliamentary instability in the prewar era was heavily criticized, and after the war, government stability based upon executive strength and policy was finally accepted by the majority. This allowed Finland to progress along well-established lines without sudden shifts and provide continuity that would help keep the Soviet Union at ease. Paasikivi's presidency was overwhelmingly oriented to foreign policy.

His successor in 1956, Urho Kaleva Kekkonen, continued the same general policy lines Paasikivi established. Indeed more stable times had finally arrived: the reparations were paid; Helsinki hosted the 1952 Olympics; and the Soviets had relaxed in their attitudes toward Finland. The traditional democratic process survived the tests of war and rehabilitation, and Finland could develop with the measure of security provided by the new guidelines in the knowledge that it had preserved its national independence and status.

CHAPTER 3

ENVIRONMENT AND POPULATION

The northernmost country on the European continent, Finland covers an area of 130,128 square miles, the size of the New England states, New York, and New Jersey combined. It shares borders on the west with Sweden for 335 miles, on the north with Norway for 447 miles, and on the east with the Soviet Union for 788 miles. About 688 miles of coastline on the Gulf of Finland (south), the Baltic Sea (southwest), and the Gulf of Bothnia (west) is deeply fragmented and studded with islands (see fig. 1).

One-third of Finland lies north of the Arctic Circle, and the geography of the country reflects its northern situation in many ways. The surface of the land was scoured and gouged in recent geological times by glaciers that left thin deposits of gravel, sand, and clay.

In the south these deposits dammed the drainage systems, and the depressions north of them filled with water to form tens of thousands of lakes that occupy more than 9 percent of the country. The land in the south is relatively low—altitudes range from 200 to 400 feet above sea level—and rises gradually from the southwest to the northeast.

The severe northern climate is moderated by warming effects from the Gulf Stream along the Norwegian coast, from the waters of the interior lakes when they are not frozen, and from the dense coniferous forest that covers more than two-thirds of the land. Continental high-pressure systems sometimes prevail, however, and result in exceptionally cold winters and hot summers. Snow cover lasts up to ninety days in the Ahvenanmaa Islands off the southwest coast and up to 250 days in the north. Precipitation ranges from twenty-seven inches a year in the southwest to sixteen inches in the northwest.

Finland's population, stabilized in the 1950s and 1960s at somewhat more than 4 million people, was reported in the 1970 census to be roughly 4.7 million. The total was expected to decline slowly throughout the remainder of the century. Growth patterns, both overall and regional, had been greatly affected by external and internal forces, by spontaneous spreading as well as sponsored group colonizing, and by forced as well as intentional retreating of settlement. In the early 1970s the country was experiencing an internal reversal of population spread from a historic direction northeastward to a contemporary one southwestward.

PHYSIOGRAPHY

Landforms

The Finnish landscape is characterized by a rather asymmetric distribution of hills and plains with the highest elevations (4,344 feet) in the extreme northwest. The higher landforms are often referred to locally as mountains. Most of the northern mountains have rounded ridge tops averaging between 1,500 and 2,500 feet above sea level, but there is a major interruption around Lake Inari, which occupies a plain at elevations of 300 to 600 feet.

More than half of eastern Finland is hilly country. Most of the area has local elevation differences of 150 to 600 feet, but in the southern third the differences range only from sixty to 150 feet. The gradual southward descent and decreased relief are reflected in other elements of the landscape, particularly the drainage and vegetation.

Paralleling the coast of the Gulf of Bothnia there is a belt of plains about sixty miles wide with elevations ranging from fifteen to sixty feet. The separation between these plains and the hills is rather sharp in the north, but in the southwest the change is gradual.

Drainage

Drainage patterns are directly related to these surface features. The north, except around Lake Inari, is drained predominantly by rivers more than 200 miles long. The principal ones are the Muonio River and its tributary the Tornio River along the Swedish border and the Kemi River and its many tributaries. The Kemi has been developed into Finland's major source of hydroelectric power by a series of dams along its main course. Both rivers flow generally southward into the head of the Gulf of Bothnia.

In the central part of the country, streams become shorter. The Oulu River is of medium length and is important for hydroelectric power generation, but most of the other rivers draining the plains area follow parallel courses northwestward to the Gulf of Bothnia over distances of sixty miles or less. These rivers are more sluggish than the longer ones of the north, and they often flow across land that must be ditched before it can be used agriculturally.

In the southeastern quarter of the country is the lake district. Its water bodies are generally long and narrow, oriented northwest and southeast. They were formed in valleys that descend slowly southward and are dammed by the great east-west double ridge called the Salpausselkä. The ridge is roughly forty miles inland and runs parallel to the Gulf of Finland coast eastward from Helsinki.

The area south of the lake district and westward along the coast is drained mostly by a series of short streams seldom longer than about forty miles. This area of low hills and scattered plains is marked by many small lakes and pockets of poor drainage.

Soils and Vegetation

Vast areas of the country are covered by soils that are stony, infertile, or generally lacking agricultural possibilities. These same soils, however, can support lush forest growth, and it is estimated that forests cover some 70 percent of the land area. Pine, spruce, and birch, respectively, are the predominant species. Because these species have adjusted to the climate and soils of the region through centuries of growth, much of the forested area replenishes itself through natural regeneration, a circumstance giving Finland an advantage over European countries farther to the south where seedlings must be planted. The many lakes and rivers provide thousands of miles of log-floating routes, used to carry timber to mills and seaports. Woodworking industries are a dominant element in the country's economy (see ch. 13).

POPULATION

Dynamics

The post-World War II era began with about 4 million people (see table 1). The 1950 census was the country's first, previous counts commonly being based on total enrollments in all church and civil registers.

Table 1. Finland, Population Growth, Selected Years, 1749–1970

Year	Total Population (in thousands)	Year	Total Population (in thousands)
1749	420	1920	3,147
1808	900	1930	3,463
1843	1,500	1940	3,695
1879	2,000	1950	4,030
1890	2,380	1960	4,446
1900	2,656	1970	4,707
1910	2,943		

Source: Adapted from A. Sømme, *A Geography of Norden*, Oslo, 1960; and Päätoimisto Tilastollinen, *Tilastoliedotus*, Helsinki, January 1970.

By 1960 the population reached 4,446,000 people, reflecting an average growth-rate per year of 0.9 percent in the decade of 1950 to 1960. By 1965 the estimated population was only 4,596,000, evidence that a falling birth rate (22.1 per 1,000 in 1950 to 16.7 per 1,000 in 1965) and emigration were taking effect. The declining rates of growth continued through 1969 when Finland's maximum total population was 4.7 million.

During the early 1970s the country's total population declined under nonwar conditions for the first time since the 1866-68 famine. It fell from 4.7 million in January 1970 to 4.6 million in late 1971.

By early 1972 the birth rate was down to 13.7 per 1,000, and the death rate was nine per 1,000. Both were somewhat lower than the averages of births (sixteen and fifteen per 1,000) and deaths (eleven per 1,000) in northern and western Europe. Finland's overall growth rate of 0.4 percent for 1972, however, was the lowest, with Sweden, in northern Europe. This reflected emigrational strains as well as other elements of slow growth.

Distribution

The settlement of Finland has progressed generally northward. It began with the earliest people known to be present coming from the south and southeast about 7000 B.C. Though the principal centers of this prehistoric settlement were in the southwest, some signs of early inhabitants have been found all over the country. By early historic times Finns were in much of the southern fifth of the country and along the Bothnian coast; it was there that Swedes mixed with them from the eleventh century on. The Swedes remained near the coast in two areas while the Finns spread northward.

By 1550 the southern fifth of the country, including the south coast, the Bothnian shores, and inland around Oulu Lake, was settled. Agricultural settlement spread rapidly to the north in the seventeenth century, continued slowly northeastward in the eighteenth century, and reached the northern border by the mid-nineteenth century.

In early 1973 nearly half the population was concentrated in the southernmost portion of the country, and most of the remainder was distributed south of the sixty-sixth parallel. The south, where urbanization had proceeded rapidly, contained the largest cities with the highest population densities as well as a majority of rural dwellers. Since 1910 the center of population had remained at a point roughly 175 miles north of Helsinki.

Most Finns lived on or near the water. Areas of population concentration lay along the southern and Bothnian coasts, in the lake district, and along the rivers.

National Aspects

Southern Finland developed before the northern part for several reasons. First, Finland's trade has been largely with European countries in relatively heavy or bulky goods so water routes from the southern and southwestern parts have been the main lines of trade. Second, agriculture-forestry and agriculture-fishing were the principal early occupations for trade and support of the people, and third, Swedish and Russian administrative centers were located in that area.

Also contributing to the concentration of settlement in the south were certain elements of the landscape—lower elevations, good soils, and other glacial outwash features. The outstanding glacial relic is the long double-ridged Salpausselkä, the recessional moraine of southern Finland that dams the south-flowing streams into many lakes. South of the moraine the land is lower and flatter.

Climatically, as well, southern Finland has some advantages over the northern part; summers are longer, and winters not as cold. January and July mean temperatures in Helsinki are 23°F and 64°F; in Lapland, 10°F and 59°F. Annual precipitation measures 24.5 inches in southern and central Finland; 20.5 inches, in the north. Unfortunately for farmers and tourists the seasonal distribution of precipitation throughout Finland is uneven; usually it is dry in June and July and becomes wet in August. Snow usually covers the ground for about three months in the extreme southwest and more than seven months at Rovaniemi in Lapland.

One result of these physical characteristics is a more valuable forest cover in southern than in northern Finland. In particular the area southwest of a line from the Soviet coastal border to the city of Oulu is characterized by great cuttings of spruce and pine, heavy use of rivers and lakes for floating, and concentrations of woodworking industries along these ways and at coastal stream mouths.

Regional Aspects

On a regional scale population distribution is explained more clearly by cultural characteristics than by physical ones. Much of the linearity of settlement, for example, is a reflection of transportation routes. Originally these may have been rivers, but now they are land lines. In the patterns of both railroads and roads one sees first a general north-south orientation and then connections from inland toward a coast (see fig. 2). The railroads were developed (during Tsarist times) to handle internal domestic exchanges by the producers, processors, and consumers of bulky and heavy goods and to support foreign trade, so they connect the larger inland places and principal ports.

Although roads supplement the railroads in facilitating the distribution and collection of heavy, bulky goods and materials going in and out of a region, they serve a more significant pupose in supporting the movement of people and goods between regions or within one. Finns are quite dependent upon buses for movement within a region or the country. Thus the roads impart a continuous linearity of settlement; the main routes are oriented in a north-south direction both within and between regions.

Occupations have broad regional concentrations. Agriculture is spread most continuously in the southernmost strip; fishing extends primarily along the southern and southwestern coasts (and some in the lake district); industry is scattered about the southern half; and most productive forestry is in the southwestern fifth. There are also discontinuous occurrences of agriculture, industry, and forestry all over the country.

Within the industrial south there are tendencies toward areas of specialization. Most metallurgical plants are located there, particularly in the southwest. The plants use both domestic and imported ores and fuels so they need to be near the Baltic Sea. Nearly all of them are

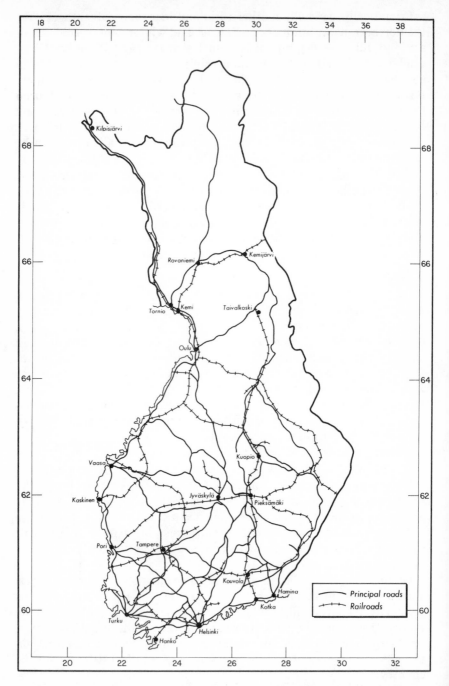

Figure 2. Finland, Major Routes of Transportation

south of a line connecting Imatra, Tampere, and Pori. The major manufacturers of transport equipment are further concentrated southwest of a line from Helsinki to Tampere to Pori. Within that area too are

40

the main plants for plastics, rubber goods, and textiles. Glassmaking and porcelain making are limited to the small section from Karhula, through Helsinki and Turku, to Lahti. Each of these areas continues to attract more people.

The regional concentration of agriculture in the south is certainly related to the physical character of the soils there. Much of the lower and flatter land near the Gulf of Finland coast is predominantly clays and silts. Where they are better drained, or have been made so, they have become the more desired soils for the raising of crops and animals.

As a result of the scattered distribution of occupations, there are intraregional differences in trade. Regional processing centers for milk are also the extra-regional shipping points for milk products bound for southern domestic or foreign markets. Wood and metal manufacturing towns serve similar functions. All attract people and play a major role in Finland's postwar conversion to more sophisticated production for foreign markets, so the larger multifunctional centers will get still bigger.

The administrative function also has attracted people to certain centers. Political hubs for regions, the twelve provinces (each with a governor), and communes (each with an elected council) draw people in for governmental actions and supplement other attractions. In some cases the administrative function has been added to a centrally located place after it attained some size from commerce or industry but, in others, administration preceded the growth.

Among major cultural characteristics influencing regional differences in population distribution is war-induced change. The losses of the three eastern sectors and movement of the displaced persons is one example of settlement increases. Persons killed or missing in the combat areas of the eastern border represent demographic losses. But the major war damage was that done by retreating Nazis in Lapland; Rovaniemi has been rebuilt and is now a city of about 30,000 people; most bridges have been replaced, but some of the destruction of rural buildings was not repaired. Thus, much of the settlement of Lapland looks much newer than it really is.

Some faunal distributions may have affected settlement distribution. Historically, for example, furs were a major attraction of early settlers to southwestern Finland; among the animals taken were fox, beaver, lynx, wolverine, wolf, and bear. They were scattered through all the forests with some tendency to concentrate in the north and east.

Baltic herring catches are of major importance (more than 50 percent of the total catch) along the coast from the Soviet border to Oulu. The herring catch is supplemented by whitefish and perch. In the lake district the more important fish taken are lake herring, perch, pike, and bream.

Some domestic foxes have been raised, and domesticated reindeer are concentrated in Lapland in the extreme north. Thus, fishermen and Lapps are tied to the location of animal resources, but the number of persons involved is small because of the limited resources.

Some regional gathering of population is related to the presence of water bodies. Early settlement in the lake district is one. More recently, though, the development of waterpower along certain streams has been a significant attraction for both industry and people. The most notable locations are in the southeast along the Vuoksi River at Imatra and the lower Kymi River in the southwest on the lower Kokemäki River, and in the north on the Oulu and Kemi rivers. As in Sweden, the north is likely to be the major source of electric power for the growing industrial areas in the south. Hydroelectric power, of which Finland produces only about one-third as much as Sweden or Norway, is nevertheless the country's primary energy source because mineral fuels are lacking.

Mineral deposits have resulted in population growth at a few places. Most important are the government-owned copper deposits in the southeastern Outokumpu area, discovered in 1910. Iron ores are widely distributed, its mining loosely concentrated in the southwest, near Oulu Lake, and the Ivalo part of northern Lapland.

Local Aspects

On a local scale, physical elements of the landscape are commonly more important than cultural factors in explaining population distribution. This is particularly true where settlement patterns are based on agricultural-forestry occupations.

One element of major significance to Finns in locating a farm is drainage. Some 30 percent of the country is swampy as a result of drainage interrupted by glacial deposition. Distinguishing the different kinds of swamps and draining them within reasonable limits of area, time, and cost have become as fine an art in Finland as in Norway. Techniques have been developed for draining some kinds of forests to improve production.

Closely related to drainage is soil type. Finnish farmers use the drained swampy soils for haymaking and the morainic soils (of rock, gravel, sands, and silts) for such crops as oats, barley, and potatoes. On the better soils in the south are grown spring and winter wheat, rape, and sugar beets as well as oats and barley. The difference between swampy and morainic soils is recognized easily; it costs three to five times more to clear the latter for cultivation. Local roads commonly follow the uphill side of the break between the two soils so the farmstead is near both types of production as well as the road. As a consequence settlements are arranged in a clearly linear fashion.

Vegetation is also of major importance in the selection of farm sites. Different kinds of swamp vegetation indicate various potentials of production. Similarly, different kinds of trees signal varying growing conditions, but these differences are even more important with respect to a farmer's income. Not only is the quality of a species significant but also whether the stand is mostly spruce, pine, or birch for conversion to lumber or paper products.

Local differences in elevation are of major consequence. Frosty air is heavier and collects in lowest spots locally. Therefore, the better locations for growing grasses for haymaking are the drained swamps and for potatoes are the morainic soils upslope from swamps or lakes. Houses a short distance upslope from lakes are also warmer. It is often assumed that south-facing slopes are preferred for settlements because they receive more direct sunlight, but conscious selection of such locations has been rare anywhere in Finland.

The details of both local climate and surface configuration, therefore, are important to Finns. Where the land has been glaciated it is essential to place fields and buildings very carefully. Depressions may be cold, wet, and difficult of access; hilltops are so much better that they are the predominant location for settlement in the southeastern quarter of Finland. Seldom is there a Finnish farmer who is not aware of the combination of detailed physical features found in each field; this knowledge is basic in an area where conditions for crop growth may drop below critical levels at any time during the growing season.

Every rural Finn also is aware of the importance of the road network to settlement patterns. Materials and machinery must be moved to a site; the equally bulky and (or) heavy products of milk and wood must be moved out. The farmer must consider not only interregional transport capability but also how local roads (or lake or sea lines) tie to them.

In the rural areas individual farmland ownership patterns are directly related to the distribution of settlement. By tradition farms are composed of scattered parcels of land, some of which may be over five miles from the farmstead to which they belong. The scattering came about originally so as to equalize among heirs the inheritance of differently valued types of land. The result is that the farmsteads themselves tend to be clustered rather than widely scattered.

Movement

Emigration

All Finland has been affected by an emigrational trend for several decades. Finns became part of a common labor market with other Scandinavian countries and Iceland when Finland joined the Nordic Council in 1956. From that time forward Finns could travel or take jobs in any of the member countries without passports or work permits. For Finns, Sweden was the dominant attraction, taking nearly half the émigrés in the 1950s and three-quarters of them between 1961 and 1965.

This movement took place for a number of reasons. Sweden was the nearest economically well developed and free nation. It has been neutral since 1809, and many Finnish children were sent there during

World War II. There were traditional ties between the two nations as well—ties deriving from the historic period of Swedish rule.

Besides these reasons, there were internal forces behind emigration, such as a field reservation program to discourage certain forms of agriculture. Under these circumstances those Finns who have moved to Sweden have been predominantly single adult males, single adult females, and children under fifteen years of age—usually in that order. Among emigrants, rural persons exceeded urban dwellers in 1970 and 1971, but in 1972 the rates were reversed.

Rural-Urban

Finland's internal rural-urban migration has been a longtime movement but has accelerated since World War II. For example, at the beginning of the twentieth century the country was predominantly rural, and in 1930 and 1940 only 18 and 23 percent of the people were urban dwellers. This went to 32 percent in 1950, more than 40 percent in 1960, and about 49 percent in 1968. At the end of 1970 the urban numbers exceeded the rural 2,393,000 (51.1 percent of the total population) to 2,287,000.

Economic developments have encouraged rural-urban migration. Industrialization was accelerated after World War II; emphasis was first on forest products and later on machinery and design goods, especially for foreign trade. The increased economic sophistication was demonstrated geographically by rural commune changes. From 1950 through 1955 there were scattered population decreases in the southern half of Finland mixed with areas of population increase but migration loss; from 1956 through 1960 most of the southern communes lost population, but a few had population increases in spite of migration losses; and from 1961 through 1965 nearly all of the southern communes experienced population decreases—but the bigger cities continued to grow. Government efforts to reduce agricultural overproduction and uneconomic farm size with such actions as a field reservation program have combined with high unemployment, especially in the north, to add impetus to internal movements of the Finns.

SETTLEMENT PATTERNS

Scattered dwellings constitute the prevailing form of settlement pattern in the inland regions of southern and middle Finland as well as the extreme north. In two other regions linear distribution dominates. One of the regions is small and in the central southwest, inland from Turku. The other and larger is a strip, about seventy-five to 125 miles wide, extending from the middle western coast northeastward to the middle north. Concentrations along the rivers in both areas are sharply defined (see fig. 3).

Clusters of dwellings in oval or amorphous shapes characterize much of a southern coastal strip that extends from the Karelian border to the

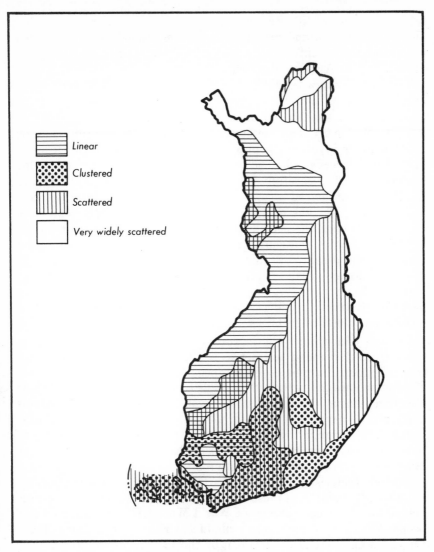

Figure 3. Finland, Dominant Settlement Patterns, by Region

western coast in irregular widths. Further, in the Helsinki area and northward the clusters are mixed with areas of scattered residences, and in the western section clusters and lines are interspersed.

On a large-scale map detailed differences in settlement patterns are apparent. The variations are greatest in the south where a relatively small area may contain a city like Jyväskylä with 59,000 people as well as short lines of rural homes along water bodies or roads or scattered single farms at the ends of short access roads. Local preferences for nearness to water or to transport routes, for flatter land, for lower elevations, for particular types of trees, and for specific exposures are easily seen, but great variations in people's values and desires are reflected by wide differences in their homesites. Apparently many kinds of conscious and unconscious site selection factors have been used through the centuries of settling. The results are spots, lines, and areas of variously spaced dwellings.

Variety also characterizes Finland's city layouts. Nearly every urban area is on water, and some have two shorelines if they are situated between two lakes, on a peninsula, or combine stream-mouth and coastal locations. Otherwise street plans range from rigidly square, like downtown Jyväskylä, to biaxial rectangular, as in central Helsinki, to various degrees of planned and unplanned irregularity in outlying communities. The carefully planned community of Tapiola, west of the Helsinki urbanized area, is an excellent example of attractiveness and functionalism where, in addition to a large commercial center and some smaller ones, there are single-family residences and several kinds of multiple-family ones arranged in subcommunities. Other center cities are composed of a mixture of multistoried buildings, usually commercial-residential or only residential structures, with nearby light and heavy industry, some old blighted spots, areas of new very modern construction under way, and the noise and smell of buses, streetcars, ships, and factories.

Patterns of settlement in the rural areas range over the whole spectrum from unplanned settling over the centuries to contemporary planned groups in colonies. Unplanned settlements are found all over Finland and are characterized by single farms, clusters, or lines, which are often associated with the edges of water bodies. These distributions developed through time with a gradual increase in a rural population engaged in farming-forestry or farming-fishing. The resulting patterns represent earlier settlement oriented toward water bodies and more recent settling associated with roads.

Most characteristic of new rural settling since World War II are the colonies. The majority of these are made up of resettled Finns who were among the displaced persons of World War II. They totaled 420,000 people who chose to move into Finland as a result of the ceding of four Finnish areas to the Soviet Union by the 1940 Treaty of Moscow and again (after recapture) by the 1947 Treaty of Paris. The three main sectors of loss were on the eastern border: Karelia at the southern end, Salla-Kuusamo in the middle north, and Petsamo at the northern end.

Many of the people went to cities, but others went to former farmland or new rural colonies. Each colony was a group settlement primarily on state-owned land and, in the north, represented a regional advance northward of rural settling until 1970. The total result of colonizing was to increase densities in the south, but in the north many blank spots on the population map were filled in.

LABOR FORCE

In general the employed population has increased in concert with the total population. For example, the total labor force was 2.08 million in 1959, reached a peak of 2.21 million in 1966, and remained near that figure with 2.20 million in 1971:

Division of the employed labor force by economic sector discloses some major changes between 1938 and 1971. Whereas in 1938, 51 percent of all employed persons were engaged in agriculture and mining; by 1971 this percentage had declined to less than 20 percent. Changes in distribution reflected steady growth of industry in the towns and cities. But the real significance of manufacturing is shown by its providing more than 31 percent of total 1971 wages and salaries while agriculture-forestry accounted for a little more than 5 percent.

The major geographic differences between southern and northern Finland give rise to an additional one, unemployment. In 1971, for example, there were about three times as many unemployed in northern Finland as in the south. This factor contributed to the gradual population drift back southward that was occurring in the early 1970s.

FUTURE GROWTH

As a result of the many changes in distribution of population the Finnish government has instituted measures to carefully assess both present and future populations.

Finnish population decline is expected to continue. By the year 2000 the forecast is for total numbers to drop 5.5 percent from the 1970 figure to about 4,360,000. This estimate is based on measures made from 1965 to 1969 and on the assumptions that: fertility will decline rather strongly to 1978 and then will be constant; mortality will remain the same as at the end of the 1960s (because no trend was detected); emigration excesses will occur until 1985 (when the total excess is expected to be 185,000 people); and internal migration will remain the same as the last of the 1960s.

CHAPTER 4

SOCIAL SYSTEM

In Finland language is the badge of ethnic identity. The country's population is predominantly Finnish speaking (more than 90 percent in early 1973) and has a Swedish-speaking minority. A high proportion of Swedish-speaking persons, known as Swede-Finns, are bilingual in Finnish, but relatively few Finnish speakers know Swedish well. Both groups are Lutheran and share values and attitudes deriving from their common faith.

Besides these two large groups, there are a number of tiny minorities, the most important of which are the Lapps. Cultural differences in addition to language distinguish the Lapps and other peripheral groups from the main body of the population.

Both Finnish and Swedish are official languages. Both are taught in the schools—Swedish as a second language in Finnish-speaking schools and Finnish in Swedish-speaking schools. Both, by law, hold equal place as the language of government in general and of the courts in particular. Here the equality ends, however, for Finnish, as the native tongue of the great majority of the population and as the speech of daily life, has been gaining greater popularity since the end of the last century.

The geographic and cultural isolation of the Finns is reflected in their language. Unlike Swedish and Norwegian, which belong to the Indo-European family of languages, Finnish is grouped with Estonian, Hungarian, and other tongues in the Finno-Ugrian family. Linguistic identity became a rallying point for rising Finnish nationalism in the nineteenth and early twentieth centuries.

The family in Finland differs from that of the Western European pattern only in detail and in the direction and rate of contemporary change. The effects of World War II, which reduced the male population, as well as the effect of industrialization, urbanization, and ideological struggle, have weakened family ties, especially in the cities. Only slight variations exist between the patterns of the Swedish-speaking and the Finnish-speaking family. They exist primarily, if at all, among the urban groups.

Despite the weakening of family ties since World War II, the Finn still has great loyalty to his family. His ties to his close kin are those of acknowledged obligation and often of deep affection stemming from experiences and aspirations shared throughout life.

The needs of the family have come to be accepted as the central issue of social policy and are given priority over all others. The government plays a dominant role in family welfare; the major family welfare programs were introduced during and after World War II, when an increase in the birthrate lessened the concern felt in the 1930s about a decline in population (see ch. 5).

The strength of the family has contributed to the unity and stability of society as a whole. Social distinctions based on various criteria, including language, occupation, and economic well-being, exist; but they are bridged at many points by family ties, by the common values inculcated in a highly literate people through an excellent system of universal education, and by a shared sense of Finnish identity and an intense national patriotism. For most Finns, despite economic and political alignment, loyalty to country is a uniting force that transcends social differences.

ETHNIC GROUPS AND LANGUAGES

The Finns

The origins of the Finns are obscure, but their ancestors probably were farmers and hunters living in what was to become central Russia. Although they mixed with Germanic and Slavic peoples, they maintained their linguistic identity. Moving northward, they gradually occupied the Finnish peninsula and displaced the aboriginal Lapps on their way.

With a long tradition of freedom as independent farmers, hunters, and fishermen, the Finns maintained a rich folk heritage throughout seven and one-half centuries of Swedish and Russian domination. Regional variations of Finnish language and culture are relatively insignificant.

The Swede-Finns

The Swedish-speaking minority traced its origins to persons who came to Finland as administrators and colonists between the twelfth and nineteenth centuries, when Finland was under varying degrees of Swedish control (see ch. 2). In Finland the Swede-Finns came to be the dominant political and economic group, a position they retained for several centuries. Swedish was the only officially recognized language and was used in church services and as the medium of instruction in schools. All government business was conducted in Swedish.

The influence of Swedish culture is strongest in the Ahvenanmaa Islands off Finland's southwest coast. In the area of Turku, on the southwest coast of the mainland, Swedish manor houses of the sixteenth and seventeenth centuries still stand. Eastward, along the Gulf of Finland, the industrial Swedes met the agricultural Finns to establish Helsinki as the country's administrative center early in the nineteenth century, and it is here that the two cultures blend.

A sense of common identity and interest began to develop among Swedish-speaking Finns in the early twentieth century. At that time Swede-Finns whose ancestors had been Finland's economic and administrative elite came together with Swede-Finns of lower socioeconomic status in organizing a new political party to pursue their common aspirations. The new party, known as the Swedish People's Party (Svensk Folkpartiet—SFP), included among its members Swede-Finn farmers, laborers, businessmen, and intellectuals in a common effort to ensure the perpetuation of their culture and language. This continued to be the primary objective in subsequent decades, but the wide range of interests of party members proved to be a formidable obstacle to developing effective political and social programs (see ch. 10).

Rapid industrialization after World War II accentuated the divergent interests within the party and exacerbated social differences already present. Swede-Finns in the upper income group began turning to other political parties, either conservative or progressive, that had better articulated goals. Farmers and blue-collar workers saw some form of socialism as more to their advantage. Although the SFP was still active in the 1970s, its diminished representation in Parliament directly reflected a growing weakening of political cohesiveness among Swede-Finns. Despite their diminishing political cohesiveness, however, Swede-Finns have continued identification with their linguistic heritage, sending their children to Swedish schools.

The Lapps

North of the Arctic Circle, in Lapland, live roughly 1,000 or 2,000 Lapps. The Lapps preceded the Finns to Scandinavia by many centuries. Until the mid-twentieth-century incursions into their territories by Finnish roadbuilders, schoolteachers, and engineers, Lapps followed two simple life-styles. Mountain Lapps migrated with their reindeer each spring to grazing grounds and back again each fall to their winter quarters. Forest Lapps lived in permanent homes and supplemented their reindeer economy by farming and fishing. Contact with the Finns has led to a decrease in grazing lands and to an increase in dependence on a money economy. In the past the mountain people traded reindeer skins and meat for cottage-industry products made by forest Lapps. Present-day Lapps sell their reindeer for money in order to buy manufactured goods.

Some Lapps are giving up their traditional life-style and are accepting Finnish customs and life-styles. Acquiring a formal education requires learning Finnish, which leads to further familiarity with Finnish culture. Young Lapps may leave their homeland for higher education in the southern cities, may marry non-Lapps, and are often reluctant to return to a life in the frozen wilderness.

Other than the wealth represented by the number of reindeer a man owns, traditional Lapp society affords few levels of status for ranking individuals. There is no formal political organization nor are there any wide variations in wealth.

Kinship is reckoned through both parents and is the primary means for identifying oneself outside the local settlement. Because relatives tend to cluster in the same area, many neighbors may be related through both males and females. Strangers are asked not where they come from but to whom they are related. Because family names are associated with specific territories, kinship ties also serve as geographic locators. The ideal household consists of the husband and wife and their unmarried children. Married children traditionally lived near their parents, but a continuing shortage of land, and a combination of influences from Finnish culture, have made this custom difficult to maintain.

Great emphasis is placed on neighborliness, hospitality, pleasant demeanor, and practical economic cooperation. Families join together for mutual assistance in hunting, in fishing, and in reindeer herding. This cooperative effort is directed by a council consisting of one man from each family, with an elected council chief.

The council's duties are primarily concerned with economic matters, but some jurisdiction is assumed over infractions of social codes. The authority of the chief is subject to the approval of the council members and, in turn, to the approval of their families. The chief's power does not go beyond the cooperating community.

Languages

After Finland was ceded to Russia in 1809, a controversy developed over the continuing use of Swedish as the only official language. Swedish had long held a preeminent position and was the tongue used by the educated elite. Growing nationalist sentiment in the 1840s and 1850s, however, resulted in a strong push for the adoption of Finnish as an official language, with the issue becoming the focus of an impassioned controversy (see ch. 2; ch. 8).

Advocates of this position were rewarded by the adoption of the Language Decree of 1863, placing Finnish on an equal footing with Swedish as an official language. Nevertheless, nationalists continued to argue that a nation's identity depended on its people's speaking a common language and that, in the case of Finland, Finnish was clearly the proper choice. The Swede-Finn minority was seen as a disfranchised population whose duty it was to become real Finnish citizens by adopting the majority language.

In 1883 the courts were ordered to use Finnish in their transactions in all districts where it was the predominant language. Supporters of these actions hoped for a voluntary acceptance of the Finnish-language culture by the Swede-Finns. This finally came, at least in token form, in 1906, when on May 12, the centenary of the birth of the foremost nationalist, Johan Snellman, some 16,000 families changed their Swedish names to Finnish.

The rapid social changes that took place after 1945 pushed the language controversy into the background. The larger question of national reconstruction, like World War II before it, made interethnic rivalries seem trivial. In any case, the supremacy of Finnish over Swedish was already more or less established.

In the early 1970s the Swedish language enjoyed equal official status with Finnish, and the national education system, from primary to university levels, provided separate schools for Swede-Finns. Swedish was also the only language other than Finnish employed as a medium of instruction in any institution belonging to the state school system.

In the early 1970s, groups that spoke languages other than Finnish or Swedish were few and insignificant. They included a few thousand Lapps, Russians, and others. Since World War II, English had replaced German as the most widely known third language.

SOCIAL STRATIFICATION

The growth of industrialization in the nineteenth century, combined with the constitutional and land reforms of the new republic in the twentieth century, broke up the traditional four estates—nobility, clergy, bourgeoisie, and peasantry—into which society had been divided since the Middle Ages. By the early twentieth century there were only remnants of the old Swede-Finn nobility, and the hereditary sanctions of the past had been swept away by modern economic and social imperatives. The Finn who could do so looked back with pride on a distinguished family line; but whereas heredity once determined the individual's lot in life, social identification was now increasingly being determined by capabilities, education, and occupation.

Lacking the clearly stratified patterns of the traditional social order, Finnish society of the early 1970s exhibited a high degree of integration and homogeneity. Nevertheless, significantly different segments of the society could be distinguished on the basis of ethnicity and contrasting rural-urban patterns. Crosscutting these culturally defined groups, moreover, were other broad social groupings: one whose members dominated the life of influential urban circles from positions of political power and economic authority; another also urban based but made up of persons with fewer economic resources and less access to higher education; and a third composed mainly of persons in agricultural pursuits.

The lines between such groups were fluid, however, and social mobility was a marked characteristic of Finnish life. Official policy, as reflected in statements on educational objectives made by a high government official in the early 1970s, stressed the importance to the nation's teachers of emphasizing the dignity and worth of the individual and of minimizing social differences within the framework of the society.

FAMILY AND KINSHIP

The family unit usually consists of the husband and wife and their unmarried children. Despite the housing shortage in towns and cities, most married couples do not live with the parents of either husband or wife. By the same token, elderly parents customarily are not brought into the homes of their married children.

In the early 1970s more attractive employment in factories or in offices was causing young people to leave family farms. Housing in urban centers was confined almost exclusively to apartments, and there was not enough space to allow the perpetuation of families larger than two generations under one roof.

To maintain the integrity of the nuclear family by keeping the household free of either married children or parents, Finland developed a comprehensive system of social services (see ch. 5). Homes for old people and for homeless children have been provided through public taxes to a degree sufficient to maintain the national preference for separate households for each immediate family.

By the early 1970s about 50 percent of the married women had jobs outside the home, and for this, too, the government provided supporting social services. There were some 35,000 day nurseries and day homes for children. Supervised playgrounds are plentiful in urban communities and are used by children of working mothers instead of having baby-sitters come into the home.

The economics of running a family farm or of conducting a nonmechanized timber business encourages successive generations of family members to remain in close proximity to one another. In most of the rural areas married children usually live in homes separate from their parents but nevertheless close by. In the cities this pattern of familial clustering is approximated despite the absence of obvious economic reasons for it. Adult brothers and sisters, single or married, tend to live in the same commune. Although industrial and clerical employment rarely call for cooperation among members of a family, social intercourse among relatives living in separate homes in the city is frequent and informal.

The family farm in Finland traditionally has been an autonomous economic unit. Labor is furnished by family members, and hired workers are rarely employed. Rules of conduct, personal goals, and social values are directed toward producing individuals who are self-reliant and cooperative.

In rural areas parental guidance and discipline of children is designed to put the child on his own at an early age. A father is not only the head of a family, he is also the manager of a labor force. The sooner

54

his children can be depended upon to help with the work load, the sooner his farm productivity can be increased.

Situations in which cooperation is neither expected nor offered within the family are delineated as clearly as the cooperative ones. Sons have a privileged position in the Finnish household; they do not help their mother but are served by her. Parents do not dominate their children, but neither are they permissive. Children are expected to conform to a behavioral code that reflects both independence and responsibility.

The feminist movement that historically was responsible for much of the equal status with men enjoyed by Finnish women was revitalized in the mid-1960s. Through television, radio, and the press, equality of the sexes became a public issue. The traditional feminist movement developed into a new program aimed at changing prevalent attitudes about the social roles of women. It called for more justice and rationality so that every individual would have a chance for self-realization. Basically, the movement advocated that every woman should have the choice of either staying at home as a housewife or marrying but making her own career without the problems involved in being a wife and mother.

Beginning in the 1860s a series of special laws has been enacted, which were designed specifically to give women the right to own and inherit property, the right to government employment and, since 1906, the right to vote and to hold elected office. Women are well represented in the professions (see ch. 6; ch. 8; ch. 9; ch. 13). About 17 percent of the seats in Parliament were held by women in the early 1970s.

A woman also had some degree of independence in the realm of husband-wife relationships. For example, she could free herself of an unsatisfactory marriage by her own initiative. After a year of legal separation from her husband, she would be granted a divorce upon request.

CHAPTER 5

LIVING CONDITIONS

In early 1973 the population generally enjoyed a high standard of living. Public health, sanitation, and welfare programs, comparing favorably with those in most other Western countries, encompassed the entire population. The diet was nutritious, and a wide variety of food was available. Although there was a continuing housing shortage, government support and a number of housing programs had made comfortable housing widely available.

The country was rapidly moving toward greater urbanization (see ch. 3). Centers such as Helsinki, Tampere, Turku and Jyväskylä were expanding steadily and attracting great numbers of young Finns who preferred the efficiency, convenience, and modernity of city life to the isolation of the countryside.

Finnish life style is conditioned by the climate. During the short summer there is a mass exodus to the countryside. The long winters are endured stoically with the help of a variety of outdoor athletic activities. Sports are widely enjoyed throughout the year, and participation is encouraged both by the educational system and by various government and social agencies. Music and the theater are also popular forms of recreation.

HEALTH

Food and Nutrition

In 1970, the most recent year for which statistics were available, the average Finn spent about 26 percent of his income on food and another 9 percent on beverages and tobacco. Alcoholic beverages and tobacco, regulated as government monopolies, were relatively costly, and many Finns drank illegally produced alcoholic beverages.

The diet is simple and well prepared, although with a heavy emphasis on starches. Porridge, cereals, onion-flavored meatballs, soup, potatoes, bread, jam, and cheeses are common menu items. For festive meals there may be salmon or bits of smoked lamprey.

According to the Organization for Economic Cooperation and Development (OECD), the average person consumed 3,070 calories per day in 1970. The Finnish rate was considerably higher than the 2,500 calories judged sufficient by the World Health Organization (WHO) for a woman doing light work and slightly higher than the 3,000 necessary for a man doing average work.

The diet was sufficient in vitamins, minerals, and proteins. Meat and fresh fruit were not abundant, but frozen and tinned fruit and vegetables were available even in remote parts of the country. Finns used butter lavishly, averaging 37.4 lbs. per person in 1970, and drank an average of 300 quarts of milk per person in the same year. Finns also consumed a great deal of cheese; over two dozen varieties were on the market.

Among the traditional foods is a special Christmas dish called *lipeä-kala*, codfish soaked in lye and dried. When cooked it gives off a pungent odor, which Finns find appealing, but is a formidable obstacle for foreigners to overcome. Another common dish is Karelian pastries. There are also large rye-crust loaves of bread filled with fish, fat pork, or game. Other popular dishes are Karelian stew, or "hot pot," which consists of pieces of pork, mutton, and veal simmered in the oven for hours, and pastries. Thick, hot soups are eaten regularly in the winter, and the light, mild soups are popular in the summer. Crayfish also are enjoyed during a season that runs from mid-July to mid-September.

The Public Health Program

Public administration of health services was expanded in 1968, but by early 1973 the delivery of health services was not yet up to the Scandinavian average. The problem was minimized in urban areas by modern, efficient hospitals and trained medical personnel, but such facilities and persons were lacking in sparsely populated areas. In Lapland, especially, one doctor might serve as many as 8,000 patients.

Finland had by 1973 thoroughly socialized its medical facilities. For public health and other social welfare purposes, the country was divided into communes with a local board of health responsible to the National Board of Health. The total staff of the National Board of Health was 150 in 1968. Commune boards of health were financed by the state and by the local community. Each commune had at least one physician at its service. Communes attempted to promote health among their inhabitants by regular examination and treatment and by encouraging such healthy outdoor activities as nature walks and skiing. Communes also provided accommodation and free medical and dental treatment for old people.

Medical Facilities and Personnel

Every commune was required by law to appoint a board of health responsible for all health care, environmental sanitation, food inspection, home treatment of the sick, and operation of almost all hospitals. There were three types of hospitals: general hospitals, psychiatric hospitals, and tuberculosis sanatoriums. In 1968 these hospitals had a

58

total capacity of 65,500 beds, or one bed for every seventy-two patients. This average was slightly higher than that of Denmark, Iceland, and Norway but slightly lower than that of Sweden.

Most general hospitals provided services for internal medicine, surgery, obstetrics, gynecology, pediatrics, ear, nose, and throat, and ophthalmological services. Nurses and interns received their practical training at central hospitals. Many of these hospitals had a polyclinic functioning as an outpatient department for the district that it served.

Two types of mental hospital were in operation, one handling uncomplicated cases, the other handling cases requiring intensive or specialized care. There also were several special care institutions, such as child guidance centers and mental health centers, which provided case-finding, home treatment, and follow-up action. In general, mental health services were improving steadily and patient turnover had increased. Private and church groups also offered counseling for the emotionally ill through such organizations as family guidance centers and clinics for alcoholics.

Tuberculosis offices run by the communes function in case-finding through regular examination, home care and follow-up treatment. Photofluorographs are compulsory for the whole population, so that early detection is possible. Special sanatorium schools provide vocational training for children and adults.

In 1968 there were 4,345 registered physicians, or about one physician per 1,081 inhabitants. Of the total, 2,241 were general practitioners, and the others were specialists—324 in internal medicine, 336 in general surgery, and 212 in psychiatry.

There were 2,504 registered dentists in 1968, or one dentist for every 1,876 inhabitants. There also were 26,895 professional nurses and midwives.

Causes of Death

In the 1960s diseases of the circulatory system led to more deaths than other illnesses, accounting for some 372 deaths per 100,000 inhabitants each year. Among circulatory diseases, arterio-sclerosis and heart disease were the most commonplace. Malignant tumors also accounted for a large proportion of deaths, as did infectious and parasitic diseases and tuberculosis. The rate of mortality from accidents, poisoning, and violence was the highest of any Scandinavian country, a circumstance that may be related to the high incidence of alcoholism in Finland.

Environmental Sanitation

Finns are in general scrupulously clean. The sauna, the traditional Finnish bath, is a favorite and frequent social activity. Streets and houses look neat and well kept.

Public ordinances require individuals to clear the path in front of their houses and to keep the houses freshly painted in a color recommended by the City Planning Board. If a citizen fails to paint his house, the city or rural planning board does it for him and sends him the bill.

Food production and consumption inspection standards are rigorous. Health officials inspect every establishment at regular intervals and are strict in enforcing sanitation regulations.

Maternal and Child Health Care

Public health programs achieved their greatest success in maternal and child health care in the early 1970s. The rate of infant mortality was one of the lowest in the world. There were one or more maternity and child health centers in every commune. Most women visited the centers regularly for examination and treatment throughout their pregnancies. In order to qualify for maternity assistance, the first visit had to come before the fifth month of pregnancy. The average number of visits to the centers in 1964 was 6.9 per pregnancy. Hospital births were the rule, and only 2 percent of all babies were born at home. Such cases occurred mostly in large and isolated communes. Centers provided examinations, personal health instruction, lessons in physiology, nutrition and babycare, and a special course on relaxation to aid labor.

Child health centers existed for children under seven. They provided examinations for children and instructed parents on child health care. Nurses also made home visits. Children were supposed to be examined at least three times during their first year and at least once a year after that.

School health care continued for children from seven to fifteen years old. School health care was intended primarily for detection of early signs of mental, physical, or dental disorders, rather than treatment. Generally, a physician gave thorough examinations to pupils in the first, fourth, and eighth grades and was available regularly at least once a month.

HOUSING

Government Support

In 1970 the average Finn spent 14 percent of his income on housing, lighting, and heating. Another eight percent went to household goods and services. The relatively low amount spent on housing is owed to government expenditure of Fmk150 million (for value of the markka—see Glossary) a year in support of public building, which makes housing comparatively cheap. Despite government support, the housing shortage resulting from World War II has not been completely overcome. An estimated 50,000 houses must be constructed annually until 1976 to meet the growing housing needs.

In the years immediately after World War I, up to 65 percent of total investment was in construction. As much as 13 percent of the gross national product (GNP) was devoted to this field in an attempt to rectify the damage to buildings during World War II. The damage was exacerbated as 112,000 dwellings were lost in territories ceded to the Soviet Union (see ch. 2). National legislation made large-scale credit available on reasonable terms in order to stimulate construction. The Housing Act of 1966 provided for increased government support and established the National Housing Board to supervise planning for housing construction.

Most Finns live in flats ranging from a one-room efficiency, or *yksiö*, to six- or seven-room apartments that are usually financially feasible only for top professional people and diplomats. Houses vary greatly in size as well, ranging from one-room wooden structures in the country to elaborate modern mansions. Special attention is paid to heating and insulation and solidity of foundation. Garden-lovers face the discouraging fact that a garden is available for show for only a few months during the year, being covered with snow much of the time. In return, grass is left mostly uncut, as though the Finns would not begrudge life to any weed in the few short months it has to grow.

An average two-room apartment with a kitchen may cost roughly Fmk30,000. Such a flat will be warm, light, and have all the modern conveniences—kitchen with double sinks, refrigerator, built-in cupboards, electricity, and gas. There also will be a small bathroom; extra storage space on the roof of the apartment building; laundry facilities, including washer and dryer; and a communal sauna in the cellar.

Building and Buying

The system for building new apartment houses is similar to a condominium—a company is formed. The company has shares held by a bank or insurance company. Prospective tenants buy shares in the company, and in effect each shareholder owns an apartment.

Would-be buyers can obtain as much as 50 percent of the purchase price as a bank loan. The government also has a loan scheme—the Arava Plan—which provides money for new housing at low interest. The Arava Plan is restricted to people who can show that they have lived in the town for some time and who are going to live in the house or apartment they plan to purchase. The loan is not given directly to the individual but is used to reduce the downpayment to the company or individual seller. For a two-room plus kitchen apartment on an Arava Plan loan, a couple would have to pay Fmk8,000 as a downpayment and then pay about Fmk150 per month until the charges were paid off. This is a reasonable amount, which most couples can afford.

It is common for industry to make housing available to its workers. Company housing—houses or apartments—usually have very low rents, which may come to only 7 or 8 percent of wages. Since World

War II, several industries have developed schemes to allow their employees to build and buy their own homes. Company architects draw up a plan for the building area and design the houses. The town builds the road and lays water, drainage, and electricity. The company gives a low-interest loan to its employees to buy the land, sells cheap timber, and lends equipment so the employees can build their own home in part. This can save the owner between 15 to 20 percent of the total cost.

House-building by the owners often is speeded up by the custom of *talkoo*—neighbors get together to do a job that one of them cannot do alone. When the work is done, the recipient of the *talkoo* provides food and drink, and frequently the participants have a party to celebrate the completion of the job. This custom retains importance in most parts of the country. The *talkoo* custom can save the home-builder another 15 to 20 percent of the total cost.

Furniture

Contemporary designers have made Finnish industrial design world famous (see ch. 8). Furniture is simple, functional, and mostly modern. Design has much the same characteristics as Scandinavian production in general and specializes in the kind of wooden furniture now associated with Nordic countries. Popular woods used are birch, pine, and teak. The severe simplicity and functionalism of the design can be traced to the influence of older styles of peasant furniture. Designs inspired by the rural tradition are still popular today.

The impact of the bold, brightly colorful, and elegant patterns that has made Marimekko fashions popular all over the world has been felt in interior design. Drapes, curtains, tablecloths, and bedspreads are frequently found in brilliantly colored, informal, bold and challenging Marimekko patterns. The *ryijy* rug has also become a common household item. Originally it was a heavy and coarse blanket used by seal trappers and deep sea fishermen. Today *ryijy* rugs form gay wall decorations and valuable heirlooms. A typical *ryijy* design has a recurring pattern of small figures.

Furniture in town differs from that used in the country. Town furniture is often modern, gay, light-weight and easy to care for. Furniture in the country may still resemble the heavy, wooden, traditional peasant styles.

SOCIAL SERVICES

Social Insurance

The first social insurance (employees' accident insurance) was introduced in an 1895 act. General, statutory old-age and disability insurance appeared with the National Pensions Act of 1937. In the early 1970s the Finnish system for social security included plans for old age and invalidism, sickness, family, and children. The cost of social insurance was divided among employers, employees, the state, and local authorities. Employers contribute the equivalent of 2 percent of each employee's pay. The state and local authorities pay the rest.

All citizens are entitled to old-age and disability pensions. Old-age eligibility begins at the age of sixty-five, and any person between the ages of sixteen and sixty-four who is unable to work owing to illness or injury is entitled to a disability pension. The basic pension is Fmk70 a month. This is a small amount, and if the insured has no other income, he may also receive an additional support pension, support allowance, and a housing supplement, which represent his major source of income.

The National Survivor's Pensions Act took effect on October 1, 1969. Survivors' pensions were not dependent on past earnings and were paid to the widow or widower and to dependent children of any citizen.

Unemployment insurance in the 1960s and early 1970s was still governed by the National Unemployment Funds Act of 1934. Unemployment insurance was voluntary, and unemployment funds were organized on a vocational basis. Approximately 37 percent of all employees participated in unemployment funds in 1968. Unemployment funds charged membership fees, which supplemented state and central government subsidies, and could grant daily, clothing, travel, and rent allowances. The maximum daily allowance for members with dependents was Fmk19 and for others Fmk15. In no case could it exceed two-thirds of the daily wages of the insured. Payments could begin only after six days of unemployment, and no one member could receive more than 150 days of assistance in a calendar year.

Universal statutory sickness insurance was introduced by an act of July 4, 1963. It covered citizens resident in Finland, every person working on a Finnish vessel, and every Finnish national employed by the country's foreign service. Compensation was given in two forms; 60 percent of the cost of medical treatment was repaid upon presentation of a doctor's receipt, and a daily allowance was given for each day of sickness. There were also special maternal allowances.

Social insurance covers much of the cost of maintaining health. In 1968 a total of Fmk 1.3 billion was spent on the Public Health Program. Although patients who go to a physician can get a part of their expenses back, this is seldom more than 60 percent of the cost except in certain chronic illnesses. The method of payment may further inhibit some poor people from visiting a physician as often as they need to because the 60 percent credit is not deducted from the physician's bill but is reimbursed by the local social welfare office upon presentation of a receipt from the physician. On the other hand, those who have no money may obtain assistance from the local social welfare office.

The Accident Insurance Act of 1948 was still in effect in the 1960s and early 1970s. It was compulsory, and all employers were obliged to compensate their employees for bodily injury suffered at work. The act stipulated compensation for medical care, daily allowances, annuities, and all the increases that go with them. Lump-sum compensation could be paid. The deceased's family could also receive funeral benefits and a pension. Anyone who was receiving or had received a daily allowance or annuity also could be given rehabilitation training. Persons rendered helpless by accidents could receive permanent care in special establishments. Daily allowances, annuities, and pensions were calculated according to annual earnings. If these totaled less than Fmk4,400 a year, the injured person's compensation was based on this amount.

Social Allowances

Social allowances are subsidies paid from public funds. They supplement social insurance and are paid irrespective of the beneficiaries' employment past or present. They are intended to eliminate or alleviate the factors that endanger the social security of certain groups. Unlike social welfare, social allowances call for no separate consideration of individual cases but are usually paid out automatically, by law.

Family assistance includes maternity benefits, child allowances, family allowances, housing subsidies, and tax relief. Maternity benefits are Fmk50 per child and are contingent upon the expectant mother's having visited a health center for a medical checkup before her fifth month of pregnancy. Each child is allowed Fmk5 per month. Special child allowances for orphans, disabled, or mentally subnormal children can go up to Fmk92 per quarter. Family allowances are about Fmk70 a year for every child after the first three. These family allowances are paid wholly in kind—for example, bed, clothes, books, or other necessities.

The Vocational Training Assistance Act of 1944 was part of a comprehensive program launched after World War II to promote vocational training. This included the establishment of new schools, the improvement of teaching methods and school administration, and the organization of training for teachers. Under the act, persons of small means are entitled to training grants and interest-free loans for study at vocational schools owned or supported by the state. The usual grant is 30 to 60 percent of whatever the state estimates are reasonable training expenses for the particular school concerned.

Persons wishing to receive vocational training through apprenticeships rather than vocational schools are also eligible for state aid. The direction and supervision of training by apprenticeship is in the hands of the Ministry of Education and its National Board of Vocational Training. Local supervision comes under the communes. Apprentices receive free theoretical training and such benefits as food, textbooks, and study requisites. Apprentices not resident at the place of training are also paid lodging costs, travel subsidies, and a daily allowance. Married apprentices receive a family support allowance.

Social Welfare

Social welfare is a measure supplementary to social insurance and allowances and is geared primarily to fulfilling individual needs not covered by other forms of social services. It is principally a public enterprise, as are most other forms of social services in Finland. The only private efforts are the small-scale family counseling and assistance programs initiated by church groups (see ch. 6). Individual treatment is given in every case and the nature and amount of assistance is determined by the particular needs of the applicant and his family. Social welfare comes under local self-administration and is thus financed mainly by local taxes. Special attention is given to family welfare.

The Child Welfare Act of 1936 generally defines a child as a person under sixteen years of age, although in some cases seventeen- and eighteen-year olds can also come under child welfare. The act stipulates that the Social Welfare Board must take steps to secure the care and education of a child if he is neglected, orphaned, deserted, or if he has committed an offense against the law or otherwise has shown signs of maladjustment or need of special care or attention not provided by the parents.

If for some reason the Social Welfare Board feels that the parents are not taking proper care of the child's education and upbringing, the board can appoint a personal supervisor to advise and guide the parents. In extreme cases the board may decide that the parents must relinquish their rights, in which case the child becomes a ward of the board. Wards of the board may be placed in foster homes, children's homes, or special schools for severely maladjusted children. Child welfare laws are strictly enforced.

Care of the mentally subnormal is the joint responsibility of national and local welfare, health, and education agencies. Special attention is given to providing the maximum amount of education possible. Primary schools have special classes for the educable mentally retarded. Moderately and severely subnormal children are exempt from compulsory school education. There are eighteen institutions, with 3,600 places that provide centralized medical, social, and educational rehabilitation for the mentally subnormal. Most subnormal children are entitled to special child allowances. They are also eligible for disability pensions after the age of sixteen.

Child welfare includes the provision of day-care centers, crêches, day nurseries for preschool children, and day homes for school children. Communes also run playgrounds and other arrangements for outdoor care and recreation. Kindergartens also are a function of social welfare, not of education.

Public aid is the last resort in Finland as in many other countries. The commune is obliged to provide maintenance and care to all persons who have no practical means of livelihood. There are no restrictions on public aid as to nationality, race, religion, or age. The aim of public aid is to promote the client's ability to support himself. The three main forms of public aid are aid at home in cash or kind, placement and care in another private household, and institutional care.

Communes also are responsible for the care of the aged. To this end every commune alone or jointly with another commune must maintain an old people's home, a home for the sick, or a similar institution. Nearly all the inmates of the communal homes receive old-age pensions, but additional aid for their maintenance is given under the Public Aid Act.

Finland has laws making the care of vagrants and alcoholics a matter for welfare and not for the courts. A vagrant or an alcoholic (or drug abuser) is identified according to guidelines established by the Vagrancy Act of 1936 and the 1961 Act on Welfare for Abusers of Intoxicating Substances. Once identified, the person is turned over to the local welfare board, where the client is given guidance, counselling, and practical assistance to help return to a regular life. Stronger measures include commitment to a workhouse or even to work in a special institution.

Labor Protection

Labor protection began with measures to safeguard children from dangers at work and excessive fatigue. The Decree of 1889 on Workers' Protection in Industrial Trades was the first statute. It stipulated the appointment of factory inspectors to ensure that the regulations were observed. Since then, legislative progress has been continuous, and in the early 1970s Finnish labor protection was well up to international standards. Working conditions were generally on a level with requirements of the law. The forty-hour workweek rule applied to almost all vocations except agriculture. The small size of many farms rendered it difficult to accord farm laborers benefits equal to those of other employees. Agricultural employees enjoyed equal labor protection with respect to occupational safety, however.

The Working Hours Act of 1946, as amended in 1965, is equally applicable to any company, organization or employer with one or more employees. Regular working hours are limited to eight a day and forty a week. By agreement between employers and employees, the regular working day can be temporarily extended by a maximum of one hour, provided the regular working time for not more than three weeks is evened out to an average of forty hours a week. Vocations that require a more flexible arrangement of working hours can arrange working time so as not to exceed 120 hours in three weeks, or eighty hours in two weeks.

According to the Annual Holidays Act of 1960, the annual-holiday year begins in April and ends in March. An employee receives 1½ working days' holiday per year for each calendar month in which he has worked for at least sixteen days during the annual-holiday year. If an employee is paid by the week or a longer period, he gets the same pay during his vacations. In general, vacations are taken at one stretch during the summer months.

The Occupational Safety Act of 1958 concerns nearly every form of work except self-employment. It requires at least ten cubic yards of air space per worker in any place of employment. Lighting must be adequate. The act also deals with ventilation, temperature, humidity, dust, smoke, excessive noise, gases, steam, and dangerous substances.

Employers are obliged to provide adequate measures to prevent accidents and ill health. Where necessary, personal protective devices such as helmets, goggles, eye shields, and safety ropes must be made available. The employee is obliged to wear or use this equipment and to keep it in good order.

Women are entitled to the same labor protection as men. There are also special provisions for women. Employers are not permitted to dismiss women employees during pregnancy. At childbirth women in industries get four weeks off with pay, and women in shops and offices get six weeks off.

The Labor Inspection Act of 1927 requires labor inspectors to check on compliance with all regulations on labor protection. There are communal labor inspectors in nearly all towns, boroughs, and rural communes. They are subordinate to the Ministry of Social Affairs and Health and work under the supervision of the state labor inspectors. They inspect factories, farms, agricultural enterprises, shops, offices, restaurants, hotels, cafés, and subsidiary temporary projects. They also inspect employees' housing where employers are responsible for the housing provided. Each place of work must be inspected at least once a year.

PATTERNS OF LIVING AND LEISURE

Dress

Clothing is largely dictated by the climate. Extremely heavy overcoats, scarves, gloves, and hats must be worn for most of the long, arduous winter. Homes, offices, and public buildings are kept very warm, however (up to 77°F), so only light clothes are needed indoors. Finland is not known for its haute couture. But in the 1970s Marimekko fashions, brightly colored dresses with bold patterns, designed in Helsinki, were quite popular all over the world. Although ordinary European dress is worn for everyday occasions, a few national costumes are preserved, especially in Lapland. Special events such as the Ritvala Helka Folklore Festival at Sääksmäki (north of Hämeenlinna) bring out exotic national costumes.

Sauna

The sauna is the traditional Finnish hot bath. The simplest form is a log hut with a large, stone-covered stove in the center. The stones are heated, and the temperature in the room may rise as high as 280°F. Steps lead up to a slatted wooden platform along one side of the room, and here naked bathers lie or sit in the hot air under the roof. While perspiring, bathers beat themselves with leafy birch branches, then wash, and sometimes plunge into a nearby lake or roll in the snow outside. Then the bather rests and allows the body to cool down fully.

The sauna is more than just a bath. It is a weekly ritual to be performed every Saturday with family or friends, with joy and even reverence. Men and women bathe separately. It is considered rude to talk loudly or move boisterously in the sauna. It is supposed to be a revitalizing experience from which both mind and body emerge cleansed and renewed.

Sports

Finns are great sports enthusiasts. Walking, running, skiing, rowing, archery, skating, sailing, boxing, ball games, racing, and various tests of strength are popular activities. Violent or bloody games such as bullfighting or football, however, have little appeal for Finns. The memory of Paavo Nurmi, the great runner, has never left them since he astounded the sports world in the 1920s and 1930s, and every year thousands of young Finns take up various sports in the name of health, recreation and national spirit.

All kinds of physical culture are promoted by activities and organizations, such as school physical education programs, sports and physical education organizations, and training institutes. School physical education programs include compulsory and voluntary forms of exercise. The compulsory requirements are gymnastics, folk dancing, running, skiing, orientation (a kind of cross-country hiking), swimming, basketball, volleyball, and Finnish baseball. Voluntary activities may include track and field, skating, wrestling, weight lifting, ball games, dancing, hiking, rowing, or tennis.

The most important sports organizations are the Finnish Central Sports Federation and the Workers' Sports Federation. These organizations perform extensive educational and public relations work in order to raise the prestige of sports and physical education. State aid accounts for 55 percent of the funds used by national sports organizations. The other 45 percent of their revenue is raised from competitions, publications, social and other functions, membership dues, commercial activity, and donations.

Sports academies are an unusual feature of Finnish sporting life. Planned and financed by sportsmen themselves, they are located near lakes and are fully equipped with gymnasiums, saunas, and swimming pools. There were fifteen academies in the early 1970s.

Recreation

Besides sports, Finns are fond of music, theater, reading, television, and radio as other forms of entertainment (see ch. 7; ch. 8). In 1970 three out of four families owned a television. Radio programs were especially popular in the more remote areas where houses are isolated and neighbors few and far between.

Holidays

Finns celebrate many occasions, such as Christmas, Shrove Tuesday, Easter, Midsummer, Flag Day of the Finnish Armed Forces, Independence Day, namedays, birthdays, and weddings.

February 5 is Runeberg Day, commemorating the national poet, Johan Ludvig Runeberg. His statues in Helsinki and Porvoo are visited and decorated with lighted torches and garlands of spruce and flowers. "Runeberg cakes" are made and sold all over Finland to commemorate the cakes his wife used to bake for him.

Kalevala Day commemorates February 28, 1835, the day Elias Lönnrot completed the manuscript for the *Kalevala*, the national epic. For school children this date also marks the beginning of their ten-day skiing holiday. Celebrations similar to the Runeberg Day activities are carried on throughout the nation.

Lapland has special church festivals on Lady Day (a Sunday at the end of March), at Easter, and early in September. Lapps attend church in their brilliant national costumes. Services are followed by a program of events such as lasso-throwing competitions and ski-racing behind reindeer on the frozen lakes.

Walpurgis Night, also called Vappu, is celebrated on April 30, in the manner of a carnival—with balloons, paper streamers, and colorful paper decorations and hats. In Helsinki students gather at Market Square at midnight and one of them climbs a statue and places a student cap on the statue's head. May Day is a continuation of Vappu. For organized workers it is the big day of the year, and for all it is the sign of spring fast approaching.

CHAPTER 6

RELIGIOUS LIFE

Freedom of religion is guaranteed by the 1923 Act on Freedom of Religions; religious life nevertheless is characterized by the central position of one large denomination—Lutheranism. The Evangelical Lutheran Church of Finland, or Church of Finland, is the state church. Its bishops are appointed by the president, and the part played by the president and Parliament in the enacting of church law is one of the significant ties that binds together the state and the church.

Attendance at Sunday services is rarely greater than 2.5 percent of the population. Sunday services, however, have not traditionally been of paramount significance in religious life. Other forms of participation in the affairs of the parish are considered at least as important as church attendance. Youth work, Sunday school, and home prayer meetings are only some of the church-related activities in which an estimated 15 to 20 percent of the members of the congregation are actively involved. Sociological field studies reflect a positive attitude toward the church even in those church members who do not actively participate in church life.

Nonetheless, the church in Finland, as elsewhere in Scandinavia and, indeed, all over the Western world, is undergoing a crisis of indifference. Changing times and social mores have raised fundamental questions regarding the status and role of the church in society and its relations to other institutions and to patterns of behavior. Although a conventional adherence to the church goes unchallenged, outward manifestations of piety and devotion are largely absent. Criticism of the church has increased in many quarters, and its connections with the state have been seriously debated.

RELIGIOUS IDENTIFICATION

In 1972 about 93 percent of the population belonged to the Church of Finland, and 1.6 percent were members of the Finnish Orthodox Church. An estimated 0.1 percent belonged to the Roman Catholic Church, 0.6 percent adhered to other religions, and 4.6 percent of the people were listed in the civil register, which means that they adhered to no religion.

The Coming of Christianity

Both the Eastern and Western branches of Christianity were

represented in Finland before the Crusades. Most of the inhabitants of the region of Karelia became connected with the Eastern branch, and the tribes living in the wide area between the Baltic Sea, the White Sea, and Lake Onega, joined the Western branch.

The most famous name in the founding of Christianity in Finland is Bishop Henry, an Englishman who came to the country in 1155 with a crusading party led by King Erik of Sweden. Bishop Henry of Uppsala and his followers stayed behind to consolidate the new religion after King Erik's departure. Bishop Henry was murdered by an irate Finnish peasant on the ice of Lake Köyliö and subsequently became the patron saint of the Church of Finland and the apostle of Finland.

The Protestant Reformation

The Finns accepted the Protestant Reformation, or Reformation, with relative equanimity; evidently the ideas of the Reformation and Martin Luther's rugged individualism suited well the rigors of developing life patterns in the Finnish forests. The reformer of the Church of Finland was Mikael Agricola, who studied under Martin Luther at Wittenberg. A fundamental feature of the Reformation was the translation of the Bible into indigenous languages. In accordance with this view, Agricola translated all of the Old Testament and almost a quarter of the New Testament into Finnish.

Agricola was also the developer of literary Finnish and early established the concern of the church that the people learn to read in order to be able to interpret the word of God (see ch. 8). In 1686 a church ordinance was passed requiring all who wished to marry to learn Luther's Small Catechism. In the eighteenth century preparation for confirmation was made compulsory for all young people. The emphasis the church placed on education and the steps taken to educate the people made literacy general throughout the country by the end of the nineteenth century.

THE EVANGELICAL LUTHERAN CHURCH OF FINLAND

Lutheranism is distinguished from other forms of Christianity in three ways. First, the most fundamental Lutheran concept is that of justification through faith alone, acquired directly from the word of God. Thus the preaching of the word of God is central; and this idea resulted in the emphasis placed on the translation of the New Testament into local languages. Second, formal liturgy is reduced and deemphasized as compared with the formality of the Eastern Orthodox and the Roman Catholic churches, and more personal forms of worship are encouraged. Hence, only two of the seven sacraments of the medieval Roman Catholic Church are preserved—baptism and Holy Communion. It is stressed that even these two sacraments are retained only as symbols to strengthen faith and have no inherent redemptive value. Third, Luther proposed a doctrine of two realms—the spiritual realm where Christians communicate directly with God, without priestly intervention, and the secular realm where the government embodies a legitimate civil authority distinct and separate from the spiritual authority of the church. The doctrine of the two realms, with its dialectical acceptance of both the separateness and the interconnections between church and state, prefigured the contemporary relations between church and state in Finland.

Organization

The church is divided into eight dioceses. Each diocese is divided into deaneries, of which there are sixty-eight; deaneries in turn are each divided into parishes. Despite the apparent episcopal nature of church organization, in essence the Lutheran Church places great emphasis on congregational life, and local parishes are quite independent.

A diocese is the territorial jurisdiction of a bishop, who is appointed by the president from a group of three candidates who have been elected by the clergy and a committee of laymen. According to church law the bishop has surveillance over the purity of church teaching, the correct administration of the sacraments, the proper conduct of the church services, the Christian instruction of young people in schools and parishes, Christian morals, care of the poor, administration of church property, and the life and conduct of the clergy. The bishop is also supposed to visit every parish in his diocese at least once every five years, but he frequently delegates this duty to his subordinates.

The country's eight dioceses include seven Finnish-speaking and one Swedish-speaking diocese. Each is headed by a chapter composed of the bishop as chairman, the dean, and three assessors. The dean is the rector of the cathedral parish (which is the seat of the bishop) and represents the bishop. The assessors assist the bishop in his official work and act as consultants to the parish pastors. The chapter is the managerial center from which the work of the whole diocese is supervised. Every five years the bishop calls all the clergy of his diocese to a conference, the main function of which is to examine issues in preparation for the Church Assembly.

Dioceses are divided into deaneries, each of which is headed by a so-called rural dean appointed by the chapter from a list of leading pastors nominated by the clergy. The dean of the cathedral, by appointment, is also the rural dean of the deanery to which his parish belongs. The dean is an assistant of the bishop, and vice chairman of the chapter. He has to see that the parish clergy obeys the stipulations of church law and the instructions of the chapter. In practice, he is the liaison between the chapters and the parish clergy. It is he, rather than the bishop, who visits the parishes and holds regular meetings of the parish clergy.

The parishes are both administrative areas and living religious communities. For the parish, the parish council and the parish plenipotentiaries are the deciding organs, and they are both selected at a parochial

73

meeting. A parochial meeting is a meeting of all clergy and confirmed adult members of a parish.

The only source of income for the parish is the church tax. The parish plenipotentiaries determine the amount of tax to be paid after accepting a rating scheme. The average amount of church tax is 1 percent of taxable income. Joint-stock companies and firms must also pay church taxes. Since 1960 this tax has been deducted at the source of income and passed through the government finance department to the parishes. The parishes pay about 7 percent of their earnings to the central church fund.

The leadership of the parish is the responsibility of the rector. He is the chairman of the parochial meeting, the parish council, and the parish plenipotentiary. The chaplain usually supervises the youth work and association activities in the parish. Curates are sometimes appointed by the chapters to help rectors of large parishes. Since 1944 the parishes have also had to employ a deaconess, who performs nursing and social work for the poor of the parish.

The three main administrative organs of the church are the Church Assembly, the Enlarged Bishops' Conference, and the Ecclesiastical Board.

The Church Assembly is the highest ranking ecclesiastical body of the church. It is responsible for approving new liturgical books, hymnals, revised versions of the Bible, and catechisms. It also proposes amendements to existing church laws and proposes new laws, which must be approved by Parliament in order to be legally binding. Generally, the assembly meets every five years, and a three-quarters majority is necessary for a draft to be carried. The result of these requirements is to make the procedure of the Church Assembly rather slow—a decision on a motion takes at least ten years—usually much more.

The Enlarged Bishops' Conference consists of one bishop, one assessor, two laymen from each diocese, and the members of the Ecclesiastical Board. The archbishop, traditionally the bishop of Turku, presides. The functions of the conference, which generally meets twice a year, are many. Among other things, it selects members for the Ecclesiastical Board when a vacancy arises in that body, and it supervises their work. It controls the central funds and determines the amount to be paid by the parishes. It makes recommendations to the government on matters of interest to the church and arranges ecumenical contacts. Since its inception in 1943, the conference has initiated a large number of committees to guide and encourage ecclesiastical youthwork, the diaconate (or official body of the deacons) of the church, religious instruction in the schools, and the training of youth leaders.

The Ecclesiastical Board is the permanent organ of the Enlarged Bishops' Conference. It consists of six members—one theologian, one jurist, one administrator, two laymen, and the archibishop who presides. One of these members must come from the Swedish-speaking diocese. The board is a purely administrative body that carries out the directives of the Enlarged Bishops' Conference and administers the central funds of the church.

There are two Lutheran mission societies—the Finnish Missionary Society and the Lutheran Evangelical Association of Finland. The former has 120 workers in Southwest Africa, Tanzania, the Republic of China (Taiwan), Israel, and Pakistan. The Lutheran Evangelical Association has about ten missionaries in Japan. Mission work is funded by donations, not by church taxes.

Relation of Church to State

The Church of Finland is a national church with links to the state. Its status is defined in the constitution and in common law. Collaboration between church and state seeks to preserve the independence of the church while continuing the special relationship with the state. Thus, new church laws or amendments to existing laws must be approved by Parliament before they become legally binding, but Parliament itself cannot propose new laws or even slightly alter existing laws.

Another indication of the link between church and state may be seen in the fact that every session of Parliament and every sitting of law is preceded and concluded with a religious service. Furthermore, the bishop preaching the parliamentary sermons is able to raise questions of internal politics. The annual four days of prayer and thanksgiving are celebrated under the protection of the state.

Questions concerning the state and the church equally are called "mixed matters." This term refers to laws concerning the relationship between church and state, or church and other religious organizations, as well as laws relating to marriage, divorce, oaths, the care of the poor, and religious education. The government is required to consult the Church Assembly on issues touching on these matters. The state also has the right of decision in important questions relating to church administration. The president appoints bishops (as vacancies occur) from a list of three names selected by the clergy and the representatives of the laity. Usually he appoints the candidate with the largest number of votes; but he is also entitled to use his own discretion and occasionally does so. The government decides whether new dioceses and parishes should be founded and whether new churches should be built. The president and the minister of education always participate in such notable church occasions as consecration of bishops and church jubilees.

In practical matters, church and state also cooperate. The church keeps the records of births, deaths, and marriages of all its members and cares for most of the country's cemeteries. The parish registers supply material for the official census statistics, thus taking a financial burden off the state's hands. For those who have withdrawn from the church there is a civil register, but this applies to only about 5 percent of the population. These non-Lutherans can register either with their own church or in the civil register. On its side, the state pays the salaries of the theological faculty of the National University of Finland and its chapters; it provides chaplains and religious instruction for various denominations in the army, navy, prisons, and hospitals.

The nature of church-state relations has been seriously debated in the light of modern trends toward secularization of government and public life. Nonetheless, surveys of the country's voters show that a majority of people support a continuing official connection between the church and the state.

Ecumenical Relations

The Church of Finland has always received stimuli from Sweden and Germany, the home of the Reformation. The Finns have been interested in the Church of England, perhaps because two of Finland's first bishops were English. The Church of Finland's ties with its Scandinavian sister-churches are also quite strong. Bishops from Sweden, Norway, Denmark, Iceland, and Finland assemble every three years in the Northern Bishops' Conference. The associations of clergymen of these countries seek greater contact with each other. The Church of Finland also maintains friendly contact with the Evangelical Lutheran Church in the United States.

The general movement for world church unity had no impact on Finland until the end of World War I. In 1919 Finns took part in the Conference of the World League for Church Cooperation. Soon after that the first Ecumenical Committee of Finland was founded and grew into the Universal Church Committee in 1933. The functions of the committee were to foster peace activities, to support minorities in different countries, to observe the ecclesiastical movements over the world, to prepare for Finland's participation at the worldwide ecumenical conferences, and to publish and distribute the results of these conferences. This committee eventually evolved into the Finnish Ecumenical Council.

In 1953 the Enlarged Bishops' Conference was empowered to arrange contacts between the Church of Finland and other churches. A foreign affairs committee was formed, which recommended the appointment of a National Committee of the Lutheran World Federation. The committee sustained sufficient interest in ecumenical affairs to the extent that representatives of the Church of Finland attended every subsequent world conference based on the Lutheran Confession. This brought together the Church of Finland with sister-churches in Scandinavia, Germany, and the United States.

The Revivalist Movements

The influence and activity of the Church of Finland can to a great extent be attributed to the revivalist movements of the nineteenth century. Unlike most rewakening movements, the impact of the revivalist movements in Finland did not lead to a break with the official church. In the beginning there were many differences, but gradually the ideas of the revivalist leaders penetrated the church and molded its vision of Christianity.

All of the movements remained distinctly Lutheran. They all adhered to the doctrine of justification by faith as the center of preaching and teaching. They made clear demarcations between the Kingdom of God and the material world. Worldly pleasures were generally decried. Emphasis was placed on varying degrees of abstinence, faith, abnegation, confession, and prayer.

Four of the revival movements are vigorous and attract a growing number of advocates annually from a varied segment of the population. Each of the movements has a central organization, its own newspaper, and magazine. Each movement holds a summer convention, which may at times attract up to 20,000 people.

An uneducated peasant, Paavo Ruotsalainen (1778–1852), nevertheless became a renowned spiritual leader and founder of the Finnish Pietist movement. The core of his belief lay in the recognition of God's greatness and man's insignificance. Man, he proclaimed, is inept and can only spoil his efforts; only God redeems and heals. Hence man's primary and all-encompassing duty is to abandon his own works and trust only in God.

Pietists remained on good terms with other Christians, never calling attention to a distinction between themselves as believers, to whom grace belongs, and the rest of the world, which is unrepentant. Pietist worship services, generally held at the home of an adherent, are supposed to supplement, not substitute for, Sunday services at church.

The Evangelical movement was founded by Fredrik Gabriel Hedberg (1811–93), a Pietist who turned away from the mainstream of the movement. Hedberg believed that the Pietist's agony over his sins detracted from the assurance of salvation that a Christian has in faith in Christ's righteousness. The movement stresses infant baptism, as its adherents believe the whole of salvation is given through baptism.

Henrik Renqvist (1789–1866), founder of the Praying movement, placed great emphasis on prayer. Supporters of this movement pray as often as twenty times daily, and some of these prayers can last for hours. Adherents of the movement, sequestered almost entirely in a small area in the southwest, acknowledge the authority of the church and attend church and celebrate Holy Communion with the rest of the congregation of the parish to which they belong; however, they place special value on knowledge of the Bible and on private confession. The conservative character of the movement inhibits its extension among contemporary youth.

The Laestadian movement, named after its founder, Lars Levi Laestadius (1800-61), originated in Lapland. A particular feature of the Laestadian movement is the stress placed on the concept of the visible congregation and on absolution given to the members of the congregation after confession.

Like the Evangelical movement, the Laestadians stress the certainty of salvation for the Christian, but they draw a sharp distinction between Christians and unbelievers, whom they expect to be doomed. Intolerance of nonbelievers has caused several rifts within the Laestadian movement itself. Nonetheless, it is the largest of the revival movements and numbers an estimated 200,000 people.

OTHER CHURCHES

The Finnish Orthodox Church

The Finnish Orthodox Church is a member of the International Orthodox Church Federation, whose nominal head is the ecumenical patriarch of Constantinople. For most purposes the church in Finland is autonomous, and its general administration is directed by its bishops and a central board. The church is divided into two dioceses, Karelia and Helsinki.

The Finnish Orthodox Church, although much smaller in membership than the Church of Finland, is also recognized by the state for tax and other purposes. At the end of World War II, the Finnish Orthodox Church lost most of its constituency when the greater part of Karelia, the eastern region of Finland, was ceded to the Soviet Union, but it received considerable compensation from the state. Since then it has been slowly rebuilding its membership. In 1968 the membership of the Finnish Orthodox Church numbered 1.3 percent of the population, and in 1972 it numbered 1.6 percent.

The head of the Finnish Orthodox Church, the archibishop of Karelia and all Finland, has his see in the middle of the new orthodox settlement in Kuopio. The Finnish Orthodox Church administration and the theological seminary are also located in Kuopio. The seminary is very small, usually having about fifteen students. There is no higher educational institution of orthodox theology in Finland, so many students continue their education in Romania, Greece, France, the Federal Republic of Germany (West Germany), and the United States.

Other Religious Groups

The strong hold of Lutheranism on the majority of the population has limited the rise of other religious groups. At the end of the nineteenth century the Methodist, Baptist, Seventh-Day Adventist, and other denominations spread in Finland. The total membership of all these groups, however, is only 15,000 people. The Pentecostal movement has had the greatest success. It is estimated to have around 30,000 followers. But as the congregations of this movement are not officially registered, it is difficult to ascertain the number. The Jehovah's Witnesses and the Mormons also carry on missionary activities, but they have not had any major impact on the population. The Roman Catholic Church has about 2,000 members, most of whom are descendants of foreign immigrants. None of these religious groups has substantial influence on the social or political life of Finland.

RELIGION AND SOCIETY

Criticism has been leveled at the church from the youthful segment of society for its alleged failure to adjust to the social changes accompanying industrialization and urbanization. Although there has been no decrease in the enrollment of students of theology, a number of them have been unwilling to take up traditional parish work as their life's calling after graduation. The delay in permitting women theologians to become pastors is irritating to some circles. Attempts have been made by church officials to reform the church at every level, administrative and substantive.

For the most part the church has responded to these calls for reform. The cumbersome apparatus of the church administrative and legislative bodies, however, has a delaying effect on the execution of reforms. Among other things, the church has attempted to modernize by encouraging youth work, family counseling, and other forms of social welfare activity calculated to bring parish members into closer and more frequent contact with the church.

Religious Education

Religious education is supervised by the Commission on Education of the Enlarged Bishops' Conference. Education is provided through Sunday school, confirmation classes, or religious instruction in elementary and secondary schools.

The Sunday School Association provides teaching materials and is partially responsible for the training of about 25,000 lay volunteers who teach about 300,000 pupils in Sunday schools. Children learn about church services by singing hymns and songs and participating in short liturgies.

Almost all youth around the age of fifteen attend some form of confirmation classes during the day, in evening classes, or in special summer camps. Confirmation classes teach doctrinal material such as Luther's Small Catechism, the wider catechism, and Christian doctrine. Church history, knowledge of church affairs, biblical material, and familiarity with the use of the Bible is also emphasized. Confirmation classes usually last two to three weeks and cover 100 to 125 lessons.

The teaching of religion in regular schools is under the supervision of the National Board of Schools, which operates under the auspices of the Ministry of Education. Children may be excused from religion class if the parents object. In this case the children are taught church history instead. If there are at least eight pupils belonging to the same faith who are freed from receiving Lutheran teaching, they may be given religious instruction according to their own denomination if their parents want it. Two to three hours of religious instructions per week are customary. Morning prayers are also held in most schools. They usually last five to ten minutes and include hymn singing, a short sermon, and prayer.

The education of clergymen and women theologians is provided by the theological faculty at Helsinki University. The ordinary degree for a clergyman takes about five years of study. For honors, several more years of study are required. The training of organists and cantors (choir leaders) takes place at the Sibelius Academy at Helsinki and at the Parish Institute of the Church of Finland. The institute also trains Sunday school teachers, youth workers, deacons, and deaconnesses.

Church Social Work

Modernization efforts within the church emphasize youth work. Each diocese has a youth pastor. Many churches have their own youth club rooms and parish organizations, maintain more than 100 training centers, or summer houses for youth. Parishes also support junior clubs for children seven to fourteen years of age, boy scout and girl guide groups, and activities for older youth, aged fourteen to twenty.

One of the most popular forms of youth meetings is the so-called open house evening. Approximately 50,000 youths participate annually in such meetings, where such subjects as the Bible and the work of missionaries are discussed. Through this sort of activity, church leaders hope to bring the younger generation closer to the church and to have a stabilizing influence on their growing years.

The Board of Family Affairs of the Church of Finland supervises the family counseling and family education work of the church. There are eight Family Counseling Centers, financed by the local congregations. Half the workers are clergy, the other half are social workers. Each center has a psychiatrist and a lawyer as part-time consultants.

The consultations between the counselors and family members usually concern infidelity, alcoholism, and marital disagreements. Such services reach a much wider segment of the population than just the active members of the congregation.

CHAPTER 7

EDUCATION AND MASS COMMUNICATIONS

Compulsory, high quality education and an extensive mass communications network have diminished the geographic and linguistic differences in Finnish society. Educational reforms are sensitive to the potential effects of the mass media on students in and out of the classroom, and it is widely recognized in a country of substantially total literacy that the media are exceptionally important in the formation of values and attitudes.

Regional imbalances pose the greatest problems for the creation of a national educational and mass communications infrastructure. Schools have been plentiful in the populous and relatively rich southwest, but Lapland and the low-income northeast have been less favored because of their rural situation, distance from Helsinki, and diminishing population. In the late 1960s and early 1970s a number of universities were founded in major cities in central and southern Finland. University expansion is not planned for the north, however, and the lack of facilities encourages migration to the southern university towns. In the early 1970s there were more students at the University of Helsinki than at all the other universities combined.

Newspapers have thrived primarily in large cities where significant concentrations of readers exist. For instance, in the early 1970s only one daily newspaper with a circulation of 28,000 was being published in Rovaniemi, the Lapp capital, whereas fourteen dailies with a total circulation of approximately 900,000 were published in Helsinki. On the other hand, radio and television broadcasting has universalized news dissemination and provided the first medium for reaching the entire country.

Historically the use of Swedish in education and the press has been proportionately greater than the population ratio of Swedes to Finns. Until 1888 Swedish-language newspapers were more numerous than Finnish and had a higher circulation. Swedish continues to be used in the press and broadcasting to a greater extent than the size of the Swedish-speaking minority (about 7 percent) would seem to justify. Swedish has constitutional protection as the second national language. It is the language of instruction at certain elementary and secondary schools and at certain faculties of the University of Helsinki. There is also one Swedish-language university (see ch. 2; ch. 4; ch. 8).

The use of Swedish in elementary schools has not caused much

81

friction because the Swedish-speaking population is concentrated in the western and southwestern coastal areas, and schools in which Swedish is the language of instruction have been established in these major centers alongside Finnish schools, each school stressing the other language as a second tongue. The proportion of Swedish elementary schools in 1969 (310 of a total of 4,600) was roughly the same as the Swedish-speaking percentage of the population.

The rapid development of university centers after 1917 was also Swedish oriented. Of the four major schools founded in the decade after independence, only the University of Turku was Finnish speaking. By the early 1970s, however, Finnish was the principal language of instruction in nearly all Finnish institutions of higher learning.

Reform of the primary school and its impact on the rest of the educational system reflect the basic premise of educational thought—that educational opportunities must be open to all segments of society. For this reason the emphasis on a strong education budget has been widely supported. In 1970 education and culture accounted for 17.3 percent of the national budget.

As in the rest of Scandinavia, Finnish public education has stressed a liberal-arts-oriented curriculum rather than one emphasizing practical studies to meet the demand for technically trained manpower. In fact, Finnish educators have fought vigorously against the trend toward technical training at all levels. This partly explains the continued existence of parallel private and public schools. Private schools often have opted for a technological curriculum and have received state subsidies. Consequently the private schools have been more responsive to the manpower needs of the economy than has the state educational system.

EDUCATION

Administration and Policy

Before independence educational policy was dictated from Stockholm or Saint Petersburg. Although the first major literary work in Finnish, the *Kalevala*, appeared in 1835, the first secondary school teaching in the national language began only in 1858. Five years later the Grand Duchy of Finland was officially made bilingual, although effective use of Finnish in the state administration took a generation (see ch. 2; ch. 8).

Russian objections scuttled the first attempts to make education compulsory, and a formal law to this effect was delayed until 1921. Paragraphs 79 and 80 of the Constitution of 1919 clearly call on the state to provide or subsidize schools, declaring that "instruction in the primary schools shall be free to all." The state therefore took responsibility for financing and supervising elementary education but delegated the burden of actual school construction and administration to communal authorities.

In the late 1960s general education policy was initiated by the Ministry of Education and its committee, the National Board of Schools. Expert committees on particular problems were appointed by the ministry. More indirectly, however, the mass media and citizens' groups influenced educational policy. The Finnish Population and Family Welfare League and the Union of Rural Municipalities were among the most active in educational policy formulation.

In the early 1970s the state owned over half the institutions of higher learning and provided subsidies covering approximately three-fourths of the operating expenses of the private institutions. Curriculum requirements for both public and private institutions, therefore, were set down by the government under a fifteen-year development program that began in 1970. This program provides for minimum increases in expenditures, minimum increases in student places, areas for curriculum expansion, and improved student-teacher ratios.

Education in Society

Traditional problems in Finnish education, such as language differences and the rural-urban imbalance, have receded in recent years, and there are now equal educational opportunities for women, who make up roughly 50 percent of the students in higher education. In place of these issues, new ones have arisen as the points of contention among several social, economic, and political groups.

The primary school reforms are a case in point. For years the socially progressive forces in Finnish society had urged the democratization of the school system. Once the general concept was accepted, the curriculum itself was disputed at every level. In particular, the reform forces challenged the teaching of religion in secular schools, but an alliance spearheaded by church leaders successfully forced the inclusion of compulsory religious education at all primary and secondary school levels.

The discrepancy in the availability of education to students from poor rural backgrounds as compared to those from other segments of the population is most apparent at the highest level. Students of middle and upper class backgrounds account for approximately two-thirds of the student population in the universities, although these groups make up only one-quarter of the total population. Regional discrepancies are also most acute at the university level; in 1965 about 37 percent of the university population was from the province surrounding Helsinki.

Increasing awareness in the late 1960s of the chronic imbalances in Finnish life, expressed particularly in the mass media, has prompted student action for reforms. The National Union of Finnish Students in particular has been responsible for obtaining greater loan and scholarship opportunities for poorer students and for other steps toward democratizing the system.

Demands for qualified manpower in a technological age and the need to emphasize the social sciences in spite of the new era have produced conflicting views as to the goals of higher education. Private interests and the government want more qualified people to fill management and technological posts. Political groups on the Left attack the system for putting too much emphasis on future productive capabilities of students.

The Evangelical Lutheran Church of Finland, to which 93 percent of the population belongs, is active in the field of educational planning. Although it has no official role, certain church requirements have been met by a degree of cooperation between the National Board of Schools and the Lutheran leaders. For example, anyone desiring to be married in church must have taken a confirmation course; therefore, such a course is taught at the expense of the church in all secondary schools. The political tactics of church leaders have also been important in education. Tireless lobbying by Lutheran leaders and laymen was responsible for keeping obligatory religious education in all primary and secondary school classrooms in the reformed educational system instituted in 1968.

Educational Reform and the Comprehensive School

On July 28, 1968, a thorough revision of primary and secondary education was enacted in the Comprehensive School Act. The bulk of the reform is to be fully implemented by 1986, and strict rules for its adoption have been laid down to guide municipal and regional authorities.

The existing two-channel school system selected students at age eleven for entry into two fifth grades: one led to junior, then senior secondary school and eventually, the university; the other, to a four-year "civic" school and ultimately vocational training. The majority of secondary schools were private, however, and charged tuition that many students who passed the secondary school entrance examination were unable to afford. The system discriminated against poorer students and had been attacked since its inception for leading to educational blind alleys for the majority of Finland's youth.

The reform, coming into force on August 1, 1970, called for a nine-year compulsory primary school, giving free, equal, and high-quality education to all. As in other Scandinavian countries, primary schooling was to begin at age seven.

The curriculum itself has been marked by a realization that aesthetic and physical education must be emphasized. For this purpose, at least one-third of the schooltime at any grade level is devoted to art, physical education, music, and practical skills.

The upper grades, five through nine, allow for some choice by the individual student in formulating a study plan. Students are given a choice of concentration among environmental studies and between languages and mathematics. Furthermore, students may pursue subjects at advanced, intermediate, or low levels. This system is expected to allow students to progress rapidly in subjects that interest them without suffering major setbacks in less interesting subjects. It is also aimed at reducing the number of students repeating a class, which is generally seen as a psychological obstacle to further educational development.

Secondary School

The reform program did away with the junior secondary school—the separate grades five through nine that led to the senior secondary school. Upon completion of the nine-year comprehensive school, students are absorbed into either senior secondary schools (grades ten through twelve, sometimes called the gymnasium) or vocational schools.

Curriculum reform in the secondary school has not been prescribed. Students specialize in either languages or mathematics and accordingly take a heavy load of courses in their special subjects. Throughout the educational system Swedish is taught as the first foreign language in Finnish-speaking schools, and Finnish is taught as the first foreign language in Swedish-speaking schools. English is the predominant second foreign language, followed by German, Latin, Russian, and French.

The majority of senior secondary schools are private. In 1969, 364 of 514 such schools were privately owned by local associations of individual citizens, although they were accredited and supervised by the National Board of Schools. State-owned schools charged Fmk50 (for value of the markka—see Glossary) per semester, although in extreme cases of hardship this fee could be waived. Tuition in private schools was often considerably higher, especially when facilities had been expanded without government subsidies, that is, beyond the limits of the National Board of Schools development program.

Vocational Training

The parallel system of post-comprehensive school vocational education was centered on the general vocational schools and a complex of technical and commercial colleges. A 1959 law on vocational schooling required each municipality to participate in the creation and maintenance of a vocational school. Ten years later, 168 state-sponsored schools were providing a three-year curriculum to approximately 42,700 students.

In the traditional two-channel school system it was difficult for students committed to vocational training to continue their studies at universities. In the early 1970s, however, increasing flexibility in educational policy was making it possible for examinations of the same level from different kinds of institutions to be accepted equally by higher institutions.

Equally important for the country's overall commercial and technical development were the approximately 170 schools and colleges giving specific training in commercial and technical fields. The schools provided an initial two- or three-year training period after completion of the comprehensive school. The colleges offered two- to four-year programs for more advanced instruction—in engineering or management, for example.

These institutes usually were privately run under the supervision of the particular ministries whose national responsibilities related to the kinds of training offered. Business schools, for example, were supervised by the Ministry of Commerce and Industry. By the end of the 1970s, however, it was expected that parliamentary action would consolidate supervisory control of vocational institutes under the Ministry of Education. In the early 1970s approximately 60 to 75 percent of the operating expenses of the technical and commerical institutes were covered by government subsidies.

Teacher Training

Primary school teachers were usually trained at one of the eleven teachers schools or four teachers colleges. The former provided a four- to six-year course for graduates of the comprehensive school. The latter offered a two-year program after completion of the secondary school matriculation examination. Ministry of Education committees dealing with the training of teachers have set as a goal the requirements of passing the secondary matriculation examination and completing a four-year teachers college course for teaching in the comprehensive school.

Secondary school teachers were required to have a university degree and a one-year training course. Business attracted the bulk of such highly qualified people through higher salaries, however, and only 55 percent of secondary school teachers had the prescribed credentials.

Higher Education

In 1972 degree courses in higher education were being offered at sixteen university centers, and a seventeenth university, in Kuopio, was to open in the mid-1970s. In 1969 more than half the students in higher education were enrolled at the University of Helsinki. This figure was expected to level off at 45 percent by 1981, when 17 percent of Finland's university population would be studying in Turku, 30 percent at Oulu, Tampere, and Jyväskylä, and 8 or 9 percent in the new complex of higher institutes in eastern Finland.

All university students are required to pass university entrance examinations. The demand for higher education meant that acceptance was not guaranteed on the basis of the secondary-school-leaving examination alone. In 1969 approximately 17,000 students passed the matriculation examination, but total admissions to higher education were just under 10,000. Ministry of Education projections indicated that, by

1981, 70 percent of secondary school graduates were expected to enter the university system. In 1972 there were approximately 55,000 students enrolled in higher institutes. This number was expected to jump to 74,000 by 1981.

In 1972 more than half the university students were studying the humanities, social sciences, economics, law, physical education, or theology. Roughly one-fourth of the student population (12,000 students) were studying mathematics, natural sciences, agriculture, or forestry. Approximately 11,000 students were studying technology, engineering, or medicine.

From 1967 to 1981 the number of students in higher education was expected to grow by 3.6 percent a year. Emphasis was being placed on medicine and technology at the expense of the social sciences and humanities. In fact, the number of technology students was expected to grow by approximately 5.5 percent a year. Studies in 1970 projected over 12,000 technology students in 1981, compared to 7,200 in 1972. The rate of increase in the liberal arts was not expected to surpass 1.2 percent a year.

More than half of the higher education centers were state owned, but all received state subsidies covering the major portion of their budgets. The universities were tuition free, and subsistence funds (outright grants and low-interest loans) were available to needy students.

It generally takes five to six years to obtain the first academic degree, three additional years for the master's degree, and an additional three years for the doctorate. It has been calculated that from 65 to 90 percent of the new students each year never finish the first degree.

Adult Education

The largest system providing adult education is that of state-subsidized folk high schools, which conduct six-month courses in literature, history, and sociology. Parallel to these schools are the physical education centers where social studies and current events supplement the athletics curriculum. Both types of institutes are state financed and provide boarding facilities for course participants.

Evening courses have been widely recognized as the best way to provide continuing education. The municipally administered civic and workers' institutes offered courses at 229 locations throughout the country in 1970, and almost a quarter of a million people participated in them. The state also provided evening courses for adults to study part time for the secondary school matriculation examination. These courses and the vocational courses organized by the state shared the facilities of secondary schools. A total of more than 20,000 adults participated in one or more courses.

The third major attempt at a structured adult education system is undertaken by the universities. Although a sprinkling of evening courses is offered, the emphasis is on the "summer university" program. This involves the establishment of summer institutes that offer credit courses for university students and anyone who applies. It was estimated that in 1969 roughly 30,000 people attended these "open-air universities."

Broadcasting also provided facilities for adult education. In 1970 an adult education section was created within the Finnish Broadcasting Corporation (Oy Yleisradio Ab), and in 1972 it was producing four major television programs a year. Language courses on television and radio were much more numerous.

Methods of Education

The full effects of the reform of primary education had not been fully felt as of early 1973. At that time about 58 percent of primary schools had only one or two teachers, and teaching usually followed traditional methods—that is, an authoritarian teacher and learning by rote and "fact" rather than "thought" learning. Creative thinking, free experimentation, and a reduced emphasis on classroom competition were planned but were not yet the rule.

The mass media also were affecting educational methods by supplementing the traditional teacher-student relationship. Broadcasting often was the first outside influence on a child, in rural as well as developed regions. It was a child's first teacher and thus reduced the gap between children growing up under very different socioeconomic circumstances.

Radio and television were playing an increasing role in classrooms, where programs could reach very large numbers of students simultaneously. Prerecorded programs also supplemented the teacher to a great extent.

MASS COMMUNICATIONS

In 1968, 98 percent of Finnish households had radios, and 76 percent owned television sets. Eighty-five percent of the adult population read at least one newspaper a day, and the same number read at least one periodical a week. Seventy percent read books, averaging three or four per person during the year.

The press has found such a wide readership partly because the population is almost 100 percent literate. Widespread interest in the media has also stemmed from the political content they have had since the years preceding independence.

Until World War II the printed media monopolized mass communications. Newspapers and periodicals flourished, particularly in the densely populated southwest, and books of all types were published. Radio and television broadcasting, on their initial appearance, only temporarily muted the appeal of printed material for the reading public.

The Press

Finland's first newspaper, in Swedish, was published in 1771. Toward the end of the 1840s, the first successful Finnish-language newspaper was established in Helsinki. Nonetheless, the educated elite continued to read the Swedish-language newspapers, and in 1860 circulation for Finnish-language newspapers still was less than half that of their Swedish counterparts. In the early 1970s few newspapers of national scope were published outside Helsinki, and journalistic activity continued to be strongly centralized in the capital. There were no newspaper chains and only a handful of evening newspapers.

The number of newspapers reached a high of 123 in 1930, although 60 percent of these put out only three editions weekly. In 1971 there were eighty-eight newspapers, of which a large number were published at least thrice weekly. Their total circulation remained relatively constant at about 2 million through the 1960s and early 1970s. The size of newspapers increased tremendously, however, in the 1960s. The consumption of paper by newspapers totaled 67,000 metric tons in the early 1970s, a jump of 40,000 tons over the figure a decade earlier.

The trend toward concentration in the south has not hurt the local newspapers. The geographic distribution of newspapers in 1970 shows that publishing in the northern areas is underdeveloped, and this has always been the case. Helsinki newspapers still account for one-third of the entire industry's circulation, but their growth has stagnated for over two decades.

Periodicals other than newspapers have always been an important alternative for municipal and regional communities without the resources necessary to publish daily. The development of periodicals has been uneven at best, particularly in wartime, when economic austerity and paper rationing first hit the less well-to-do local publishers. Nonetheless, the number of periodicals in 1970 was approximately 1,750, or nine times the figure for 1900. The biggest boom in this literature came in the 1950s with postwar prosperity and the proliferation of trade and professional journals.

The privately owned commercial press depends on advertising income to meet publishing costs. Half the daily press and almost all of the periodical press is commercial. The country's largest newspaper, the *Helsingin Sanomat* (circulation, 277,500 in January 1971), is a Helsinki-based national commercial daily. The commercial press is nonpartisan but, like most of Finland's industry, it has a conservative bias.

The Political Press

The emergence of a political press began when the nationalist movement swept the country in the 1860s, and Finnish newspapers became platforms for elevating the role of the Finnish language. Russian censorship moved the Finns to fight harder, and the news media became the battleground between the conservative, Swedish-speaking elite and the nationalists. New journals were founded as the movement grew more radical, and the first modern party and workers' press emerged at the turn of the century with the publication of *Työmies*, aimed at the new industrial working class.

The party press boomed, and the number of party-backed daily newspapers increased to 105 in 1918. Then the newspapers were hit hard for both political and economic reasons. During the civil war of 1918, the country was geographically divided; the leftist press could not print in the south, and the rightist press was banned from the north. In 1930 the Finnish Communist Party was censured and with it the communist press, only to be replaced by extreme rightist propaganda for the Lapua Movement (see ch. 2). By 1971 the number of political newspapers had declined to thirty-nine (see table 2).

Table 2. Number of Newspapers Published by Political Parties in Finland, 1971

Publisher	Issues per Week					Total
	7	6	5	4	3	
Finnish Social Democratic Party	1	3	2	1	3	10
Finnish People's Democratic League	1	–	2	–	3	6
Finnish Rural Party	–	–	1	–	–	1
National Coalition Party...........................	6	1	–	–	–	7
Center Party	6	7	1	–	–	14
Simonist splinter of the Social Democratic Party	–	–	1	–	–	1

Source: Adapted from Torsten Steinby, *In Quest of Freedom: Finland's Press 1771–1971*, Helsinki, 1971.

In 1970 more than half (approximately 1,028,000) of the total volume of newspaper circulation was party affiliated. The National Coalition Party and the Center Party together controlled three-fourths of all party-supported newspapers; each also received about 18 percent of the popular vote in the 1970 general elections and controlled a similar percentage of the entire newspaper circulation in that year. In contrast, the circulation of Left-oriented newspapers (combined Finnish Social Democratic Party, Finnish People's Democratic League, and Communist Party) fell short of 250,000, or just 10.9 percent of the total newspaper circulation in Finland. The leftist parties, however, captured over 40 percent of the popular vote that year. These figures are the basis for claims by the Left that moderate conservative forces control over 89 percent of the press in Finland.

Radio and Television

Administration and Financing

The Finnish Broadcasting Corporation is the sole licensed broadcasting company. It began full-scale operation in 1926, but television programming did not emerge until 1958. About 93 percent of its shares are state owned, and its activities are supervised by an administrative council composed of members of Parliament. This council selects a nine-member board of directors and names a director general. Therefore, the higher administration usually reflects the ideological balance existing in Parliament.

There are three programming councils, one for Finnish radio, one for Finnish television, and one for all broadcasting in Swedish. The councils set program standards, which are implemented by the program sections in cooperation with the engineering, administrative, and economic sections. Programming sections are in charge of producing material in specific areas, such as education, culture and art, and news. Swedish programming is dealt with separately on all levels and is guaranteed by law a position relative to the size of the Swedish-speaking population. In 1973 the Swedish share of the total budget was almost 20 percent, although the Swedish-speaking population numbers about 7 percent of the entire country.

A long-range planning and research staff was created in 1966 by the board of directors. This staff outlined a set of goals for the media in 1967, and in 1968 it put forth a development scheme to be implemented by 1980. The annual budget for research and administration was Fmk588,000, the equivalent of US$140,000 in 1969.

Broadcasting funds derive from two major sources: radio and television license fees and commercial advertising. A radio license costs Fmk20 per year, and the television fee is Fmk80 per year. The fees are collected by the Post and Telegraph Administration, the government revenue service. With approximately 1.7 million radio licensees in 1970 and 1 million television sets, this kind of funding covered about four-fifths of the company's operating expenses.

Commercial television programs account for the other fifth of the total revenue. A private company, Oy Mainos-TV-Reklam Ab, is licensed to buy program time from the public company for showing on the second national network (only used for commercial television). Roughly one-third of the daily programming on Finnish television is produced by commercial television; these programs are primarily for entertainment, and a maximum of 15 percent of the air time can be used for advertising. Most of the foreign television films and serials are broadcast on commercial television, although Oy Mainos-TV does produce original programs by renting facilities from the public company.

In 1969 an average of 365.4 hours of radio and 63.5 hours of television were presented weekly, a larger volume than anywhere else in Scandinavia. Color transmission began in 1967 and by 1972 reached an average of twelve hours per week.

Programming

In 1968 about 40 percent of radio broadcasting time was devoted to light entertainment, particularly music (36 percent); about 27 percent, to arts, letters, and sciences; 23 percent, to information (news, public affairs); about 3 percent, to educational broadcasts; and 7 percent, to religious, children's, and other programs. During the same year, 43 percent of television time was devoted to information programs; 34 percent, to light entertainment; 10 percent, to children's and religious programs; 7 percent, to arts, letters, and sciences; and about 6 percent, to education.

Educational Programming

The Finnish Broadcasting Corporation has been concerned with the educational and cultural content of its programming since its inception. School radio began in 1934; school television, in 1962; media language instruction, in 1963; and adult education programs, in 1965. It was not until 1966 that all educational programming came under a single department, the Education Programs Section.

There are four major production units in the Education Programs Section: school radio, school television, language instruction, and adult education. Planning is very important, especially if the programs are to supplement classroom instruction. The Education Programs Section maintains contacts with individual educators as well as teacher and parent organizations. Long-range planning is conducted by the corporation's staff. In February 1972 a joint policy board was set up to institutionalize contacts between the Ministry of Education and the Education Programs Section. Beginning in 1973 the ministry will subsidize programming intended to complement classroom teaching in particular subjects.

School programming is transmitted in the morning, and language and adult education programs are shown during the evening. School programs are limited to twenty or twenty-five minutes and aim at specific age groups. The Finnish Broadcasting Corporation broadcast in 1970 a total of 198 hours of educational television programs and 373 hours of educational radio programs. In 1973 about 22 percent of the total broadcasting budget went for Swedish programming, and Swedish programs accounted for about one-third of the total school broadcasts.

Educational discrepancies between north and south were expected to be a prime target of the Education Programs Section through the 1970s. Similarily, the corporation's long-range planning staff was planning for a decentralization of broadcasting, so that regional centers eventually might cater more to the needs of particular regions. The economic constraints on such a development in the 1970s were prohibitive.

Full-scale production of education video cassettes and similar devices was expected before 1980. In the early 1970s the Finnish Broadcasting Corporation could only supplement its aired programs with a small volume of printed material. Taped programs, however, would revolutionize Finnish education; first, because emphasis could be placed on overcoming regional deficiencies; second, because a program could be shown at an appropriate time in the day's curriculum; and last, because the economic constraints of expensive broadcast air time would no longer apply. The use of such programs in classrooms would be under the control of the Ministry of Education. The Finnish Broadcasting Corporation wanted to be able to plan its own programming with the new technology and had applied for sole rights to produce educational video cassettes. The private sector, which had already begun developing the necessary instruments, was fighting for an equal share of the future market. In 1972 it looked as though the private interests would triumph, primarily because of the increasingly strained relations between the government and the broadcasting company.

Media Impact and Preference

The few authoritative surveys that have been taken, primarily at the University of Tampere, show that public preference for a particular means of mass communication is rooted in education; the more formal and lengthy a person's educational background, the more time he spends with newspapers for general knowledge and with books and films for entertainment. Contact with the media is inescapable; less than 1 percent of the population goes for a week without encountering the media.

Less than ten years after its inception in Finland, television broadcasting had become an important medium for entertainment and instruction. Although it may be too early to judge the impact of television on Finnish society, broadcasting in general has not greatly reduced the importance of the printed word. The press remains the primary source of news and current events, whereas the electronic media supplement the cultural pastimes. The actual importance of each medium is difficult to estimate. It is widely recognized, however, that the newspaper strike of 1967 caused the public much greater discomfort than the 1966 television strike.

The Foreign Presence

The quantity of foreign films, magazines, television shows, and recordings is substantial. Approximately 40 percent of all television programming is foreign made; 95 percent of all films shown in Finland come from abroad, as do 60 percent of the phonograph records. There is a preponderance of material from the United States and Western Europe, although Soviet and Eastern European films have cornered a respectable 30 percent of the film market. The American influence is felt primarily in films, records, and broadcasting. On television an average of three American series are broadcast each season. Furthermore, the Voice of America can be received more than fifteen hours a day in most parts of Finland.

Sweden also remains an important media exporter for Finland, particularly in the entertainment field, followed by Great Britain, the Federal Republic of Germany (West Germany), and France. The size of this foreign presence is a reflection of the constitutional guarantees of press freedom. In cases of extreme political sensitivity (as for the publishing of Alexander Solzhenitsyn's *August 1914* in Finland), the government has been known to delay publication until a high degree of international acceptance makes the impact less crucial.

Conflicts and Freedom of the Media

Freedom of the press was a basic tenet of the Constitution of 1919, which guaranteed that no advance censorship by government could be placed on written material. The provision still holds true, although on moral grounds the government may censor in advance the visual media, such as films.

There is also a 1948 provision for punishment in the case of journalistic defamation of foreign states. This supplement to the criminal code of that year has never been invoked; it was passed as a reminder to the press of the delicate balance to be maintained with the Soviet Union (see ch. 2; ch. 11). In fact, the media has been characterized by a general reluctance to criticize the Soviet Union; there are no restraints on criticism of Western countries.

The large amount of political publishing has made the Finnish press vulnerable to charges of mudslinging in the past. A "code of honor" for journalists was initiated in 1957 by the Finnish Association of Journalists. It was not until 1968, however, that the Board of Opinion for Mass Media was created to hear and act on complaints of mistreatment by the media. The Finnish Broadcasting Corporation, journalists, publishers, and the public are represented on this board. If a complaint is deemed justified, all contracting parties agree to publish a reprimand of the culpable party.

The major conflicts in mass communications in the late 1960s and early 1970s were confined to the emergent broadcasting media and the path chosen for their development. Under a Left-dominated Parliament, the Administrative Council of the Finnish Broadcasting Corporation and the board of directors opted for an active participation in the broadcasting media in the national life. The tenets of their development programs have often been reiterated; that is, that although "radio and television should not try to implant any particular theory of life in the mind of the audience, . . . broadcasting ought to be a live and active factor in the community to which it belongs, consciously inspiring discussion." This activation of broadcasting meant a new emphasis on education, current events, and political discussion, away from the staple entertainment emphasis of the media.

The champions of activism recognized that it would entail a politicization of the media, giving an equal balance to all political biases. To certain broadcasters this meant that a political balance should be established in the mass media in general and that a leftist slant in broadcasting would be justified because conservative forces controlled the bulk of the printed media.

The radical line became most prominent in cultural programming, particularly in television theater. Public opinion became polarized, and Finnish Broadcasting Corporation surveys show that public trust in broadcasting increased among left-wing voters from 1965 to 1970 and decreased among conservative voters.

The so-called information war reached a climax at the March 1970 general elections. The conservative elements, backed by private industry, the church, and small farmers, made the Finnish Broadcasting Corporation an electoral issue; in that year the slide to the Right, and the rise of the Finnish Rural Party, clearly showed that the public responded unfavorably to the corporation's reforms. A new, more conservative Administrative Council has cracked down on so-called radical broadcasting, even to the point of reprimanding the long-time director general, Eino S. Repo, for allowing a sharply political news broadcast to be aired.

The information war continued into the early 1970s. The influence of the media, like that of the educational system, was just being fully explored. Awareness of socioeconomic discrepancies increased as the communications network expanded, and it appeared likely that education and the mass media, in the name of democratization, would continue to be battlefields for the political forces in Finnish society.

CHAPTER 8

ARTISTIC AND
INTELLECTUAL DEVELOPMENT

Finnish artistic and intellectual development achieved a truly national style and a momentum of its own by the latter half of the nineteenth century. The nationalist movement was the primary catalyst in stimulating the arts and letters, which had been dormant during Finland's 600-year subordination to Sweden. It has been aptly observed that "Finnish art has a long past and a short history." A vigorous and anonymous folk art had existed for thousands of years, but conscious and independent artistic activity developed only after release from Swedish domination and strengthened as russification was imposed. The headway made by nationalism and cultural development during this period strongly supported the claim for independence in 1917. In fact, Finnish culture and nationalism reinforced each other to such a degree that Finnish arts and letters matured directly from infancy into a golden age, whose influence prevailed a century later.

The appearance at the right moment of gifted and inspired individuals was more responsible than broad-based movements for the cultural flowering, which was marked by the effort of Finnish artists and intellectuals to develop a national idiom. Although artists took on quasi-political roles, their works were not parochial or limited in their appeal to Finnish audiences.

The Finnish disposition to individuality, combined with geographic, commercial, and cultural isolation from the mainstream of both Western and Eastern cultures, has allowed Finnish artists to choose from outside influences and to cultivate the Finnish taste for the simple and the functional. Until the economy became fully industrialized in the mid-twentieth century, there was no firm economic basis for the continuing support of creative work. The state has generally been encouraging but has been limited in the support it could offer, and private sources of patronage and support have been lacking. Finland does not have sizable cities or a café society, which in Europe were the forcing grounds for art. In Finland, then, the artist has been relatively unencumbered by artistic canon and has had a measure of artistic freedom rarely found in other civilized and established societies.

Although some artistic activity has become institutionalized with the establishment of government and university departments and juries awarding state prizes, Finnish arts and letters have only occasionally become overtly political in message or purpose. Artists and intellectuals were so valuable to the nationalist movement that opting for the creative life is considered a natural, and not an effete, aspiration. Artists and intellectuals of the post-World War II period have been departing from the nationalist tradition, which they sometimes dub *tuohityö* (birch-bark work), but they do not fully reject it. Since nationhood was achieved and a coordinated artistic effort was no longer necessary, the cultural atmosphere has been more open to influences from outside and to artistic experimentation and intellectual debate at home.

THE KALEVALA

The national epic, the *Kalevala*, which recounts the struggles of the men of the earth—farmers, fishermen, smiths, and magicians—in primeval Finland, exerts a pervasive and traceable influence on all the arts and occupies an enduring place in the public imagination. The *Kalevala* is not an epic in the conventional sense—an episodic tale of ancient authorship glorifying the action world of demigods—but it is a synthetic epic welded together by the nineteenth-century intellectual, Elias Lönnrot, from existing vernacular lore. It unites Finns of all generations in its tragic sense of life, its ironic humor, and its praise of hospitality and of intelligence over force. Except for occasional disparagement by the youth, the Finns still venerate the *Kalevala* as a timeless creation of art and life symbolizing the qualities that have enabled them to survive. Despite the many passages of incantations and magic, the *Kalevala* abounds in practical anecdotes and is infused with the light of common sense. Its spirit, if not democratic, is at least antiaristocratic.

The origins of the word *kalevala* lie in ancient folklore. Variants of the tales that compose the *Kalevala* were passed by word of mouth and elaborated since pre-Christian times by bards reciting runic poetry.

The majority of the poems of *Kalevala* are about the relations, both in peace and war, between two tribes, the Kalevala and the Pohjola. The leader of the Kalevala tribe is the old and steadfast bard and shaman, Väinämöinen, whose plotting, wooing, and enchanting constitute one-third of the poems. Other principals are the amorous adventurer and reckless warrior, Lemminkäinen, and the mighty smith, Ilmarinen. The Pohjola in the Northland is led by an autocratic woman, Louhi, who has a daughter so lovely that she is courted by the sun, the moon, the stars—and Väinämöinen. The tribes struggle with each other for possession of the sampo, a talisman. One of the most grisly, and yet touching, stories deals with Lemminkäinen's adventures and death by hacking at the hands of the Pohjola. His mother, a popular symbol of maternal love, pulls her mutilated son from a river, pieces his body together, and with spells and supplications to the Almighty, restores his life. Another episode tells of the tragic Kullervo, who drives his sister to suicide, makes war on family members, and dies by his own hand.

Compiling of *Kalevala* material into a single epic began in the 1820s. Careful recording of the performances of chanters was undertaken by Finns of all walks of life, including students who devoted summer vacations to it. The activity was promoted by contests, among those collecting this poetry, and it was inspired by the trend in nineteenth-century philosophical thought that sought to base the national culture on a great epic embodying folk consciousness.

The most avid and scholarly collector was Elias Lönnrot, a country doctor who trekked into eastern Karelia as far as Archangel to record the living oral tradition, which by then had weakened in western and southern Finland. Originally convinced that the poems were fragments of a homogeneous epic narrative along the lines of the *Iliad*, Lönnrot later discovered his mistake and collated the fragments into a body amounting to 23,000 lines having only a minimum of connecting material written in. In Lönnrot's conception, the *Kalevala* begins with the creation of the world and ends with the birth of Christ. The denouement tells of the departure of Väinämöinen, who sees himself as an anachronism with the advent of Christianity.

The *Kalevala* was published in 1835 and has been translated into more than thirty languages. The rhythm of the work, in English translation, resembles Longfellow's *Song of Hiawatha*, which in turn was inspired by a German translation of the *Kalevala*.

With the publication of the *Kalevala* the general citizenry as well as the intelligentsia grew increasingly proud of their literary heritage and confident of their cultural future, impressed by the fact that the creation sprang from a popular and unlettered, rather than a narrowly intellectual, source. The Finnish language—and thereby, Finnish literature—gained a new appeal in its viability and color. Creative artists drew inspiration from the old motifs, and politicians and educators saw in the epic a rallying point for the nationalist movement, especially as russification was more intensively imposed at the end of the century.

LITERATURE AND POETRY

Publication of the *Kalevala* reassured the Finns of the quality of their heritage of oral poetry, but the possibilities of a creative literary language were yet to be realized. Finnish and Swedish critics were skeptical. Until the middle of the nineteenth century, Swedish was the predominant language of all cultural life.

A radical change, however, came with the publication in 1870 of *Seven Brothers* (Finnish title, *Seitsemän Veljestä*), by Aleksis Kivi. Kivi, a self-educated man, traveled within only a few miles' radius of his home; he suffered long, disabling periods of depression and finally became psychotic. Yet it was he who set Finnish literary standards by developing style; he created characters and dialogue that have entered the popular consciousness. Kivi's highly allegorical work galvanized the Finnish-language movement and the nation-building process, exemplifying Ezra Pound's idea that "literature is language charged with meaning." *Seven Brothers* is the most cherished novel in Finland.

The story tells of seven brothers who react against the narrow discipline of village life—and its compulsory education—to opt for life in the forest. Back in nature they develop their own economy, but each gradually becomes convinced of the need to civilize himself by becoming a solid citizen and a dutiful father. *Seven Brothers*, which has been translated into English, was not only the starting point of modern Finnish literature, but its realism and its humorous tone were revolutionary departures from the growing tendency to idealize the Finn. Kivi's influence and position in Finnish literature has been compared to that of Mark Twain in American literature.

The church was of paramount importance in promoting literacy and inculcating respect for the printed word among the peasantry. The requirement that all candidates for confirmation and marriage be able to read and write, albeit in an archaic form of Finnish, was largely responsible for the strong generalized response to the national movement when it came. Moreover, because the vocabulary of Finnish is relatively simple, even the classics are accessible to every reader.

Women have made important contributions to Finnish literature of the modern period. Two of the best known women authors are Maria Jatuni, whose works include short stories, novels and plays; and Arno Kallas, whose works have been translated into English.

The chief proselytizer of the Finnish language was Johan Snellman, who stimulated the nationalist movement in the 1840s with his literary journal *Saimaa*; like most Finnish-language organs, it was periodically proscribed by the government. Later, as a statesman, Snellman was a key figure in the passage of the Language Decree of 1863, which put Finnish on equal footing with Swedish.

Even the two men most instrumental to the nationalist movement, poet Johan Ludvig Runeberg and educator Zachris Topelius, wrote exclusively in Swedish. Runeberg achieved great renown because of his patriotic poems; Topelius made his greatest impact through children's books. The best known of the latter's works was entitled *A Book About Our Country*, which earned him the endearment, "Uncle Topelius."

Themes important in the last decade of the nineteenth century occupy the attention of writers and readers living in a decidedly different world nearly a century later. A timeless theme in Finnish belles lettres and poetry is man's closeness to, even oneness with, nature. Industrial man, who made his first appearance in Finnish literature in the 1930s, is treated as an endangered species who stands to lose his vital ties with nature. A related theme treats loneliness and spiritual isolation, the rigors of which frequently lead to insanity, alcoholism, or suicide. Another theme focuses on the inner Dostoevskian man who achieves consciousness only through suffering. Some writers protest social and political ordering, often to an antisocial, anarchic degree. There is a genre of literature that portrays the frustrations of the worker. The political and social debate, coming to a head in the 1970s, over women's rights had been forcefully advocated as early as the 1890s.

The subject of the civil war of 1918 has come under literary and scholarly scrutiny only since the end of World War II. During the year of the conflict, however, Frans Eemil Sillanpää, a realist and pacifist, in his book *Meek Heritage*, took a typically Finnish look—"with both eyes"—at the two sides. His monistic view, representative of many other realists, saw man as part of nature and subject to its laws; hence, the differences that made men enemies were only artificial. At the time of his death in 1964 he was a patriarchal figure, even though his productivity had slackened considerably by 1939 when he was honored with the Nobel Prize in literature.

The weakening of anti-Russian feeling stemming from the nineteenth century has allowed literary energies to be directed inward to self-criticism. Novelists and historians of the post-World War II period have shown no reluctance to investigate another sensitive period of Finnish history—the period between the two world wars. Some writers of the "new" history consider the interwar period to have been a reactionary time when fascist tendencies and nationalism permitted eventual cooperation with the Germans against the Soviets in the Continuation War from 1941 through 1944.

The publication in 1954 of *The Unknown Soldier*, by Väinö Linna, sparked a feud engaging the entire population in what has been called "Finland's Literary Continuation War." His criticism of the platitudes and pedantry of officers and front-line Lottas (women volunteers) is expressed through the communication between the young draftees of a machinegun platoon. Linna presented the image of individual and national prowess in desperate circumstances, but he depicted the Finnish soldier as man and not hero, in a spirit similar to that of *The Naked and the Dead* by Norman Mailer. Linna, born in 1920, won the Literary Prize of the Nordic Council in 1963, the second year it was awarded.

The highly critical attitude of many young writers, particularly since the 1960s, has prompted a retrenchment of literary criticism and a tightening of state censorship. Paavo Rintala came in for harsh attacks questioning his patriotism when his rather unflattering portrait of Carl Gustaf von Mannerheim was completed in trilogy form in 1962. Rintala and other protagonists of social change arouse a sometimes hostile reaction from the public, which does not tolerate ideas even faintly Marxist-socialist. The first charge of blasphemy lodged since 1927 was brought against Hannu Salama and his publisher, Otava, in 1964. The charge was made by members of the Conservative Party and by the archbishop of Turku; they alleged that certain passages of Salama's *Midsummer Dances*, mainly about youth agonizing between city and country, offended the religious feelings of Christians. Despite the support given him by the literati, Salama was convicted and imprisoned.

The continuing study and collecting of folk poetry began in the 1760s. Henrik Gabriel Porthan—historian, man of letters, and professor at Turku Academy—published one of the first scholarly works on folk poetry, *De Poesi Fennica*. Two centuries later the Finnish Literature Society's folk poetry archives, which include tape recordings of live recitations, were among the largest in the world. Independent creative poetry in Finnish, however, developed with difficulty. Finnish poets of the nineteenth century were still shaping and refining the written language which, although rich in metaphor and having many vowels, did not lend itself easily to borrowed meters and rhyme schemes or to the unrhymed trochaic meter of native folk poetry. By the turn of the century, however, the craftsmanship and intellectuality of poet Eino Leino had rendered the literary language more manageable and lyrical.

Modernism, with its imagery and unrhymed free verse, was introduced in the 1920s by Swede-Finn poets. The experimentation of the Finnish modernist group, along with the inflow of international influences, combined to produce an increase in volume and improvement of quality in Finnish modernist poetry. The country caught up quickly to the movement that had been current in Europe for thirty years. Since the 1960s a number of experimentalist poets have become even more spontaneous and colloquial in style and more political and social in orientation. The title of Pentti Saarikoski's important work is "What Is Really Happening?" One of his poems conceives of political Finland as a big bird flying backwards, cawing "Kto Kovo, Kto Kovo"—Russian for "Who Whom, Who Whom?" Saarikoski himself is unique—he is the first Finnish writer of completely urban origin.

Modern Finnish poetry (dating from the 1950s) generates unusual pride among a people with a long tradition of oral folk poetry. It has been called "the secret treasure of contemporary European literature," an allusion both to its quality and to its linguistic isolation.

Generally conceded to be the foremost poet of the post-World War II period is Paavo Haavikko, whose work first appeared in 1951 when he was twenty. In being less consciously bound to Finland than other artists, Haavikko has had immeasurable impact on postwar poetry, and his nine-poem cycle, *Winter Palace* (1959), is considered the most important volume of poetry published in the past two decades. About half of Finland's writers and poets are women, and one of the most important is Eeva-Liisa Manner, whose subject of study is the nature of the human ego.

Such is the interest in poetry that most poets can reasonably expect to see their work not only published as small volumes but run for several editions. Consequently, aside from the influential bimonthly literary magazine *Parnasso*, there are relatively few "little" literary reviews, which elsewhere serve as stage and audience for poets. Perhaps this accounts for the relatively underdeveloped function of literary criticism.

The volume of book publishing in Finland, for a country of its size, was enormous. In 1972 the industry brought out 4,500 titles, in a combined total of 20 million copies. In proportion to the population, this was one of the highest rates of production in the world. Three book publishing giants are distinguished by their size. The three largest, Werner Söderström and Otava and Tammi, release as many as 1,800 titles each annually. Many serious works are serialized in the popular magazines.

Because of the complexities of the Finnish language, only a few dozen titles of fiction and poetry have been translated into English. American readers are familiar with *The Egyptian* and *The Etruscan* and other novels by Mika Waltari, world famous historical novelist and member of the Academy of Finland since 1957. More works are translated into German, which is resuming its pre-World War I role of prime mediator of all the Scandinavian languages. Important foreign works are readily translated into Finnish, frequently by writers and poets themselves.

Public demand for literature is sizable and constant. In addition to their nearly 100-percent literacy rate, the Finns, along with the Icelanders, claim to be the heaviest buyers and readers of good literature in the world. The country has more than 700 bookstores, and one of the many book clubs has 170,000 members, the equivalent of more than 10 percent of all households. It is not unusual to find 100 volumes on the shelves of a worker's home. In literature, as in other arts, amateurs ply publishers with their creations. Books are sold everywhere, from the largest bookshop in Europe—the Akateeminen Kirjakauppa (designed by Alvar Aalto), which serves the University of Helsinki and the city—to the remotest village and the quietest railway station..

THEATER

From its inception, theater in Finland has been created by the people for the people's entertainment, and—owing to the remarkable liveliness of the amateur theater movement—it has been in large part a theater in which acting is performed by the people. This state of things is a logical outgrowth of conditions existing in the 1830s when the Finnish-language theater was germinating and in the 1860s when real growth got underway.

Theater and music were ready outlets for the early expression of national feelings. Finnish-language plays and the growing number of companies with Finnish actors directly reinforced the general efforts at establishing the Finnish language as the vernacular while at the same time the Swedish-speaking minority fostered its own theater.

The first Finnish-language professional theater, known simply as the Finnish Theater, heightened general cultural and linguistic consciousness by touring the country from 1872, the year of its founding, up to the early twentieth century. The organization lengthened its name to the Finnish National Theater in 1902. The founding of a national theater before a theater tradition had developed is the reverse of the sequence that usually occurs in other countries.

At the turn of the century the growing workers' movements and the youth club movement enthusiastically supported the theater. The workers and the students have been as avid as the intellectuals in their attendance and in their willingness to act onstage. Because almost all theaters have been subsidized and box-office considerations therefore have not been determinative, the Finnish theater has been able to present an unusual number of premieres and experimental productions.

The civil war of 1918 divided the sentiments of the population into two camps. This division of society was maintained through the interwar period and was reflected in the coexistence of a bourgeois theater and a workers theater. Following World War II most of these theaters merged for economic reasons and became city or municipal theaters. In the industrial city of Tampere, however, the Tampere Workers' Theater survived and has been a major influence in the Finnish drama world. With its new ideas in production and themes, Tampere also has been unique for its open-air Pyynikki Summer Theater, which uses as a backdrop its beautiful surroundings of water, forest, and hillside by rotating the audience on an electrically powered turntable. This successful innovation was the first of its kind in the world.

Amateur theater has been funded by subsidies, receipts, and, importantly, private individuals. Most amateur groups have been affiliated with three central organizations of their own, which have supplied them with scripts and teams of directors and coaches. That the theater never has been an elitist amusement is shown not only by the existence and vitality of the amateur movement but also by the cooperation between professional and amateur actors, most readily seen in the semi-professional theaters having a permanent staff of two or three full-time members, backed by a host of "evening actors."

The Finnish theater had its antecedents principally in the seventeenth and eighteenth century tours made by foreign troupes from Sweden, Germany, Russia, and France. In 1872 a polemical piece by playwright and journalist Kaarlo Bergbom stimulated local interest in drama. Bergbom sensed the significance of Aleksis Kivi as the first writer and dramatist working in the Finnish language, and thus he included in the Finnish National Theater's repertoire all of Kivi's stageable plays. Most of them, such as *Kullervo* (a tragedy based on the *Kalevala*), *The Country Cobblers*, and a dramatized version of Kivi's novel, *Seven Brothers*, dealt with Finnish themes. Bergbom was also instrumental in promoting the realist plays of social-minded Minna

Canth (1844–97), whose plays continued in the early 1970s to be in the repertoire of most major and minor theaters in Finland. The characterizations and themes of these two dramatists have endeared themselves to Finnish audiences and have continued to receive fresh productions.

The Finnish public early displayed an affinity for Shakespeare's works, and by 1912 Paavo Kajander had translated into Finnish all of Shakespeare's thirty-six plays. Only in the 1950s were efforts made to produce new versions. Other foreign favorites have been Friedrich von Schiller, Molière, Henrik Ibsen, Nikolai Gogol, and Anton Chekhov.

Topical comedies and musicals, as well as gallows humor, gained in popularity in the postwar period, soon followed by a greater receptivity to the drama of Arthur Miller, Tennessee Williams, Jean Anouilh, and Bertolt Brecht. The plays of major contemporary world playwrights have been staged in Finland very soon after their world premieres; the plays of Samuel Beckett and Eugene Ionesco and the theater of the absurd were being performed in Finland even before they found international acceptance.

About half the plays produced in any given season have been by Finnish playwrights, encouraged in part by competitions, government drama prizes, and the four drama schools. In the post-World War II period Finnish dramatists writing for both professional and amateur theaters have tended to stress the social function of drama. They have focused on national self-analysis. In general they have examined the effects of war and its aftermath, and in particular they have taken a closer look at the civil war of 1918. In the 1960s and 1970s political cabaret, documentary plays, and the theater of fact grew in popularity, launched by the 1966 premiere of the amateur production of *Lapualaisooppera* by left-wing poet Arvo Salo. This scathing satire about political ambivalence and fascist tendencies in Finland in the 1930s provoked widespread controversy and public discussion in the mass media.

Finnish drama has long been characterized by seriousness and emotional intensity, but with more and more poets and novelists trying their hand at playwriting, a greater lyricism has been introduced. Finnish acting has long been characterized by histrionic exaggeration, but under the influence of director Jack Witikka there has been a greater concentration on understatement and levity. Colloquial speech has given way to a more personal expression. Music has been increasingly used for a specific stage effect, and such musicals as *My Fair Lady*, by Allan Lerner and Frederick Loewe, always draw big audiences.

As of 1971 there were thirty-four professional theaters, including four Swedish-speaking groups, all operating on the repertory system with actors on two-year contracts. In the 1960s regional theaters began to offer the service of either transporting audiences to performances or going on tour in the region. In the 1970s there were fifty theaters with a half-professional, half-amateur staff. Financing derived from three sources: ticket sales, which provided about half the expenses; local and municipal subsidies, which have been increasing sharply since the 1960s; and state funds, which have been decreasing. State allocations were given to the theater because it was considered to be an educational institution. Free, or players', theaters were steadily receiving more state grants, although such support lagged behind that given in Sweden.

Amateur groups function in almost every town, no matter how remote. A village of 100 inhabitants, and even hospitals and prisons, could muster at least one amateur group. In the early 1970s some 8,000 amateur groups gave a total of some 20,000 performances yearly. This dynamism, plus the fact that in the 1971-72 season almost 2 million tickets were sold for professional performances, indicated that theater was a truly consuming national passion. Television only temporarily preempted activity in the amateur movement and in the 1970s had not gained the ascendancy it enjoyed in other countries.

MUSIC

To many people, Finland evokes the music and formidable image of Jean Sibelius. At times inspirational and romantic, at times mournful and austere, but always original, his music expressed national feelings that Russian oppression prevented from being spoken. Although his music is uniquely Finnish, it evokes a warm universal response. Finland had a tradition of religious and folk music, but, until Sibelius, symphonic music was undeveloped. When he died at age ninety-one in 1957, he was a legend.

One of the reasons for the lack of composition and performance of formal music was the absence of court life, which in Europe provided the composer with an audience and with support—both intellectual and financial. Neither before nor after the Reformation did the church establishment foster new music; the Roman Catholic Church in Finland before the Reformation was not wealthy enough and the Evangelical Lutheran Church of Finland, or Church of Finland, thereafter was not disposed to elaborate ceremony. Nor were there enough rich individuals to patronize the arts. Towns were small and far removed from each other, and even further removed from European influences. The genius of Sibelius could flourish because it appeared at a time when other factors crucial to musical life—professional musical training and a competent orchestra—had been firmly established.

Elements of contemporary Finnish composition have been partially inspired, however, by a body of church, school, and folk songs. Centuries ago musical instruments were scarce, so a tradition of solo and choral singing developed. Still extant is an edition of medieval church songs, the Turku Diocesan Liturgy, compiled about A.D. 1330 from several religious festivals honoring local saints. Among the songs is the Finnish carol to King Wenceslas, which is often mistaken as being of Bohemian origin.

Folk music takes the form of song, incantation, recitation, and other forms of vocal expression. The mood and brilliance of songs vary from one province to another. The Lapps have continued to sing simple chants, the text of which consists of snatches of humor, praise, or mocking comment; the pentatonic melodies are sung with many repetitions.

The greatest influence on composers has been the *Kalevala*. As folk music it was conveyed by the melody of the *runo* (rhyme or verse), whose striking feature is its rhythm of five beats to the measure. As many as 100 verses are chanted in couplets in one song session. The early Finns gathered around a bonfire to hear a reciter and a repeater (a single accompanying *runo* singer or a chorus), swaying to the accompaniment of the *kantele*, a stringed instrument. The *kantele*, a national folk symbol, originally had five strings, corresponding to the tonal range of the melodies of the *runo*, but through the centuries the number of strings evolved to about thirty. In the eighteenth and nineteenth centuries the violin and clarinet replaced the *kantele* as the accompanying instruments to songs and dances, as well as to wedding music. They in turn gave way to the one- and two-row accordion.

Differing in concept and structure from the melodies of the *runo* are the song melodies with rhyming lyrics that emerged in the seventeenth century and flowered in the nineteenth. Some of the most admired were composed by Sibelius' contemporaries, Leevi Madetoja and Oskar Merikanto. The songs are more topical than their narrative predecessors and deal with nature, love, and sorrow, rarely with work. The plaintive quality of many of the songs and of much singing itself reflects life's rigors and sorrows, which are never otherwise expressed. The most festive music is associated with weddings. In eastern Finland vocal music is preferred, whereas instrumental music commonly is played at weddings in the west.

Musical activity became organized in 1790 with the founding of the Turku Musical Society. By 1795 women were allowed to perform in the programs. In less than twenty years the society's membership swelled to 900. The majority of the members were foreigners, however, and this state of things prevailed well into the nineteenth century. The organization's purpose of cultivating the musical arts was met not only with concerts but also with musical training, which was provided free to indigent youngsters. The society's library of 2,000 scores was reputed to be the most comprehensive in Scandinavia.

A tradition began when Finnish students at the Swedish University of Uppsala brought their own male choir to Turku. Choral singing since then has constituted the principal musical activity at universities. The standards achieved by the Helsinki University Men's Choir have been such that the group has made recordings and extensive tours at home and abroad every year.

In September 1827 fire almost completely destroyed Turku. The university—and cultural activity—moved to Helsinki where real growth occurred. In 1835 the German-born violinist and composer Fredrik Pacius assumed the post of principal teacher of music at Helsinki University, where he set up stringent standards in music education. His activity as teacher, conductor, choir master, violinist, and composer contributed to the excellence of Finnish music in the last two decades of the century. Pacius composed the Finnish national anthem "Maamme" (Our Land) to words by Runeberg.

The possibility for creative growth lay in the confluence of the innovative activities of two important men. Martin Wegelius, in disagreement with the methods of Pacius' establishment, founded the Institute of Music (now the Sibelius Academy) in Helsinki. Wegelius traveled abroad to recruit qualified teachers and, dissatisfied with available textbooks, published his own. His efforts were complemented by those of Robert Kajanus, who founded the first professional symphony orchestra in 1882 and remained for fifty years at the head of the oldest concert orchestra in northern Europe performing on a permanent professional basis. For musicians this development signaled the possibility of living and working exclusively as musicians. And indeed, Sibelius was working on the music that his friend Kajanus was soon to champion and definitively interpret to international audiences.

Sibelius' work, the occasional dissonance of which represented a departure from the Viennese classicism prevailing at the time, had an epic quality and seriousness of purpose that evoked popular admiration. After several years spent in Berlin and Vienna, where he studied composition, orchestration, and the violin, Sibelius conducted the premiere of his five-movement Kullervo Symphony (inspired by the tragic figure in the *Kalevala*), which established Sibelius as a hero and a composer.

The world took note of Sibelius and the cause of Finland when the composer's "Finlandia," among other works, was performed by Kajanus at the Paris World Exhibition in 1900. In 1914 Sibelius conducted "The Oceanides" (of Homeric inspiration) at the Norfolk Festival in Connecticut. In 1953, on his eighty-eighth birthday, Sibelius galas were staged, and in his native country fifty towns renamed streets and parks in his honor.

Styles in Finnish composition in the postwar period range from national romantic to electronic music and jazz. A number of composers have a special talent for compositions for stringed instruments, choral music, and speech choirs. Premieres of new music are anticipated and discussed.

Finland's singers—especially women—and professional choirs have achieved international fame. In the 1970s Helsinki had two large symphony orchestras and a third orchestra, affiliated with the Finnish National Opera. There were almost as many amateur musicians in village, factory, and office choirs as there were amateur actors. This development partially derives from the encouragement parents give their children to learn an instrument or to sing. Musical evenings in the family setting or in the civic orchestra are common.

Foreign troupes began performing in Finland in the mid-nineteenth century, and in 1911 Aino Ackté, a singer of international reputation, founded the Finnish National Opera, the country's first and only opera company of professional status. A favorite opera has been Tauno Pylkkänen's "The Wolf's Bride," which won the coveted Prix Italia in 1950. The Finnish Ballet, connected with the opera, was established in 1922. The government supports both enterprises, and the opera receives additional support from the state lottery. The Savonlinna Opera Festival, also inaugurated by Ackté, performs on an open-air stage in the Great Courtyard of the Savonlinna fortress.

The greatest public holidays have been choral festivals, held regularly since 1884, when they were originally staged for unifying purposes. In 1935, the *Kalevala* jubilee year, a massive choral festival involving nearly 4,500 singers was mounted. Helsinki has arranged a Sibelius Festival every summer since 1951. The Savonlinna Festival, first held in 1955, has devoted itself to lieder. The Turku Festival of Music, held annually since 1960, has featured chamber music. The Pori International Jazz Festival, initiated in 1966, has drawn enthusiasts from the United States and Europe. The village of Kaustinen is the site of the Kaustinen Folk Music Festival, whose core of participants has been the population of the village. The Vaasa Festival has presented avant-garde music; the Jyväskylä Arts Festival has drawn many to its seminars. London's Camden Festival has evolved into a principal agent for launching new Finnish music onto the international level.

PAINTING

Although no major Finnish painters have appeared in the world's great art museums nor does a lasting Finnish school influence international style, Finnish painters have sustained themselves by satisfying the constant popular demand for original art. Except for folk art and some church frescoes adapted from German and French models, painting has had only a modest indigenous tradition in Finland. The graphic arts have had none. It was not until the early nineteenth century that painting acquired the status of an independent fine art when a number of amateur painters turned out portraits of Finnish society in Empire dress; others produced landscapes, peasant scenes, and bird paintings. The educator, Topelius, encouraged book illustrations in an effort to define a national image. In general, however, the output of the unschooled painters of the 1800–50 period was small, even though the

Finnish Society of Fine Arts and its drawing school were instituted in the 1840s.

The 1880-1910 period marked a happy coalescence of trained artistic ability and self-confident nationalism, resulting in painting that was definitely Finnish and highly creative, naturalistic, and symbolic. Many artists reached their technical maturity with study in France and Germany. The romantic influence of karelianism affected many painters with its motifs of folk and Byzantine inspiration. Art nouveau and symbolism influenced some painters, notably Hugo Simberg, a miniaturist. Another important artist of the period was Helena Schjerfbeck, who painted quiet interiors and thoughtful portraits. Although she had little influence on her contemporaries, she was "rediscovered" by art critics in the 1930s, who ranked her ultimate influence in the Scandinavian art world just behind that of the Norwegian expressionist Edvard Munch, one of the pioneers of modern art.

Competitions often have elicited the best from Finnish creative artists. A competition arranged in 1891 by the Savo-Karelian Students' Union to find an illustrator for Lönnrot's *Kalevala* more satisfactory than the preceding foreign artists brought forth Akseli Gallen-Kallela. Conscious or not of the "back to nature" impulse, which carried Vincent Van Gogh to Arles and Paul Gauguin to Tahiti, Gallen-Kallela took to the backwoods of Karelia and there worked out his highly decorative and symbolic style, which eventually became known as the Kalevala style, and which every Finn instantly recognizes. Most of his artistic career centered on the *Kalevala.* His work, along with the music of Sibelius and architecture of Eliel Saarinen, first came to international attention at the Paris World Exhibition of 1900. Gallen-Kallela's influence on architects and craftsmen, as well as on his fellow painters, ranks him as Finland's foremost artist.

During World War II painting still concerned itself with the regional, the patriotic, and the representational. Surrealism and dadaism, which were popular elsewhere during the interwar period, and abstract art, which developed later, made virtually no headway in Finland. With the supply of consumer goods effectively depleted, there was more private spending on paintings, especially for the ever-popular romantic landscape. The Fine Arts Academy of Finland was reorganized during this time and subsequently became the center of art education while taking responsibility for the Ateneum, the state art collection.

As Finland recovered, artists traveled more, aided by state funds administered through the Society of Finnish Artists organized in 1952. Meanwhile, more foreign exhibits came to Finland. Although a number of figurative and expressionistic works were still being done as late as the early 1940s, surrealism gradually took hold in Finland, most strongly in Turku. Abstract expressionism made a delayed entry and gained steady influence during the 1950s. By that time art had become internationalized. Contemporary Finnish painting combines the primitive and the progressive, the melancholy and the humorous; a dark palette is used, with an occasional accent of bright color.

SCULPTURE AND DESIGN

The contours, textures, and economy of line that characterize Finnish sculpture and design—and that characterize what has come to be known as contemporary Scandinavian design—are the result of an intuitive understanding of the properties of natural materials, deriving from a centuries-long tradition of working with wood, stone, iron, clay, wool, and flax. Until the twentieth century, wood was the primary material in making weapons and tools, houses and ships, skis and sleighs, housewares and simple art works. Early artisans achieved not only artistic but practical results by splitting wood according to its grain and working with the varying hardnesses. Wood-carving has always been a favorite activity throughout the Baltic countries. The most frequent subjects of early Finnish carving were bears and moose, made probably for a magical purpose.

Stone, especially granite, worn smooth by water and ice, was sculpted into animal heads. Finland's oldest work of art is a stone elk head dating back four to five thousand years. The Lapps ascribed magical powers to *seits* (figurative shapes) seen in decaying tree trunks or in natural rock formations, which they individualized by stacking or marking in some way. Even the *Kalevala* mentions this oldest of art forms. Twentieth-century sculptors maintain the ancient preference for wood and granite worked organically into smooth shapes.

A modest tradition of church statuary, particularly of madonnas, established itself during the Roman Catholic period but was considerably restricted and simplified by the succeeding Church of Finland. Finnish style—derived from basic values, severely limited resources, and in reaction to European and Russian ostentation—has always tended to equate beauty with simplicity and utility. Only faint echoes of Renaissance grandeur and baroque opulence reached Finland. In fact, modern churches are conspicuous for the absence of almost all statuary or decoration. Rather, the accent has been on dynamic form, on the exterior and the interior.

As was painting, sculpture was relatively slow to respond to the demands and possibilities of the national awakening in the nineteenth century. With the achievement of independence in 1917, however, sculpture came into its own with Wäinö Aaltonen in the vanguard. Again as did painting, sculpture achieved success by responding to the need for nationalist symbols. The new republic demanded war memorials, heroes' graves, and statues of Finland's great figures. The style was generally classical, typified in Aaltonen's famous marble bust of Sibelius and his bronze statue of the Olympic champion, Paavo Nurmi.

Sculpture stagnated in nationalism and classicism in the 1940s and

111

1950s, but the close of World War II brought a huge demand for war memorials. Materials were scarce, but resourceful sculptors resorted to birch bark and parts of destroyed aircraft. In the late 1950s nationalism was losing its influence, and by the 1960s the real break with traditional classicism came to a head—with many traditionalists themselves leading the way. An example of one traditionalist who made the shift is Aimo Tukiainen, who had created more war memorials than any other sculptor. In 1960 his traditional equestrian statue of Mannerheim, which had required eight years' work, was unveiled to great public and critical appreciation. That same year, after a journey in Greece where the ancient ruins made a deep impact on him, he created an abstract war memorial suggestive of a bombed-out bunker.

State policy stipulates that 1 percent of funds appropriated for a public building be used for sculpture or murals. Since World War II business and industry have increasingly been able to commission special sculptures. Considering the Finnish architectural concept of total design, prospects for sculpture look bright as it has been increasingly called upon for its decorative effect and to provide a finishing touch to architecture. Even small towns have raised enough money for an original sculpture in their squares.

THE APPLIED ARTS

Potters fashioning combware in the New Stone Age used clays and created forms and surfaces that inspire modern craftsmen. Simple ornaments (Finland is not rich in precious stones) dating from the Bronze Age give evidence of a talent for making jewelry that presaged the reputation nineteenth-century Finnish goldsmiths and jewelers were to attain in the capital of Imperial Russia, Saint Petersburg.

In the Middle Ages, Vikings introduced the thick, durable handwoven *ryijy* rug from Morocco and Spain, which fishermen and seal trappers quickly adopted as a means of keeping warm. By the eighteenth century, however, these rugs had evolved into creations of such intricate and colorful design that they had become valued as heirlooms and status symbols and were prominently displayed on walls. In the old Swedish areas, designs were simple and figurative; they were more fluid and expressive in Karelia. In the 1970s specialized techniques produce rugs of abstract patterns that change as the deep pile falls one way or another; various shades of blue, green, yellow, and rose are used that recall the traditional homemade vegetable dyes.

In the late eighteenth century cottage crafts developed, first in parsonages and then in peasant homes. These small-scale manufacturing centers produced rugs, cloth, linens, pottery, even silverware. Glassblowing could only be a factory operation. The tradition in glassware has developed steadily from its founding in 1793, practiced largely by Swedes; it has risen to a high technical and artistic level, exemplified in the glass sculpture case in flaming wooden molds, the innovation of designer Timo Sarpaneva, who was trained in sculpture.

The Finnish Society of Crafts and Design, founded in 1875, has become an important promoter of the industrial arts. Another organization, The Friends of Finnish Handicrafts, established in 1879, proved to be a forward-looking organization that updated traditions in weaving, embroidery, and especially rugmaking.

Functionalism, a dominant style in design and architecture throughout the Western world in the 1970s, had already attracted the interest of Finnish artists and critics by the start of the twentieth century. In 1901 critic Gustaf Strengell expressed the essence of functional design when, in speaking about a chair, he said, "If it is well-constructed, it is beautiful." The bent plywood chair, originally designed in the 1930s by Alvar Aalto and still in mass production forty years later, exemplified this concept of functional beauty.

The most expansive and creative period in the applied arts has been since the 1950s when industry joined with design to meet the needs of the Finnish and, importantly, the world market. Artist-designers initially hesitated to form the partnership, but their fears were overcome when they were provided with their own studios, excellent facilities and materials, and freedom for experimentation. Stunning reward came as early as 1951 at the Milan Triennale, the all-important international competition in design where Finnish designers, led by Tapio Wirkkala, who had been trained as an architect, won almost all the top awards. The press and the public at home treated the winners as celebrities. Government grants multiplied fivefold in the next decade. The partnership of industry and designer was thus reinforced to the extent that the small private studio is rarely to be found, except for occasional textile and metal products workshops. Even so, the well-known organization of Marimekko, representative of the revitalized textile and informal dress industry, employs 300 workers. The Arabia ceramics factory is the largest and most diversified in Europe. Asko is the largest furniture factory in Scandinavia.

Since World War II designers have produced for the smaller apartments inexpensive chairs and tables that can be either stacked or collapsed and dishware in compact nesting and stacking shapes. The colors and shapes of these high-quality goods bear out the old craftsman's insistence that everyday items can be beautiful as well as useful.

ARCHITECTURE AND TOWN PLANNING

The successes achieved by Finnish architects and planners since the 1930s and especially since the 1950s have received world acclaim. This is all the more remarkable considering that Finland does not have the models of an ancient or an ongoing civic architecture. On the other hand, the lack of tradition has permitted Finnish architects to participate freely in the functionalist movement (so-called modernism) that has prevailed in international architectural theory since the interwar period. The no-nonsense Finn came naturally to this architecture, which is called "rational" because the purpose of the building determines its form and substance.

Little remains of early peasant or municipal architecture because the majority of peasant dwellings and public buildings were built of wood. Although it is readily accessible and well suited to the cold climate, wood is easy prey to fire and war, and the history of Finnish towns is one of a succession of devastating fires. To minimize the loss resulting from fire, the example of the Russian town plan was followed—broad streets were laid out, and large spaces were allowed between buildings in order to forestall the spread of fire. Porvoo, east of Helsinki, is exceptional in having its old quarter preserved intact.

What has remained and what is being carefully preserved are the approximately eighty stone or wood churches found in villages, particularly in southwestern Finland, and which date from the end of the Middle Ages. Only Turku Cathedral, built in the fourteenth century, was constructed on the monumental scale found in European cathedrals. Most of the stone churches are modest in size and ornamented with simplicity, in part because granite is difficult to sculpt. Although each region evolved a distinctive style, the gothic and renaissance styles were introduced; however, modification of these styles resulted in churches and towers more squat and earthbound than those of Europe. The building plan was generally a plain rectangle, with the interior divided by three aisles. A free-standing bell tower, particularly from the seventeenth century on, was constructed of wood and painted pale yellow, grey or white, in contrast to the bulky granite masses. Use of brick was limited to the gables, door and window casings, internal pillars, and vaulting. A steep-pitched, shingle roof covered with black tar topped both stone and wood churches.

Reflecting the fact the Finland's nobility was never as wealthy and aloof as European nobility, the manor houses and castles are simple, austere, and few in number. They might more accurately be classified as military fortresses, recalling Finland's history as a battleground. One exception is the castle at Turku, which from the fourteenth century was the home of a ducal court and then of the governor general; the purpose of the castle was largely administrative. The most recent fortress is Suomenlinna. Built in the mid-eighteenth century to guard the seaward approach to Helsinki, it constituted the mightiest system of fortifications in Scandinavia.

Helsinki has a planned aspect and stateliness as a result of the influence of the German-born architect Johan Carl Ludwig Engel, who was appointed consulting architect in the reconstruction of Helsinki after it was ravaged by fire in 1808. Before his death in 1840 Engel had successfully executed his plan according to the Empire style, erecting neoclassical buildings in stone and brick, set on streets and squares laid out on a grid pattern and crisscrossed by broad avenues of trees.

In the 1970s Helsinki's skyline is dominated by two big cathedrals, one Lutheran and the other Eastern Orthodox, a visual reminder of Finland's position between East and West. At the turn of the century, however, when Finnish nationalism was rising, architects made a conscious effort to extricate themselves from ancient or current styles imported from abroad. As with the other arts, the aim was to create new forms by reviving traditional Finnish forms. Municipal buildings, such as the National Museum in Helsinki, and churches, such as the cathedral in Tampere, are characterized by bulky, rough-hewn granite rocks; on the exterior of the buildings flora and fauna and Kalevala motifs are carved in stone. This architecture based on popular tradition was readily accepted by the public and represents a considerable part of the Finnish scene.

Three events signaled the shift from national to international orientation. The achievement of independence in 1917 meant for architects that striving to symbolize national identity was no longer necessary. Preparation for the transition had been made earlier, however, by Strengell, who had stressed the relationship between beauty and function, and by architect Sigrid Frosterus, who speculated on the possibilities of reinforced concrete and steel, which were to become central to functionalism. Concrete can be cast into almost any shape, satisfying the functionalist's preference for a more free form. Architect Eliel Saarinen himself moved from national romanticism to a kind of functionalism, seen in his Helsinki railway station (built 1906–14), whose simple form more directly reflects its means of construction and its function, and whose ornamentation is secondary to the whole concept.

By the late 1920s functionalism had taken hold in Finland. National romanticism expanded to an even more monumental degree and neoclassicism went through another revival, best seen in the parliament building (1930). Certain functionalist features, such as asymmetry and horizontality, a free floor plan, and the discarding of ornamentation, had evolved independently in Finland. The standardization of units, mass prefabrication, and the social considerations of functionalist theory helped to meet the housing problem that had developed in the aftermath of World War I and the incipient industrialization of the late 1920s. Attention was directed primarily to construction of the worker's apartment. Differing from the functionalist tendency toward teamwork in other countries, Finnish architects tended to work on their own, although increasingly they have been constrained to work alongside engineers and other architects in laying out systematic town plans.

Functionalism in Finland was spearheaded by Alvar Aalto, a luminary in international architecture. Aalto "finnicized" functionalism by using Finland's primary resource—wood. Some Aalto innovations are the undulating wood-strip ceilings and the flooring and paneling of laminated red plywood strips first seen in his public library in Viipuri.

Functional architecture got a mixed reception from the public, which often disparaged its "packing-case" character, although judging committees, which happened usually to be composed of progressives, welcomed the new style. The flat roof favored by many functionalists particularly offended those Finnish architects who deemed the steep-pitched roof the most natural. Aalto foresaw the psychological and aesthetic problems of a potential community of barracks. In the period of reconstruction following World War II be advocated housing originating with a central unit or cell, to which other units could be added as the residents chose and as the economy improved.

Much of the reconstruction effort following World War II, directed by the national building loan department, resulted in makeshift housing construction of wood planks. This construction was an expedient rather than an aesthetic solution to the combined pressures of a population explosion, further urbanization and industrialization, the need to resettle 400,000 refugees (12 percent of the population) streaming in almost overnight from Karelia when it was ceded to the Soviet Union, and the need to rebuild areas of Lapland razed by the retreating Germans. (Fittingly enough, the Lapps have a proverb, "Rebuilding is more important than life.") The emphasis at this juncture was on single-family housing and large-scale regional projects as opposed to apartments.

On the whole, functionalist concepts have survived the regressive period of reconstruction. The postwar experience of Aalto and all other Finnish architects who spent as much time on planning as on designing has carried over to the more affluent period since the 1950s. As a result Finnish concepts and seminars in city planning, along with ideas for corporate headquarters, civic centers, and summer cottages, are instructive to the world at large. Decades earlier, Saarinen pioneered in the science of planning and used the concept of total environment even before he immigrated to the United States in 1928.

A milestone in postwar planning is the garden city concept of Tapiola, the experimental town built in the 1950s outside Helsinki, which preserves the natural setting and makes use of the contours of the landscape. In contrast to the free-flowing "antiplan" of Tapiola, which gave special consideration to the pedestrian and to motor transportation, town planning of the late 1960s and 1970s emphasized greater systematization and accessibility by reviving the grid pattern and promoting public transportation, while maintaining contact with nature by retaining green belt areas. To avoid uniformity a plan for rebuilding a city center or for constructing a satellite town may call for as many as twenty architects, each one responsible for one block. As in the other arts and sciences in Finland, architects are commissioned through the competitive system, which bases awards on concepts rather than details.

Finnish architects make perhaps their most striking departure in church architecture, done on a monumental scale with "modern" forms. Other architects have made advances in modules and prefabricated wood housing. Wood will continue to be an important building material and an element in interiors, and no right-thinking Finn would set foot in a sauna constructed from anything other than wood.

As a profession and a social group, architects of the 1970s enjoy unusually high status. Their lives and projects are topics for the popular media. Professionalism and status are reinforced by the stringent selection of applicants to architectural schools and jobs. The envy of his counterparts elsewhere, the Finnish architect enjoys creative freedom when commissioned to do a project and exercises considerable influence on the town plan. He also has a free hand in designing interiors, furniture, even lighting fixtures. Enjoying an elite status, Finnish architects have become sensitive to social problems, slowly but surely.

SCHOLARLY AND SCIENTIFIC RESEARCH

Organized scholarly and scientific research was initiated at Finland's oldest university, Turku University (established 1640). In the early years the decidedly theological orientation of the university restricted the flow of philosophical and scientific influences from abroad and, except in the field of botany, it inhibited the pursuit of scientific research. Near the end of the seventeenth century, however, a professor of poetics, Torsten Rudden, sought and won the support of the chancellor for the "liberty to philosophize," incorporating the new Cartesian theories and favoring Swedish over Latin as the language of instruction and theses. Secularization advanced only gradually: Copernicus' heliocentric theory was not accepted until the early eighteenth century; Swedish became the language of instruction only by midcentury. In line with the European response to science in the Age of Enlightenment, Turku established chairs in economics and in chemistry.

The Age of Enlightenment was as important for the humanities as it was for the sciences. Finland's great man of letters, Henrik Gabriel Porthan, was the pioneer in research in Finnish history, language and literature, and folk culture. As a central figure of the Aurora Society, Porthan was responsible for the publication of the country's first newspaper, a literary journal of historical and other humanistic research findings. Comparative study of the Finno-Ugric languages originated with Matthias Alexander Castrén in the nineteenth century. In folklore research the geographical-historical method of Julius Krohn and his son Kaarle achieved such an international reputation that the international association, Folklore Fellows, eventually set up its headquarters in Finland. Finnish and Swedish history has attracted scholarly attention away from the study of European history, although there has been a school of historians that investigates the classical and papal history of Rome. Like the other Scandinavian countries, Finland has an institute in Rome carrying on classical research.

Although much humanistic research has been directed to the study of the national culture, scientific research has been more international in scope and methodology. Scientific progress in the late eighteenth century resulted largely from the activities of chemistry professor Johan Gadolin who pioneered research in the theory of combustion and who discovered the elements yttrium and gadolinium. Gadolin's son-in-law, noted physicist C. G. Hallstrom, became the first chairman of the Scientific Society of Finland in 1838. Through its publications the society forged international contacts and promoted the exchange of information. Astronomy was an important science, as evidenced by the construction of an observatory in 1815 in Turku and by the fact that contacts with Russian astronomers (and other scientiests) continued even into the period of russification, whereas study of Russian culture and language diminished.

Basic research in the natural and physical sciences and in mathematics has been conducted chiefly at the universities and technical schools, such as the Institute of Technology at Otaniemi (established 1849) affiliated with Helsinki University, the Technical Faculty of Oulu University, and the Technical University in Tampere. Indeed, the statutes of Helsinki University favored the natural sciences, but the demands of the post-World War II "mass university" have prompted rethinking in other directions. Once effectively independent in its research activities, Helsinki University is becoming more integrated into the national pattern of research policy and planning. Owing to limited wealth and resources, most research is conducted by individuals engaged also in teaching or other professional work. At times and in some fields, conditions have been such that scientists have immigrated to countries where prospects for research and application are brighter.

University scientists have made some notable achievements in the last century. Finnish mathematicians have made a mark in numbers theory. Wood and sawing technology has become a specialty. Geologist Jakob Johannes Sederholm made an international contribution with his studies on the origin of granite. In 1945 biochemist Artturi Ilmari Virtanen was awarded the Nobel prize in chemistry for his method of preserving fodder without losing its nutrients and freshness. This practical method has had worldwide application. Despite the international eminence achieved by sociologist Edvard Westermarck with his studies of marriage and the origin and development of moral ideas, the social sciences have remained a minor research field compared with the natural sciences and technology. The social sciences have received assistance from the United States through Fulbright scholarships and other kinds of aid.

Finland has bilateral and multilateral agreements with governments and organizations in the fields of scientific and cultural endeavors. An agreement on scientific and technological cooperation with the Soviet

Union was signed in 1955; an agreement on cultural cooperation was signed in 1960. Finland participates in the United Nations Educational, Scientific and Cultural Organization (UNESCO) as well as in the work of the Committee for Scientific and Technological Policy of the Organization for Economic Cooperation and Development (OECD). The Nordic Council cultural agreement signed in 1971 contains provisions for scientific research, meetings, surveys, and publications. Finland contributes to the financing of several technological research institutes and projects coordinated by Nordforsk according to the Nordic Council agreement. As one example of institutional and individual cooperation, the Finnish Academy of Science and Letters collaborates with the ionospheric laboratory of the Max Planck Institute in the Federal Republic of Germany (West Germany) and expedites the exchange program of researchers initiated by the British Royal Society.

change program of researchers initiated by the British Royal Society.

The administration of scientific research lies with the Ministry of Education and its subordinate network of research councils (patterned after the Western European model) known collectively as The Academy of Finland. Individual research councils have been established for the humanities, the medical sciences, the natural sciences, the technical sciences, the social sciences, and agriculture and forestry, all presided over by the Central Board of Research Councils. Members of the research councils are appointed by the State Council for three-year terms; the chairmen are appointed by the president. Ministers whose departments are involved serve on the Science Policy Council, the coordinating body, and the clearinghouse for proposed projects. Its chairman is the prime minister.

The functions of the academy range from financing research to publication and includes policy planning. The academy also finances Finland's participation in international projects, such as the International Biological Program, the International Hydrological Decade, and Man and Biosphere. In its 1970 program the central board worked out long-term objectives in regard to the quality of life, including medical care and environmental research and research into the structural problems of society.

The government allocates almost all its research funds to the universities and about forty government research institutes where 60 percent of basic research is conducted. The research councils do not have their own research institutes. Applied research also is conducted at some government research institutes, the largest of which fall under the aegis of the Ministry of Commerce and Industry and the Ministry of Agriculture and Forestry. As of 1969 the government institutes employed about 800 researchers and about 1,600 assistants. Applied research in the field of environmental protection is directed from the office of the prime minister. About 130 private, nonprofit scientific societies and foundations operate government-funded institutes, such as the Institute of Parasitology of the Finnish Scientific Society.

Industrial research, devoted mainly to research and development, accounts for about one-half of the research carried on in Finland. Government financing of private industrial research is negligible, although a special semiofficial foundation, the Finnish Independence Commemoration Fund, exists with the objective of obtaining more government allocations for applied research and product development that benefit the national economy. Industry invests about 1 percent of its gross income in research, which employed about 5,600 people as of 1969.

Total national outlay of funds for scientific research and development amounted to only 0.8 percent of the gross national product (GNP) in 1972, one of the lowest figures among OECD member countries. Each year the Ministry of Education receives from government football pools and lotteries about Fmk10 million (for value of the markka—see Glossary), which are used to finance scientific publications and conferences. Distribution of funds according to discipline breaks down roughly as follows: natural sciences and technology, 69 percent; agriculture and forestry, 12 percent; social sciences, 8 percent; medical science, 7 percent; humanities, 3 percent; and miscellaneous, 1 percent. Distribution according to stage of research is as follows: basic research, 10 percent; applied research, 40 percent; product development, 50 percent. Expenditure by the Ministry of Defense on research is relatively small.

SECTION II. POLITICAL

CHAPTER 9

THE GOVERNMENTAL SYSTEM

Finland has been an independent republic for more than fifty years. Almost all Finns, except certain extremist groups on the Right and Left have continuously supported their Constitution of 1919, which distributes power among the executive, judicial, and legislative branches of the government. Supreme executive power lies in the president of the republic who makes decisions within the cabinet (also known as the State Council). Judicial power is vested in independent courts of justice. The legislative power is exercised jointly by the president and a unicameral parliament elected by proportional representation and universal adult suffrage. The Parliament Act of 1928 provides the working legal basis for all legislative action.

Finland's constitution emphasizes the primary role of Parliament, the sovereign power resting "with the people, represented by their delegates assembled in Parliament." Historical precedent, however, has superimposed a strong executive on the system. The bases of this executive power lie in the paramount importance of foreign relations and the president's prerogatives in determining foreign policy.

Independence of the courts is assured through the irrevocability of judicial appointments. The judicial branch cannot judge the "constitutionality" of a law passed in Parliament, but it may sanction individual actions of members of the legislature and the State Council or of the president in a case of treason.

The role of the State Council within the executive is primarily administrative. Since the president may make decisions against the unanimous opinion of the council, its own part in the formulation of policy has been confined to the preparation of alternatives rather than final decisions.

HISTORICAL BACKGROUND

Finnish constitutional history was inextricably linked to that of Sweden until 1809, and to a lesser extent to that of Russia until the beginning of the twentieth century. Representational government in Finland dates from the Diet Act of 1617, which limited the powers of the Swedish monarchy. The law established a national parliamentary body, the Diet of Estates, to represent the four great classes (estates) of the society: noble, cleric, burgher, and peasant. The tendency toward popular rather than autocratic rule was thwarted by a new form of government forced on the diet by the king in 1772. The greater powers accruing to the sovereign were yet again increased in 1789 with the passing of the Act of Association and Security.

With authoritarian provisions already in force, the Russian conquest in 1809 did not necessitate revamping the structure of government. The Grand Duchy of Finland, although nominally under the tutelage of the Russian tsar, exercised a high degree of autonomy, with complete freedom of legislation and finances internally. It combined executive and judiciary functions in a body called the Senate, which was controlled by Finns. The Senate's economics department held the administrative and executive reins of the country, while its judicial department represented the highest court of justice in the Grand Duchy. A Russian military presence, however, was maintained under the command of a Russian governor general residing in Helsinki. In turn, the liaison between the Senate and the Russian tsar (nominally, grand duke) resided in Saint Petersburg.

This era came to an abrupt end at the turn of the century with Russian attempts to abrogate the constitution and annex Finland as a province. This process was interrupted by Russia's military defeat in the Far East and her revolutionary ferment at home. In 1906 a new parliamentary system was adopted, but a renewed wave of oppression prevented its effective use until independence was declared on December 6, 1917.

CONSTITUTIONAL STRUCTURE

Fundamental and Ordinary Laws

Finnish constitutional law is a collection of fundamental laws and more commonplace, administrative (ordinary) laws, which together provide a legal context for public action and civil rights. Fundamental law reflects the basic theory upon which the state's institutions are based; its amendment is difficult and, with few exceptions, has been unnecessary. All ordinary legislation must be in keeping with the principles set forth in the fundamental laws.

Two fundamental laws form the working basis of the government: the Parliament Act of 1928 and the Constitution of 1919. These laws derive from the Parliament Act of 1907, which marked the first truly Finnish constitutional law of modern times. The act called for a unicameral legislature to be elected by universal suffrage and proportional representation. Thus Finland became one of the first modern democracies to recognize the equal political rights of men and women. The contents of the act remain substantially intact, with only minor changes inserted in the updated 1928 version.

From independence to the end of World War I, the prospective form of government remained a subject of heated controversy in and out of

Parliament. After the Civil War, monarchist sentiment was high, and Parliament elected a German prince to be king of Finland in October 1918 (see ch. 2). With Germany's defeat in the war, the election was annulled. The monarchist machinations gave rise to a republican backlash, however, and Parliament finally passed a republican constitution on July 17, 1919.

Two other fundamental laws have been enacted since 1919. The Act of November 25, 1922, created a High Court of Impeachment. The Act of December 28, 1951, granted internal autonomy to the Ahvenanmaa Islands.

Certain ordinary laws also remain important cornerstones for the constitution: a 1918 law created the Supreme Court and the Supreme Administrative Court; a 1922 law still governs the manpower strength for the individual ministries; and the election of the president was first delineated in a 1924 law, which was amended in 1955 to create a presidential electoral college.

Separation of Powers

The Constitution of 1919 and its contributory laws have distributed governmental power among executive, legislative, and judiciary branches. Each branch has independent functions as well as functions that interlock with the other branches.

Executive power is held by the president and his state council (cabinet). He directs foreign affairs and is commander in chief of the armed forces. He holds wide powers of decree and appoints department heads (cabinet ministers), provincial governors, the chancellor of justice, and most judges. He and his cabinet initiate legislation, he has pocket veto power, and may dissolve Parliament or call it into extraordinary session.

Constitutionally, supreme power is vested in the unicameral Parliament, which can change the constitution, override presidential vetos, and force cabinets to resign by voting no confidence in them. Its legislation is not subject to judicial review. On the other hand, it appoints the solicitor general who controls courts of law and public administration. Some of this responsibility is shared with the chancellor of justice who also serves as counsel and public prosecutor for the government in disputes between the public and the executive branch. Finally, a high court of impeachment is empowered to judge the legality of actions taken by the presidentially appointed state council and chancellor of justice.

Civil and Political Rights

The individual rights of Finnish citizens are delineated in Part II of the constitution, entitled "General Rights and Legal Protection of

Finnish Citizens." First and foremost, all citizens are equal under the law, with constitutional guarantees of their rights to life, honor, personal freedom, and property. Fundamental civil and political rights have been guaranteed by the determination of boundaries beyond which state action is forbidden, except in times of national crisis.

The right of freedom of movement encompasses residence, protection from deportation, and guaranteed readmittance into Finland. Only in special cases, as in the instance of individuals convicted of criminal activity, are these freedoms abridged. Furthermore, travel and residence in the border areas are regulated under ordinary law.

Complete freedom of religious worship and association is guaranteed, and a 1922 law reiterates this concept in greater detail. Cultural affinities of all Finnish citizens are protected in the Act. In particular, Finnish and Swedish are established as national languages. Hereditary titles are forbidden, secrecy in private communications is guaranteed, and a Finnish citizen can be tried only by a court having jurisdiction over his case.

The inviolability of the home and property are fundamental rights. The expropriation of property in times of public need is allowable, however, and determined separately by ordinary law. In the case of such a law, however, the constitution assures full compensation for any public restraint on private property holdings.

Article 10 of the constitution guarantees citizens of Finland freedom of association, freedom of assembly, and freedom of speech. Related ordinary laws were passed to delineate more precise regulations governing the exercise of these rights.

Freedom to state personal opinions without hindrance from authorities is ensured, as is the right to print and publish freely. A 1919 law on freedom of the press was based on the principle of no governmental control before publication; an action can be brought to the courts only after a breach of the guidelines on published material has been alleged (see ch. 7). In 1945, however, prior censorship of films on moral grounds was sanctioned by ordinary law. In 1951 Parliament promulgated a "right-to-know" law ensuring government openness except in cases affecting national security as determined by the president acting jointly with the State Council.

The enumeration of rights in the Constitution of 1919 omits what are called social rights. With the exception of a brief reference to "special protection by the State" for the "labor of citizens" (Article 6), no mention is made of the positive measures necessary to ensure a minimum quality of life. Social rights legislation has not been lacking, however, particularly since World War II. A substantial part of the legislation—health and safety standards, training programs, management-labor relations—is aimed at protecting the financial and physical well being of the labor force.

Constitutional Interpretation

Interpretation of constitutional law in formulating and administering parliamentary legislation is at no point delegated to a court. The constitution states only that "if a provision in a decree is contrary to a constitutional or other law, it shall not be applied by a judge or other official." This ambiguous provision reflects the early parliamentary fear of a strong, independent judiciary. Nevertheless, the need for some constitutional review in the formulation of law is recognized. Within the Parliament the Constitutional Committee, which reflects the attitudes of the entire body, reviews all major legislative proposals.

Constitutional Amendment

A unique system of constitutional amendment has evolved in Finland. To amend the provisions of any fundamental law requires a simple majority on the first reading. A second approval is necessary, and if the proposed amendments are carried forward from one legislature to another, approval by two-thirds of the votes is required.

The more delicate and uniquely Finnish form of constitutional alteration is the so-called exception to fundamental law. Exceptional laws are temporary suspensions of particular constitutional clauses. The procedure for making an exceptional amendment is the same as for fundamental amendments. If action is urgent, the Parliament Act of 1928 provides a quicker procedure in which the proposed legislation becomes an emergency bill.

An emergency may be declared by five-sixths of Parliament. The declaration then may be approved by a two-thirds majority. In practice, almost all exceptions have been enacted in this manner.

STRUCTURE AND FUNCTIONING OF THE GOVERNMENT

The Executive

The executive branch is charged with the administration and execution of all law passed in Parliament and ratified by the president of the republic. The president and the State Council have the right to initiate legislation. Furthermore, each has primary responsibility in particular areas, such as foreign affairs and regional administration.

A system of checks and balances exists within the executive. The president must approve all executive decisions in a council meeting, with the countersignature of the appropriate minister. The State Council in turn may be forced to resign in the event of an irreconcilable difference of opinion with the president, who then can try to form a new council more amenable to his programs.

In relations with the legislature, the State Council's autonomy is limited by its need to enjoy the confidence of Parliament. Conversely, the president's power relative to the council has increased directly as a result of the lack of parliamentary control over his actions.

The Presidency

The president of the republic is elected indirectly by universal suffrage to a term of six years. His term of office cannot be cut short by Parliament, unless he is found guilty of treason. In the case of impeachment, three-fourths of Parliament must vote to press charges.

The head of state may not hold any other public or private posts and, traditionally, he has severed his political party ties. In his temporary absence, the prime minister, who is the senior minister on the State Council, performs the presidential tasks. If a permanent replacement is needed, elections are held at the earliest possible moment, with the prime minister presiding during the interim.

Jointly with the State Council, the president formulates government proposals. Independent of that body he has strong personal powers, among which are the suspensive veto; the right to issue decrees; the dissolution of Parliament; primary responsibility for foreign affairs; the supervision of the state administration; civil service and particularly ministerial appointments; command of the armed forces; and the right to grant citizenship, immunity, and pardons.

The suspensive veto returns a bill to Parliament for reconsideration. The president normally exercises this right with the concurrence of the State Council, primarily to clarify bills that have been badly formulated because of partisan conflict. The Parliament must either modify the bill along lines suggested by the president or override the veto with a two-thirds majority on a second reading.

The president also has the right to issue decrees on the basis of a mandate in Article 28 of the constitution. The decrees are concerned primarily with such matters as details in the administration of bills and public property. A presidential decree, however, may not contain a change in a law already passed by Parliament. The power to change law is a parliamentary prerogative, although an emergency law may attribute this right to the presidency in times of crisis, as in the early 1940s.

The power to dissolve Parliament has been exercised only five times since 1919. Usually the possibility arises when the government requires a clear popular vote on an important issue, as after the Note Crisis of 1961 (see ch. 11). Only once has the dissolution not been approved by the State Council—in 1924, following the crackdown arrest of all the communist members of Parliament. The dissolution of Parliament remains a means by which the president can effectively threaten the legislators into action. This may help them to overcome factional divisions in the short run but does not ensure backing for the government.

The power to direct the country's foreign policy rests mainly with the president. Article 23 of the constitution requires, however, that the formal administration of foreign policy be channeled through the appropriate ministry. Top level negotiations are usually carried out by the president, with the formalities of signing agreements left to the foreign minister.

Supervision of government administration is a task of the president, but it is exercised primarily by the State Council. The head of state lacks the staff to oversee the entire governmental machinery effectively.

Various nomination procedures are used to provide names for civil service posts. All the high positions are appointed by the president. These include diplomats, provincial governors, justices on the higher courts, the chancellor of justice, military officers, and members of the State Council. In the case of the State Council the president usually abides by the results of party negotiations. On occasions when council crises have led to resignations, however, the president has appointed caretaker governments which need not consist of party politicians. This is an effective power to exclude individuals or entire parties from the State Council, although the president has traditionally exercised prudence in not using this power to an extent which would antagonize the parties.

Supreme command of the armed forces is entrusted to the president. The constitution provides for a transfer of command in wartime to a military commander at the president's request. This was the case when President Kyösti Kallio named Marshal Mannerheim commander in chief in 1939 at the outset of the Winter War.

The president can grant pardons and general amnesties; the latter must be approved by Parliament. "Clemency laws" have usually been approved in the wake of internal disorders such as the 1918 Civil War and the general strike of 1956 (see ch. 2). Individual immunity can also be granted by the president, but only according to certain provisions in the law. The granting of Finnish citizenship, as well as release from citizenship, also requires the head of state's signature.

The prestige of the presidency is both a cause and a result of the fragmentation and heterogeneity of the other organs of government. The president's power and independence are constitutionally based, and therefore provide the single most effective factor for continuity in the governmental system. So much so, in fact, that presidential decisions are tacitly regarded as above all criticism. Criticism has reemerged, however, partly with the approval of the president himself; he often uses criticism to defend his programs and to challenge publicly those who would criticize him.

The State Council

This ministerial body, appointed by the president, consists of no more than 16 ministers, including the prime minister. The permanent ministers are for defense, finance, education, justice, interior, foreign affairs, social affairs, commerce and industry, and communications and public works. The prime minister directs the State Council office.

A minister may head two ministries and, likewise, a ministry may have two co-ministers. The president may appoint ministers without portfolio, but this practice has not been followed since the late 1940s. The top government prosecutor, or chancellor of justice, sits on the State Council but has no vote in its decisions. He also differs from the ministerial appointees in that his post is guaranteed for the entire period between elections. The nonpartisan office requires a good legal background.

The prime minister is the State Council's representative before Parliament. Joint ministerial responsibility for State Council decisions binds the members to uphold its decisions, although dissenting opinions can also be formulated and published with the government proposals. If dissent reaches critical proportions, a prime minister may resign, forcing the dismissal of the entire State Council.

The duties and powers of the State Council are both administrative and legislative. The preparation of government proposals in ministries, their submission for approval by the Parliament, and their execution and supervision after presidential ratification are the State Council's primary administrative tasks. Moreover, the Council can independently legislate in those areas regulated by a parliamentary decision. State Council "decisions" are usually based on an explicit request by the legislature that more exact provisions for a law be laid down by the council. This executive power approximates the presidential decree, although unlike the latter, is not sanctioned by fundamental law and thus is dependent on Parliament's will.

The collegial provisions of Article 40 of the Constitution of 1919 insure that the majority of decisions are agreed on by all the ministers. Within the State Council, three forums have evolved for formal and informal debate of its proposals: the "evening school," the ministerial committees, and the plenary sessions.

On the eve of State Council plenary meetings, the council sits in a closed, informal session to discuss and negotiate proposals prepared in the ministries. This "evening school" dates from the late 1930s when its purpose was to speed up decisions in the plenary session. Eventually the evening session became an effective way to solve problems which, if openly discussed, would display conflict. The bargaining is easier in closed sessions, and so is particularly important in coalition governments when public votes can crack the government's unity.

There are two permanent ministerial committees which are responsible for preparatory work on important foreign policy and financial issues. The prime minister chairs both, and the foreign minister and finance minister participate on the appropriate committee. Two or three other ministers participate on each committee. Decisions made within the committees are binding on the ministry concerned, in that they set limits for a ministry's program. For example, a financial committee decision can put a limit on the spending of a ministry for any given program. If the ministry refuses to abide by the committee decision, the question is sent to the State Council. Therefore, the ministerial committees exercise an effective pre-legislative control over the individual ministries.

The effective importance of the plenary session has diminished with the power wielded in the evening sessions and by the ministerial committees. Nonetheless, final decision, by vote or acclamation, still lies in the plenary session attended by the ministers, the chancellor of justice, and other interested persons. The ministers deliver individual argument for or against, and decide by simple majority vote. In the case of a tie, the prime minister's opinion prevails. The president, however, may send to Parliament a bill that has been voted down in the State Council.

The State Council's responsibility to Parliament includes the council's obligation to answer questions or interpellations from the floor of that body. An interpellation must be cosponsored by at least twenty members of Parliament and requires that the appropriate minister respond orally on a given date. A question must be in writing from an individual member, and the appropriate minister must answer in writing within thirty days. In 1966, however, a "question hour" was introduced, during which members of Parliament can cross-examine government officials once a week.

The Legislature

Structure

The Parliament Act of 1928 fixes at 200 the permanent number of seats in the unicameral legislature (*eduskunta* in Finnish and *riksdag* in Swedish.) Elections are based on equal and universal suffrage and a proportional distribution of seats. Elections are normally held every four years, at which time all the seats are up for election. The average turnover of seats in each election is about one-fourth of the total.

Parliament is in session almost year round. Normally, it adjourns for the summer and on state holidays. Although the president may call for an extraordinary session, this power has little practical meaning since the parliament meets regularly.

There are approximately 15,000 registered voters for every member of Parliament. In 1972, about 20 percent of these representatives were women, and the average age was a little under fifty years.

Any registered voter may run for office, with the exception of military personnel. The informal eligibility requirements are substantial, however. Of these, party affiliation is the most important single factor, especially in an electoral system that favors larger political groups. Political work on the communal government level also has been of great importance as a background to parliamentary work.

While Parliament is in session, the member is granted special legal immunity, although he is still legally responsible for any criminal acts committed during the session. He cannot hold another job while serving in Parliament.

At the outset of a session following an election, the Parliament chooses a speaker who must serve on a nonpartisan basis, and a committee of forty-five electors to decide on membership in the various legislative committees. The electors are chosen for the entire period between elections, and reappoint the committees at the opening of each session. Parliamentary action begins with the individual member, with party groups, with legislative committees, or with the plenary session.

According to Article 11 of the Parliament Act of 1928, members of Parliament are not bound to follow party dictates; nor is there any specific mention of party activity within the act. Nonetheless, parliamentary groups are discernible along strictly partisan lines. Therefore, the individual is in practice bound to a party policy unless he chooses to leave his party in favor of another.

The degree of solidarity exercised within particular party groups varies according to the make-up of the membership. Communists and others on the far left tend to stick together, whereas the heterogeneous Swedish People's Party is loosely knit. In votes of confidence in the government, however, cohesion of the party groups is almost always total.

Based on the number of seats held in Parliament, each political party receives subsidies in the form of government budgetary appropriations voted by Parliament (see ch. 10). This financial aid helps to alleviate the disadvantages of the smaller, less well-off parties and groups.

Committee work in Parliament is the real basis for legislative decisions. All important bills must first pass through one or more appropriate committees, including fiscal and petitionary bills, government proposals and parliamentary legislation. In all cases concerning the amendment of the constitution or the impeachment of government officials, Parliament can act only on the recommendations of the appropriate committees. The Speaker, upon approval by the members, determines which committee will receive a bill for study. Often, statements and further study are required from another related committee, resulting in reports that join under one cover all government and individual proposals and opinions related to a particular issue.

The committees are of two kinds—permanent and extraordinary. The Parliament Act of 1928 specifies permanent committees as: constitutional, legislative, foreign affairs, finance, and banking. Extraordinary committees, which are de facto permanent in that they are reestablished every year, deal with education, agriculture and forestry, social affairs, defense, transportation, and other matters. Subcommittees are permissible by law but they are rare. Committees usually divide into sections for particular matters, then reconvene to approve a committee report. Subcommittees, if they exist, report directly to Parliament in the name of the entire committee.

A supervisory Grand Committee of forty-five members is appointed by the committee of electors to oversee Parliament's legislative process. This body usually is composed of the most experienced members of Parliament. In effect it represents the corps of lawmakers that would comprise the upper house in a bicameral legislature.

The ultimate forum for parliamentary action is the plenary session, at which the party groups are seated from left to right in that ideological order. Sessions are usually held twice a week.

The agenda is prepared by the Speaker. Proposals transmitted from the State Council always take precedence on the calendar and must be acted on before the discussion of individual bills. Discussion of all bills precedes a vote, and no time limit is placed on speeches, interjections, or replies. Members vote by standing, but when the majority is not clear, the Speaker may request a machine-recorded vote or a secret ballot.

Legislative Procedure

The president of the republic and members of Parliament can initiate legislation. Government proposals are prepared by the State Council and passed to the legislature by the president. Individual bills are the result of personal initiative and lobbying by interest groups and individual citizens.

Individual bills must be introduced within two weeks of the opening of a diet, but government proposals may be submitted throughout the sessions. Bills are presented to Parliament in one of three forms: legislative bills, financial resolutions, or petitions. Legislative bills concern the passage of a new law or the rescinding or amendment of an existing one; financial resolutions concern all requests for budgetary appropriations; and petitions concern individual requests that the government take specific actions within its scope of activity.

Committees give first priority to government bills, often leaving private bills to the end of a session when there is little or no time to discuss them. In fact, it is estimated that less than 10 percent of the members' legislative bills are approved in one session; approximately 50 percent of the proposals are never even voted on.

Administrative Activities

Outside the legislative framework, Parliament's influence extends to the supervision of governmental activities, which may involve court action over discrepancies in government administration, as well as the administration of certain public organizations. For example, the activities of the Bank of Finland are supervised at the highest level by the legislature's Banking Committee, which oversees the bank's activities on behalf of the entire legislature. Parliament also elects the bank's trustees to serve for the period between elections.

Parliament also elects the directors of the National Pensions Institute, as well as those of the Finnish Broadcasting Corporation. In the latter case, the primary reason for Parliament's administrative control is to assure nonpartisanship in the mass media (see ch. 7).

Able to initiate proceedings to investigate the legality of actions taken by the chancellor of justice, the president, or members of the State Council, Parliament also exercises legal power in cases of administrative discrepancies. Such discrepancies would include the investigation of election errors (criminal or otherwise), or of the eligibility of some elected official to sit in Parliament.

The Legal-Judicial Structure

Finland's legal structure can be summarized in terms of the four major arenas for judicial review: the supervisory offices, general courts, specialized courts, and courts of administrative law. All judicial appointments are made upon the recommendation of the courts themselves, thus impeding patronage to a great degree. The right to tenure also insures the independence of the courts from partisan or governmental pressures.

Supervisory Offices

The offices of the chancellor of justice and the judicial delegate (ombudsman) guarantee the legal rights of Finnish citizens and supervise the legality of actions by public authorities. To this end, the chancellor of justice is the top prosecutor before the highest courts and is appointed by the president. His primary task is to see that all public officials perform their duties legally, and without detriment to the rights of any individual. Within the State Council, his opinion is increasingly sought prior to adopting positions, in order to avoid conflicts of interpretation when the proposal is sent to Parliament.

On almost equal footing as protector and overseer of government actions is the judicial delegate, based on the Swedish "ombudsman" model. It was not until 1957 that an amendment to Article 49 of the constitution gave the ombudsman parallel duties to those of the presidentially-appointed chancellor. The ombudsman is elected to a four-year term by Parliament after its election. As he is concerned primarily with the protection of individual rights from injustices by the governmental machinery, the ombudsman may investigate the actions of authorities at all levels at his own discretion.

To summarize the jurisdiction of the two supervisory offices: the chancellor of justice sees to it that injustices are not committed at the centers of decisionmaking, and the ombudsman seeks to protect persons from unjust public intrusions from the standpoint of the individual. Therefore, the majority of individual complaints are addressed to the ombudsman.

General Courts

Local courts, appellate courts, and the Supreme Court are responsible for administering justice in civil and criminal cases. Judges on the local courts are appointed by the Supreme Court, whereas those of the appeal courts and the Supreme Court are appointed by the president, on the recommendation of the courts themselves. Local judges are assisted by municipally elected lay boards that serve as juries and whose unanimous opinion cannot be overruled by a judge.

The appellate courts are located in Helsinki, Turku, Vaasa, and Kuopio. They consist of several judges as well as civil servants, including prosecuting attorneys and bailiffs. The judges may overturn a local court ruling and, in important cases may consider, as a primary instance, criminal proceedings.

The Supreme Court serves as the highest court, although the right to appeal beyond the appellate courts is limited to important matters. In the case of a presidential trial for treason, the Supreme Court tries the case. The court may also consider appeals on decisions by certain specialized courts.

Specialized Courts

A number of courts have been created over the years to deal specifically with highly specialized civil and criminal proceedings. These include military, land partition, labor, prison, and water resources courts, as well as the High Court of Impeachment. The latter is the forum when a cabinet member, a chancellor of justice, or a member of the Supreme Court or the Supreme Administrative Court is charged with criminal behavior. Charges must be brought by the president of the Parliament speaking for a three-fourths majority.

The make-up of this specialized court includes: the president of the Supreme Court who chairs the high court; the presidents of the appellate courts, the chairman of the Supreme Administrative Court, a law professor from the University of Helsinki, and six at-large judges elected by Parliament's forty-five electors.

Courts of Administrative Law

There is an increasing tendency to rely on the judicial system to resolve complaints by individuals against public authorities. A 1950 law made it a civic right to protest any administrative decision, although no provisions specified to whom the protest should be directed.

Although the establishment of a local network of administrative law courts has not been possible, the Supreme Administrative Court has existed since 1918 as the highest appellate court for complaints concerning public administration. Of these complaints, tax questions fill the major part of the court's docket. A special court of administrative law remains the highest instance of appeal for civil servants concerning loss of jobs.

Finally, a 1955 law established a network of regional administrative courts that work closely with the administrative central offices to air complaints of maladministration on the local and regional level.

Civil Service

The formal eligibility requirements for entering into the civil service include a minimum age (twenty-one years), Finnish citizenship, good knowledge of Finnish and Swedish, and an appropriate educational background. As in most European countries, the latter implies legal training, although the social sciences are becoming increasingly accepted as fundamental to efficient public administration.

In general, the president appoints to high government and judicial posts, and the Supreme Court makes the lower judicial appointments. The State Council and the central and regional offices fill the remaining jobs. Appointment to the higher posts usually is based on the nomination of a single candidate, although the decisionmaker need not follow the suggestion. The majority of posts are filled, however, on the basis of application, examination, and recommendation. Usually the personnel official chooses the three best qualified applicants, from which the appointing office picks one.

Patronage appointments, as in all modern democracies, are not unheard of. The impact of this practice is most discernible in the higher administrative posts, such as the board members of large state-owned corporations. The political overtone of administrative appointments has naturally increased with the rapid pace of partisan politics but remains relatively small in comparison to most other countries.

Salary and retirement compensations are determined by Parliament. The levels are not competitive with private industry or the professions, but firm protection of work rights is an inducement to work for the government. No tenure is assured by law, except in certain judicial posts. All civil servants must retire at age sixty-seven.

Subnational Governments

According to the constitution, Finland shall remain divided into provinces, circuits, and communes for the purpose of general administration. Circuits (or counties) are strictly census units rather than centers of regional administration. Communes are effectively self-governing units, detached from the state administration, while provinces represent the direct influence of the national government on the regional level.

Provincial Administration

Finland is divided into twelve provinces: Lappi, Oulu, Kuopio, Pohjois-Karjala, Keski-Suomen, Vaasa, Mikkeli, Häme, Turku and Pori, Kymi, Uusimaa, and the Ahvenanmaa Islands (see fig. 4).

A presidentially appointed governor heads the provincial government, whose administration combines a general and a financial office. The latter is charged with disbursing government funds and overseeing the collection of national and local revenues. The general department covers all other tasks within the provincial administration's

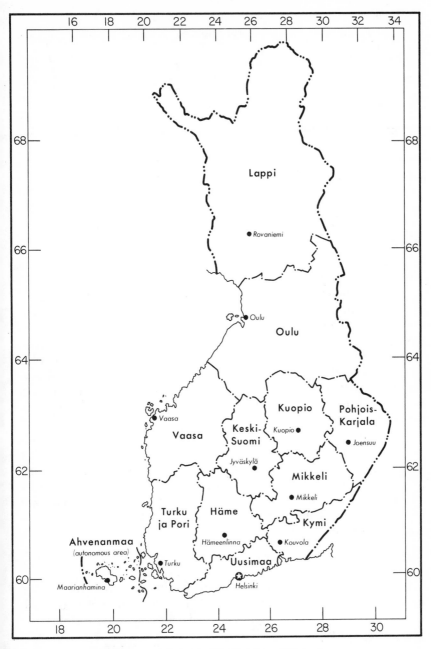

Figure 4. Administrative Divisions of Finland

jurisdiction. These include maintenance of the police authority in the province and supervision of communal affairs.

Communal Self-Government

Communal self-government was a cornerstone of the administrative laws passed after independence. It was not until 1948, however, that a single communal law was promulgated to encompass all previous provisions.

In 1972 there were forty-nine cities, twenty-nine boroughs, and 443 rural communes in Finland, each exercising a rather high degree of autonomy. Each local entity elects its own urban, town, or rural council for a period of four years. Since council members are not salaried, day-to-day administration may be turned over to a "communal board" composed of civil servants appointed by the councils.

The administrative tasks of the communal governments include: the maintenance of public utilities and a police and fire department; the collection of local business and property taxes; and numerous social tasks, including the administration of the school system and health facilities (see ch. 7). State intervention in communal affairs is usually confined to financial aid, technical expertise, and information dissemination.

The Ahvenanmaa Islands Status

Historical precedent has relegated the national government's role in the Ahvenanmaa Islands to a secondary one vis-à-vis the regional government. The Swedish-speaking province elects triennially an assembly that exercises administrative as well as legislative powers. The governor is nominally the highest authority in the region, but his role in local politics is limited to that of liaison with the national government. The assembly elects a seven-member regional board for a period of three years. The chairman, however, must enjoy the confidence of the assembly.

Any legislative action applicable only to the Ahvenanmaa Islands may be promulgated by the assembly, as long as it does not conflict with national law. The Ahvenanmaa Islands have special taxing powers beyond those of the other regions, including the right to levy an increment on state income revenues. Self-government does not include a regional judiciary; all legal matters must be settled in the state-authorized courts of law.

THE ELECTORAL SYSTEM

The electoral system remains strikingly similar to that formulated in 1906. The principle of proportional representation has been challenged at regular intervals but has survived three major reforms—in 1935, 1952, and 1955.

Parliamentary Elections

The Right to Vote

All Finnish citizens, with the exception of individuals convicted of a crime and other specified cases delineated in Article 6 of the Parliament Act of 1928, have the right to vote. In May 1972 Parliament set the minimum voting age at eighteen years. All eligible citizens are pre-registered to vote on the basis of census lists. The registers are open to public inspection, and if an eligible voter's name has been omitted from the list, he may petition to be registered.

Electoral Constituencies

In 1972 there were fifteen constituencies, with seats varying in number from twenty-two (Helsinki) to one (Ahvenanmaa Islands). The number of seats was established by the State Council prior to each election on the basis of the total population of each district. Election boards are appointed at the communal and regional levels, with an emphasis on equity participation by all party groups (to ensure non-biased vote counts).

Candidacy

Every eligible voter except military personnel can run for a parliamentary seat. Candidates are nominated mainly by the political parties, and primary elections are held to determine who will run for the seats. Individual citizens also may be nominated by groups of thirty or more voters.

Because there is a number of parties of unequal size and resources, the smaller ones may pool their votes by forming electoral alliances to limit the advantages of the larger ones. The alliances are more technical than political, however; they do not continue to function after an election.

Voting and the Ballot

Parliamentary elections are held every four years. Polls are open for two days beginning on the third Sunday in March. The candidates are listed by numbers on the list of each electoral alliance. Therefore, the voter can vote for both the alliance and the candidate by writing his number on the ballot. If only the nominee's name is filled in, the alliance does not benefit from the vote but the candidate does. Special provisions are made for absentee voting in other constituencies as well as for Finnish citizens residing or traveling abroad. Campaigning at polling places on election days is strictly forbidden and punishable by law.

Election Results

Within each electoral alliance, the candidates are ranked by number of individual votes. On this basis the candidates are ranked by a system in which comparative numbers are attributed as follows: in each alliance, the candidate with the most votes receives a number equivalent to the party's entire vote count. The second highest is attributed half of the votes for his alliance; the third, one-third of the votes, and so on. This is done for all the candidates in all the electoral alliances, based on the total number of votes for each alliance (party).

All candidates are ranked according to the comparative numbers.

Given a twelve-seat constituency, the twelve candidates with the highest comparative numbers are considered elected. Therefore, a candidate has an advantage if he runs on an alliance that has a relatively large backing.

Presidential Elections

Provisions for the election of the president of the republic are delineated in the constitution. Elections are held every six years on the basis of indirect universal suffrage. The most recent election was in 1968.

Eligible voters go to the polls to vote for electors, totaling 300 in the entire country. Voting follows the same rules as for parliamentary elections, and the number of electors from each constituency is determined by the State Council on a proportional basis of population. The public goes to the polls on January 15 and January 16 of an election year, and the electors convene one month later in Helsinki for an electoral convention.

A candidate must win a majority of the votes. If this is impossible on the first and second ballots, the two candidates receiving the most votes on the second ballot are pitted against each other for a final, majority-determined round.

A new president is inaugurated in Parliament on March 1 following his election. Exceptional provisions may be passed in Parliament to elect the president in times of crises directly in the Parliament. Such was the case of the election of Marshal Mannerheim in 1944. Similarly, the first President, K. J. Ståhlberg, was elected in 1919, and J. K. Paasikivi was elected for his first term in 1946 by Parliament. All subsequent presidents have been elected by the usual, indirect method.

CHAPTER 10

POLITICAL DYNAMICS, ATTITUDES, AND VALUES

Political participation is channeled primarily through political parties and economic interest groups, all of which aim to influence the formulation of social, economic, and political policy in the national government. Political parties are represented in Parliament, and they are often represented in other government organizations, such as the State Council, where they seek to influence policy. Three major extra-parliamentary groups, representing workers, employers and farmers, lobby in the executive and legislative branches of government and sit on a consultative committee, the Economic Council, which is attached to the State Council.

Political parties as well as economic interest groups can be classified generally as socialist or nonsocialist. The nonsocialist parties, which generally support private enterprise, can be subdivided under conservative and center labels, and the important nonsocialist economic groups protect the interests of farmers and employers.

The appeal of political or economic interest groups varies geographically. The north and east tend to be rural and poor and thus inclined to vote socialist; the south and west have long been the preserves of farm interests, but the cities in these regions have become sharply divided along class lines, with workers joining trade unions and voting socialist and the middle class tending to vote conservative.

The capacity of the political parties to take effective public action is considerably impaired by the large number of parties. In Parliament, for example, it is difficult to get a majority vote. The same thing is true in the State Council, which reflects the political composition of Parliament. In this unstable situation the votes from one or more parties can bring down the coalition in power. The State Council that was set up in September 1972 was the twenty-first since 1956.

The economic interest groups, in their approach to government legislation, confine their goals to the socioeconomic sector. Their impact on legislation derives mainly from their input into the legislative proposals drawn up by the ministries. The input comes from representation on government consultative committees as well as from lobbying. The success of the interest groups in having a say in policy formulation can in some measure be judged by the rarity of strikes. Such success, however, has not eliminated the use of threats of coercive action to support their positions.

The backup role that economic interest groups play in the political process is best exemplified during government crises, when parties cannot form a majority in Parliament. In 1962, for example, a caretaker cabinet included several trade union and business leaders. Finnish economic policy usually is drawn up by ministries on the basis of compromises worked out between interest groups, and political parties provide a stamp of approval. This reality, however, does not detract from the importance of political parties, which remain the major vehicle for popular participation in government.

POLITICAL PARTICIPATION AND COMPETITION

The Political Parties

Parliamentary strength is a good index of the popularity of the political parties (see table 3). The organization, outlook, and attraction of these parties are examined in descending order of their strength in Parliament as of January 1, 1973.

Finnish Social Democratic Party

The Finnish Social Democratic Party (Suomen Sosialidemokraattinen Puolue—SDP) changed markedly after World War I. Under the leadership of Väinö Tanner the party transformed itself from an ideologically Marxist group to an establishment party with generally socialist goals. The trend continued after World War II under Väinö Leskinen. Centralized economic planning has been the key objective; socialization of industry has been viewed as a process that should be confined to areas absolutely needing it. The short-term economic goal for the 1960s and 1970s is the bolstering of industrial production, particularly by the state-owned corporations. The social policy gives priorities to full employment, social security, more housing, and better working conditions.

The decidedly practical approach met with firm resistance within the SDP. In 1959 the extreme left-wing of the party, led by Aarre Simonen, formed the Social Democratic League of Workers and Small Farmers (Työväen ja Pienviljelijäin Sosialidemokraattinen Litto—TPSL), also known as the Simonists. Over the next decade the TPSL pointed to the lack of long-range socialist goals in Finland and called for greater worker democracy (to make production decisions) and the socialization of major industries. In 1969 the TPSL disbanded, and the SDP has successfully reintegrated most of the dissidents into its ranks.

Throughout the 1960s and early 1970s Rafael Paasio was credited with the success of the SDP, particularly in reuniting the leftist splinter group with the more moderate mainstream. In late 1972 a new leader emerged when the party secretary, Kalevi Sorsa, became prime minister.

Roughly 35 percent of the working class votes for SDP candidates.

140

Table 3. Finland, Composition of Parliament by Party, Selected Years, 1945–72

Party	1945	1948	1951	1954	1958	1962	1966	1970	1972
Finnish Social Democratic	50	54	53	54	48	38	55	52	55
Finnish People's Democratic League (including Finnish Communist)	49	38	43	43	50	47	41	36	37
Center	49	56	51	53	48	53	49	36	35
National Coalition	28	33	28	24	29	32	26	37	34
Finnish Rural	...	...	...	...	...	...	1	18	18
Swedish People's[1]	14	14	15	13	14	14	12	12	10
Liberal People's	9	5	10	13	8	13	9	8	7
Other[2]	1	...	...	...	3	3	7	1	4
TOTAL SEATS	200	200	200	200	200	200	200	200	200

[1]This party emerged in 1969 as an offshoot of the Center Party, which at that time was known as the Agrarian Party.

[2]In 1958, 1962, 1966 seats for Simonist splinter-group of Finnish Social Democratic Party; in 1970 and 1972 seats for Christian League of Finland.

Source: Adapted from Jaako Nousiainen, *The Finnish Political System*, Cambridge, 1971.

These voters are usually among the better paid workers in the south and west as the SDP has not been widely accepted in the northern backwoods areas, particularly in Oulu and Lapland.

Working class preference for the SDP over the Finnish Communist Party (Suomen Kommunistinen Puolue—SKP) is disproportionately high in areas bordering on the Soviet Union, particularly in north Karelia. The second most important support base for the Social Democrats is the urban lower middle class, which divides its votes between the SDP, the Finnish Rural Party (Suomen Maaseudun Poulue—SMP), and the Liberal People's Party (Liberaalinen Kansanpuolue—LKP). The SDP also attracts a large proportion of the professional vote. In the mid-1960s the New Left movement in Finland worked through the SDP and Simonist splinter group, not through the Communists as usually was the case in Europe. The largest share of the youth vote, therefore, is still concentrated in Social Democratic ranks.

The SDP relies mainly on membership dues for operating funds. This is typical of socialist parties, which require mass membership as part of their popular image. Fees are paid to the central organization according to income levels; the average yearly subscription is about Fmk4.8 (for value of the markka—see Glossary). The party bureaucracy has been pared down, and is recognizably smaller than the Finnish People's Democratic League (Suomen Kansan Demokraattinen Liitto—SKDL) and Center Party organizations. The SDP Council consists of fifty members; it is responsible to a party congress every three years.

Finnish People's Democratic League

The Finnish People's Democratic League (Suomen Kansan Demokraattinen Liitto—SKDL) is an electoral alliance that joins some noncommunist leftists as well as members of the SKP. The SKP has been represented in Parliament by the SKDL since 1945.

The SKDL includes the SKP, the Socialist League of Students, and the Democratic League of Finnish Women. The economic and social goals of the groups are almost identical; they chose to work for change by participating in State Council politics from 1966 to 1971. The SKDL is expressly interested in better relations with the Soviet Union, but the noncommunist members have sought to avoid ideological domination by the Soviet Communist Party.

The SKDL membership, both working-class and rural, is singularly poor. Support in the northern backwoods area is high, particularly in Oulu and Lapland. Rural supporters are primarily lumber workers and marginal farmers in the northern regions, which are most often hit by unemployment. Discrepancies in incomes between north and south also help to account for its backwoods constituency.

Membership of the SKDL (154,000 in 1965) accounts for roughly one-third of its support at the polls. About one-half of the members are also members of the SKP. After 1945 the SKDL regularly received over one-fifth of the popular vote until 1970, when the walkout of the militant wing of the SKP over participation in the State Council reduced support to 16.6 percent of the vote. In 1972, however, it regained its position as the second largest parliamentary group, with thirty-seven seats.

The SKDL relies on membership fees for financing its activities. It has the largest membership after the Center Party (Keskustapuolue) but, nonetheless, relies heavily on the government subsidies, which dropped drastically with the loss of parliamentary seats in 1970.

The size of the grassroots organization of the SKDL is second only to that of the Center Party. Seventeen regional units supervise the work done by more than 2,500 local offices. Within the sixty-member steering committee, the Communists are underrepresented. The SKP is allowed fewer representatives in proportion to its members than are the other three groups. Within the SKP a nine- to fifteen-member committee supervises relations with the SKDL. The latter is characterized by a rather loose organization, although the SKP remains internally a tightly knit organization.

There is a sharply defined dichotomy within the SKP between its adherents in the industrialized areas and those in the backwoods areas. The urban Communists are highly organized and socially active; the rural members are the contrary. "Backwoods radicals" are isolated, both from any local community and within their own class. On the other hand, industrial workers maintain strong ties within their class but are often estranged from the community. Poor northern farmers and lumber workers apparently have been voting a protest, and the populism of the SMP began to capitalize on this discontent in the 1970 and 1972 elections.

Center Party

The Center Party (Keskustapuolue) was known as the Agrarian Party until 1965 when it changed its name in order to attract nonrural voters who occupied a central position on the ideological spectrum. The party traditionally has been the single most powerful group in Parliament. From 1919 to 1970 it had not received less than 20 percent of the popular vote; however, in 1970, it polled 17.1 percent. A continuing outflow of population from the countryside, as industrialization quickened in the early 1970s, portends a continuing deflation of the party's role as a focal point in national politics.

Support for the Center Party is rural, with the exception of the rich, conservative southern provinces of Uusimaa and Häme, and the Swedish-speaking Ahvenanmaa Islands. Common interests among farmers have made of it a high-membership party, but this has not prevented the estrangement of the poorer farmers who in the early 1970s had gone over to the SMP.

In the 1966 election roughly 56 percent of Center Party votes came from party members, more than twice that of most other parties. This was in some part because of the extensive party organization throughout the country. In 1965 the number of precinct and communal offices of the party was set at 3,000, over twice the corresponding number for the Social Democrats. It maintains twenty-two regional offices. The highest organ is the biannual party congress, but the everyday leadership is vested in a 100-member party commission and a central executive board.

As is the case in the other nonsocialist parties, membership fees are nominal. The Center Party, because of its rural base, has developed a party tax in barter; the district organizations collect milk and grain from members, and the proceeds from the sale of the collections fill the party's coffers. Over one-fifth of the Center Party's operating budget is financed in this way. It also benefits from the government subsidies for party activities, roughly Fmk1.7 million in 1972.

The Center Party rejects both socialism and big business capitalism. Small-scale private enterprise, centralized economic planning, and agricultural reform were the main tenets of the party program in 1972. Attempts to consolidate a political center, however, have apparently failed. The number of seats in Parliament decreased from fifty-three in 1962 to thirty-five just ten years later. The success of the SMP in 1970 particularly cut into the membership of the Center Party. The political importance of the Center Party in forming State Councils has not diminished, but after 1970 chances of its regaining dominance within that body were poor. The party's almost constant participation in the State Council has given it a reputation as the government party and, consequently, it is blamed for unpopular gorvernment actions.

National Coalition Party

The National Coalition Party (Kansallinen Kokoonus—KOK) is the most important conservative party. It has provided an active program of conservative reform directed toward liberalizing the economic system. Espousing so-called people's capitalism, the KOK has been the leading party on the Right working to dismantle the machinery of governmental control, which the socialists would like to increase. It is the self-designated defender of private enterprise.

The KOK's consistent strength is based on a membership of well-to-do farmers from the south, businessmen, professionals, and the middle class in general. Half of its supporters are urban dwellers, and it has run strongest in Helsinki, Häme, northern Turku, southern Vaasa, and Kymi provinces. In 1966 a voter analysis showed that fully 12 percent of KOK supporters were workers, 40 percent businessmen, 20 percent farmers and 28 percent white-collar workers. As is the case in most of the parties, the KOK membership (83,000 in 1965) represents only roughly one-fourth of its supporters at election time.

Despite extreme shifts to and from the Left at certain periods in Finnish history, rarely has the KOK's electoral support gone below 12 percent of the popular vote. It is therefore considered one of the most stable political groups in the country. In 1970 the party won 18 percent of the popular vote, second only to the SDP's 23.4 percent. KOK seats in Parliament also peaked that year at thirty-seven. This election success was in great part owing to the modernization efforts of the KOK's leader, Juha Rihtniemi, who took over in 1965 but died in January 1971. The party reins then were turned over to another youthful reformer, thirty-four-year-old Harri Holkeri.

The party leader works directly with an executive board, which oversees the activities of the district organizations. The KOK maintains sixteen district offices located in well-defined voting regions. The entire organization convenes several times annually, represented by sixty members on a party council to which the party leader and executive board are responsible. KOK activities are for the most part financed by contributions, fundraising events, and other nonmandatory means.

Finnish Rural Party

The Finnish Rural Party (Suomen Maaseudun Puolue—SMP) began as an offshoot of the Agrarian Party in 1959 under the leadership of Veikko Vennamo. It gained its first seat in 1966, and by 1970 the SMP no longer represented only small farming interests but increasingly those of urban workers, small businesses, and the less-well-off in Finnish society. In 1970 Vennamo's party won eighteen seats in Parliament, reflecting a general shift to the Right in Finnish politics. Like the Center Party, the SMP rejects both big business capitalism and socialism and adds large farming interests to its grievances. By late 1972, however, internal dissension had split the party into two factions.

Swedish People's Party

The Swedish People's Party (in Swedish, Svensk Folkpartiet—SFP) exists primarily to protect Swedish ethnic culture in Finland, drawing its members from a cross section of the Swedish-speaking population, rich and poor, rural and urban alike. The general tenor of SFP programs is conservative, particularly in relation to the economy.

SFP strength is concentrated in Swedish-speaking areas—Helsinki, the Ahvenanmaa Islands, and the western and southern coasts. Excluding the Ahvenanmaa Islands, where some 95 percent of the population vote SFP, approximately 85 percent of its support comes from Uusimaa and Vaasa provinces alone.

Only about 25 percent of the Swedish-speaking people are dues-paying members of the SFP, but as many as 85 percent may back party candidates in an election. In 1970 the party received 5.7 percent of the popular vote.

The SFP maintains the smallest organization of the major parties, having ninety-seven precinct offices located in four major electoral regions. The party assembly meets annually, whereas the expanded central committee meets several times a year to discuss proposals made by the steering committee. SFP activities are financed mainly by contributions as membership dues are nominal. Local party offices are

145

responsible for raising funds to supplement the government subsidies.

Liberal People's Party

The Liberal People's Party (Liberaalinen Kansanpuolue—LKP) is substantially a middle-class party. As is the case with the SFP, the LKP favors government economic planning but upholds the need for private enterprise; that is, the LKP opposes nationalization of industries that the socialist parties would like to see come under government control. The LKP, however, concentrates on its social goals, particularly in the democratization of the educational system and in greater social security benefits.

The LKP's electorate is spread thinly throughout the country, but the bulk of its votes comes from the more populous southern Uusimaa and Turku provinces where it attracts mainly urban white-collar workers. In terms of the size of the voting population the LKP does relatively as well in the north as in the south. Party membership is very low; in 1966, 7 percent of its votes came from dues-paying members. For financing, the local offices of the party rely on membership dues, whereas the regional and national offices are operated on contributions.

Since 1951 the strength of the LKP has remained relatively stable. At times of discord within the Left the LKP has typically received votes from moderate Social Democrats whose views on social policy coincide with those of LKP members. This was the case in 1962 when the LKP representation in Parliament peaked at thirteen seats. Its popular vote has remained constant at about 6.3 percent of the national electorate. The party's leadership is delegated to an executive board, which is responsible to a sixty-six-member party council. The party congress meets every other year to review the work carried out in approximately 300 local offices scattered over fourteen electoral districts.

Christian League of Finland

The Christian League of Finland (Suomen Kristilliinen Liitto—SKL) was the smallest party represented in Parliament in 1972, controlling four seats. It was founded in the late 1960s and first gained national representation by winning a single seat in 1970. The impetus for its formation came from dissident Right elements of the Center and LKP parties, particularly over the debate concerning the role of religious teaching in the proposed educational reforms (see ch. 7). Its all-encompassing platform is to bring Christian ideals to Finnish politics.

The Interest Groups

The evolution of organized interest group activity has been very slow. Pressure groups have developed on a national scale relatively free of direct links to political parties although overlapping memberships have resulted in close informal ties.

In 1972 the Finnish Central League of Trade Unions (Suomen Ammattiliittojen Keskusjärjestö—SAK) was the largest interest group in the country, with a membership of 720,000. The only major trade federation, it represents about 35 percent of the workers in industry and agriculture.

There is no institutional link between the trade union movement and political parties on the Left, but a heavy overlapping membership has existed at the top levels of the SAK. The trade union movement has traditionally been led by SDP members, despite periodic attempts by SKP members to gain control, particularly in the early 1950s. A schism within the SDP in 1959 had a serious impact on the SAK. Unlike the party struggle, however, the leftist forces within the union were strongest, and in 1960 the more conservative member-unions bolted the SAK to form the Finnish Trade Unions Association (Suomen Ammattijärjestö—SAJ). Roughly one-third of the SAK membership went over to the SAJ. This was the first time that Finland's organized labor was not represented by a monolithic pressure group. The split, however, was mended in the wake of the conciliation of the SDP, and the SAK in the early 1970s was characterized by a more radical outlook and greater participation by Communists in leadership positions.

The Central Federation of Finnish Employers (Suomen Työnantajain Keskusliitto—STK) represents the major industrial employers, public and private. Some 2,500 firms employing over 500,000 workers belong to the STK. The combined economic resources of the participating enterprises have made the STK a potent force in the determination of general economic policy, particularly that pertaining to labor, and political ties have essentially been unnecessary.

The participation of state-owned enterprises has had two beneficial effects. In the first place, it has tended to moderate the employers' positions in labor negotiations, since government-controlled enterprises are under the scrutiny of Parliament. For this same reason, positions of the STK are more palatable to the government because of its indirect participation through the public sector companies.

The Central Union of Agricultural Producers (Maataloustuottajain Keskusliitto—MTK) represented over 420,000 farmers in 1972. As is the case with the SAK, the MTK has had a large, overlapping membership in common with the Center Party and, increasingly, with the SMP. To a great extent discord within the MTK between big farming interests and the smaller, subsistence-level farmers contributed to the rise of the SMP. Feeling outweighed within the MTK whenever conflicts arose, the less well-to-do farmers turned to the SMP to voice their protest.

Through the early and mid-1960s the MTK concentrated on tax and social legislation as well as guaranteed income legislation, which Parliament finally passed in the form of guaranteed prices on farm products. With this goal finally achieved the MTK turned in the late 1960s to agitate for regional reform. Active pressure was an acute necessity as the percentage of the working population engaged in agriculture was falling rapidly, from 46 percent in 1945 to 25.6 percent in 1964. The relatively underdeveloped northern and eastern farming regions are being depopulated for lack of a regional policy to encourage the development of agriculture in those areas. The MTK's objective, like that of the Center Party, is to stem the flow of farmworkers into urban areas.

The Central Federation of Officials and Civil Servants (Toimihenkilö-ja Virkamiesjärjestöjen Keskusliitto—TVK) is the smallest of the major interest groups, combining several unions that represent over one-fourth of the salaried white-collar population. Its membership exceeded the 200,000 mark in 1972 and included the unions of civil servants, nurses, and teachers. The TVK's varied membership in terms of occupation and socioeconomic class and, to a large extent, its links to government through its public sector employee membership (75 percent) have precluded any close links with particular political parties.

Lobbying in Finnish Politics

There is both an institutionalized and an informal system of lobbying. All interest groups maintain in Helsinki offices whose primary responsibilities are to maintain contacts within the administration where legislation is initiated. This also involves constant discussion with other groups affected by particular pieces of legislation. Besides this, the largest interest groups participate in the government's Economic Council.

Under the supervision of the Ministry of Economics, this Economic Council and its subcommittees criticize the government's economic programs and help to formulate its general economic policies. Participation is limited to government administrators and representatives of the major economic interest groups. From 1945 to 1964 a total of 410 interest group representatives sat on the Economic Council, of whom 156 came from the MTK, ninety-eight from the SAK, ninety-four from the STK, and sixty-two from the TVK. Appointments are made by Parliament so the groups with close party ties are noticeably well represented. For example, the strong Center Party from 1945 to 1964 gave disproportionate emphasis to agricultural interests on the economic committees. A similar situation occurs in recruiting experts to testify before parliamentary committees; the political makeup of the committee determines which interests will have a greater voice.

The unofficial participation of interest groups in the formulation of economic policy takes many forms. The four major groups draw strength from very different sources; the SAK and the MTK's activities are based on political and manpower resources, whereas the STK relies on its financial wealth. The TVK has neither a political nor a financial base and must rely on direct contacts with the government through its civil servant membership for whatever influence it has in the formulation of economic and social policy.

What is not achieved by working with the government on committees usually becomes the target of pressure tactics. The kinds of resources at a group's disposal to a great extent determine what these tactics will be.

The MTK exercises the most varied forms of pressure. First, with a relatively educated membership it is able to rely greatly on the results of investigations and studies carried out within its own organization. This information is an important trump card for the MTK when it is bargaining for certain demands and would otherwise have to use governmental or industrial figures. Second, it attempts to influence political decisions through close collaboration with the Center Party in Parliament, while maintaining a completely separate organization. Third, and most important, it may withhold agricultural produce from the market as it did in March 1956 when it received cabinet-level assurances that agricultural price hikes would not fall behind promised wage increases for industrial workers. Although the threat of withholding has been used successfully, it tended to hurt the long run position of the MTK; in the 1960s the union put more emphasis on negotiation. The diminished role of the Center Party in Parliament also makes bargaining with the government a greater necessity.

The trade union movement has been less cooperative than the MTK with the government. Its underrepresentation on the Economic Council and its lack of financial resources have contributed to its discontent. Strikes, though, have been relatively rare. The major strike of 1956 in which over 400,000 workers participated has not been repeated, primarily because it was one of the chief points of contention that led to a schism within the SAK in 1960. Open threats to strike were made by the SAK only four times between 1945 and 1964. One reason for this relative moderation is that general control of leftist newspapers by Communists has deprived the heretofore SDP-inspired SAK of a vital instrument for arousing public opinion on its own behalf. The reunification of the SAK in the late 1960s, which was characterized by greater communist participation in its management, markedly strengthened its bargaining position. The possibility of strikes occurring is greater in the 1970s with the more radical line taken by the SAK, and this gives the union a stronger hand in the Economic Council.

With a large reserve of capital assets the Federation of Finnish Employers controls most of the commercial press and funds private research (see ch. 7). The government depends on contracted research for much of its planning, and only the large industries can afford to maintain large staffs for research and development purposes. Lobbying at the different ministries is commonplace because the federation alone can afford to staff offices just for this purpose. Finally, the positions of the federation are usually supported by the parties of the Right in Parliament; this relationship is primarily ideological, but the influence of corporation donations to party coffers should not be underestimated.

The TVK has the least privileged basis for pressure politics. Without much money and without a homogeneous political inclination, the federation's resources are meager. The most explicit mechanism for calling attention to TVK demands is the threat of job strikes. Public employees do not have the right to stage walkouts, however, and in the past this has made mass action by the TVK very difficult. The rights of public employees are protected by law, however, and all official decisions regarding the situation of civil servants must be reached with the participation of their unions—generally the TVK.

The rise of interest groups in recent years has several explanations. First, the declining importance of Parliament has shifted the burden of policy formulation to the executive branch. Subsequently, the lack of a political consensus because of the fragmentation of political parties has made it imperative that government policy not alienate the major economic segments of the society: farmers, workers, and businessmen. The State Council, therefore, has been willing to work out proposals in close cooperation with the representatives of the major interest groups. In other words, Finland's present-day economic direction is more often based on negotiations, not among political parties, but among interest groups.

POLITICAL VALUES, ATTITUDES, AND ISSUES

Historically, the most important social cleavage reflected in political attitudes is the one between town and country, between urban dwellers and rural farmers. The gap has been widening rapidly as rural inhabitants move to the cities; by 1970, 51.1 percent of the population were urban dwellers. Migration to the towns, of course, altered the traditional role of agriculture as the predominant occupation.

There is a common feeling within the relatively small population that the survival of the country in international affairs depends to a great extent on internal solidarity. This solidarity is reinforced by Finland's sensitive international position between Sweden and the Soviet Union, between the West and the socialist countries. The neutral path that Finland chose has been itself an isolating factor. On domestic issues, however, the picture is not one of solidarity; the numerous political parties, which reflect deep socioeconomic divergences in the society, almost ensure disagreement.

Differentials in access to secondary and higher education also have important effects on political attitudes. Of the children of industrial workers and farmers, in 1965 only 10 percent attended high school; children of the same families made up only 8 percent of total university enrollment. Such discrepancies serve to perpetuate socioeconomic cleavages and probably contribute to the polarization of political and economic interests along class lines.

All the political parties accept the Constitution of 1919 as the working basis of the government. Within its limitations, however, the Communists and the SDP have called for a greater devolution of power to

Parliament. The KOK, on the other hand, has been interested in keeping a strong executive. An increasing inclination to place more power in Parliament also was suggested by the results of a 1971 survey of more than 1,000 people. The respondents saw the presidency almost unanimously as possessing too much power.

Earlier surveys in 1967 and 1969 indicated a growing tendency among the electorate to favor more direct popular participation in the political process. Selected samples of 1,500 respondents were surveyed by the Finnish Gallup Corporation to determine by what methods Finns preferred to choose their head of state. In 1967 only 36 percent of the respondents had opted for direct election. Two years later, however, 48 percent preferred that method as against 45 percent for an electoral college, 6 percent for parliamentary vote, and 1 percent giving no opinion.

The tendency to favor more direct participation in government was particularly evident among the young. Among respondents in the nineteen to twenty-four age group, 52 percent were in favor of direct elections as were 58 percent of the twenty-five to thirty-four age group. More noteworthy were the differences in opinion among various social groups. Sixty-three percent of the upper class respondents in 1969 preferred the existing system compared to an average of 43 percent for all the other socioeconomic groups.

Another sample survey made in 1969 solicited views of some 1,500 people on priorities in public spending. Respondents were asked to specify areas of expenditure in which appropriations should be decreased, raised, eliminated, or kept the same. The replies clearly showed an opposition to government support of political parties. Correspondingly, greater public spending was favored in the socially oriented job and housing sectors. Government expenditures in other major sectors were generally supported by respondents except for agriculture, which one-third of those interviewed preferred to reduce or eliminate.

A more volatile issue, according to a poll taken of 1,000 people in the early 1970s, is the political power exercised by nongovernmental groups. Big business was thought to possess too much power by respondents in all social groups, particularly labor. Farmers were wary of both big business and the trade unions.

In government in the early 1970s the power of the presidency was being challenged; yet the major political parties were in favor of substituting a parliamentary reappointment of Urho Kekkonen to the presidency in 1974 for an election whose disquiet could affect adversely the country's delicate new line in foreign policy (see ch. 11).

Parliamentary stability was at best a remote possibility, particularly in view of the decreased capacity of the Center Party to bridge the ideological gap. The heightening influence of economic interest groups, in turn, would not subside as long as a political majority in Parliament was lacking.

CHAPTER 11

FOREIGN RELATIONS

Finnish foreign policy is aimed at preserving the nation's political and territorial integrity and safeguarding the continuity of its national existence. Geographical reality (having the Soviet Union as a neighbor) and historical development (having been defeated in World War II) led Finland to adopt a postwar national security policy of maintaining its freedom of action by dissociating itself from the conflicts of major world powers. The main feature of contemporary Finnish foreign relations, therefore, is the policy of neutrality. Nonalignment as the official political doctrine has helped to establish friendly relations with other countries regardless of their political systems.

Within the framework of Finnish neutrality there are three important policy orientations: a special relationship with the Soviet Union; a traditional policy of close collaboration with the other Nordic countries—Sweden, Norway, Denmark, and Iceland; and an active policy as a member of the United Nations (UN).

FINNISH NEUTRALITY

Finnish neutrality is not derived from a long historical tradition, nor is it the result of an international treaty. It was adopted as an outlook and as official policy as a result of bitter experiences during World War II. Finland had attempted to stay out of that conflict, but circumstances forced it into a combat role, and it ended on the losing side (see ch. 2).

After the war, the country's international position was extremely difficult: it was isolated and its freedom of independent political action was restricted by terms of the final peace treaty signed February 10, 1947. The events of World War II taught the Finns some lessons, however. They realized that the main task of foreign policy was to find a modus vivendi with the Soviet Union.

In the immediate postwar period, Juho Paasikivi, prime minister from November 1944 to March 1946 and then president, stressed the importance of improving relations with the Soviet Union, a policy which became known as the Paasikivi line. Neutrality as such was seldom mentioned during the time of Paasikivi's presidency, but the policy of nonalignment and the avoidance of all conflict with Soviet interests was a necessary precondition to the subsequent adoption of neutrality as an official policy.

The Agreement of Friendship, Cooperation and Mutual Assistance, signed in 1948 by the Soviet Union and Finland, was a significant step toward neutrality. The agreement, subsequently reaffirmed in 1955 and 1970, was not a mutual defense alliance like those that the Soviet Union concluded at the time with such Eastern European countries as Hungary, Bulgaria, and Romania. According to the treaty, Finland was only obliged to defend its territory against an attack by the Federal Republic of Germany (West Germany) or by West Germany's allies and to forestall an attack on the Soviet Union mounted through Finnish territory. The agreement provided for Soviet assistance to Finland in case of an armed West German attack but only after consultation between both partners had determined that such a threat existed. On the other hand, the preamble of the agreement stated that the Soviet Union respected "Finland's desire to remain outside the conflicting interests of the Great Powers." Although the Finns did not characterize their official foreign policy as neutral until the mid-1950s, the Agreement of Friendship, Cooperation and Mutual Assistance with the Soviet Union represented the first international recognition of Finland's neutrality-nonalignment orientation.

The easing of world tension and Soviet Premier Nikita Khrushchev's policy of detente in the mid-1950s were advantageous to Finland's desire to achieve wider international recognition of its neutrality. The withdrawal of Soviet troops from the military bases in Porkkala on the southwest coast particularly strengthened the international status of Finland's nonalignment position. In 1955 Finland became a member of the UN and the Nordic Council, an interparliamentary organ of cooperation among Scandinavian countries. This membership enabled Finland to enlarge its maneuvering on the international level and created a stable condition for an active policy of neutrality.

After the death of President Paasikivi in 1956, President Urho Kekkonen succeeded in extending Paasikivi's policy of achieving international recognition of Finnish neutrality, particularly among the great powers. Kekkonen's policy, well known as the Paasikivi-Kekkonen line, has been one of active neutrality. Contrary to cautious and passive Swiss neutrality and focusing upon humanitarian activities, Finland's neutrality stresses active participation in international life.

This policy became evident particularly in the UN, where Finland in the 1960s began to follow a consistent pattern of active neutrality. Finland has avoided taking sides in issues that involve the interests and attitudes of the great powers. Finland's position on the German question and on other issues, such as the status of Vietnam, Korea, and South Africa, has been very cautious and restrained.

An example of Finnish active foreign policy was the plan of Kekkonen for establishing a denuclearized zone in the Nordic region in 1963. Another example was Finnish support for the Strategic Arms Limitation Talks (SALT), which took place in Helsinki and contributed to the

SALT agreement between the Soviet Union and the United States in May 1972. Finland did much preparatory groundwork and was host in 1973 to the multilateral preliminary talks of the Conference on Security and Cooperation with Europe (CSCE), involving the Soviet Union, the countries of Eastern and Western Europe, Canada, and the United States. As early as May 1967 Finland offered Helsinki as the site for the conference and in 1970 appointed a roving ambassador to assist with multilateral preparations for the conference.

BILATERAL RELATIONS

Relations with the Soviet Union

Mutual mistrust and hostility between the Russians and the Finns was heightened at the end of the nineteenth century when the tsarist government began to pursue a centralist geopolitical policy toward Finland—then an autonomous grand duchy—and when the Finns began their struggle for national independence. After Finland gained its independence in 1917, the Soviets feared that Finland might become a threat to the security of the Soviet Union, particularly because of Finland's proximity and because of the possibility that Finland might join an anti-Soviet coalition.

In 1939, facing a war with Germany, the Soviet Union maintained that its security, especially that of the Leningrad area, was at stake, and thus it had to prevent Germany from using Finnish territory as a base from which to launch a military attack. The Soviet intention was to establish a system of buffer states along its western borders. The Finns refused to accept the demand of Soviet dictator Josef Stalin for concessions, including bases in Finland, so the Soviets turned to military means to obtain their goals. But because the Soviet army was not able to destroy Finnish resistance during the Winter War or later during the Continuation War, Finland was the only country fighting on the German side (as cobelligerent and not as an ally) that escaped foreign occupation.

After World War II, Finland again succeeded in resisting Soviet pressure. Instead of accepting Stalin's first proposal for a military alliance, President Paasikivi offered an alternative proposal that resulted in the 1948 Agreement of Friendship, Cooperation and Mutual Assistance. Some international factors, such as the Berlin blockade, Western reaction toward the 1948 events in Czechoslovakia, and the first indications of the forthcoming Soviet-Yugoslavian dispute, contributed to the modification of the Soviet position. The Soviet Union also did not want to alter the status of Swedish neutrality and weighed other internal factors, such as the weak position of the Finnish Communist Party and the quality of the Finnish army.

The turning point in Soviet-Finnish relations was the 1955–56 period. The Soviet Union, pursuing a policy of peaceful coexistence, tried to improve its relations with Finland by returning the Porkkala bases to Finland in advance of the agreed upon date, ending objections to Finnish membership in the Nordic Council, and supporting Finland's admission to the UN.

The late President Paasikivi and his successor, President Kekkonen, have been considered by the Soviet leaders as guarantors of the continuance of a friendly Finnish policy. The Soviet leaders, however, did not hesitate to express their dissatisfaction with Finland's domestic developments whenever they felt that the continuation of the "Paasikivi-Kekkonen line" might be threatened. For example, in 1958 and in 1961 two developments strained relations between the Soviet Union and Finland. In the first case the Soviet Union responded negatively to the 1958 electoral victory of the Social Democratic Party and in particular opposed the possible nomination of Väinö Tanner as prime minister. The Soviet Union threatened to suspend trade agreements and recalled the ambassador from Helsinki on grounds of the ambassador's alleged poor health.

The strain in relations in 1958 was solved when President Kekkonen formed a new State Council. The 1961 difficulty was more complicated. Alarmed by Denmark's decision to accept a proposal for joint North Atlantic Treaty Organization (NATO) command on the Baltic Sea with West German participation, the Soviet leaders claimed this was an indication of a German threat that required military consultation according to Article 2 of the 1948 treaty. President Kekkonen personally met with Soviet Premier Khrushchev, achieved a postponement of military consultation, and regained Soviet recognition of Finnish neutrality.

The "mini" crises of 1958 and of 1961 did not cause any significant change in the relations between the two countries. On the contrary, during the ensuing 1962–72 period Finnish-Soviet relations continued to be amicable. Finland's successful policy of active neutrality in the UN and elsewhere had contributed to this trend.

Economic cooperation between the two countries is supervised by the Permanent Inter-Government Finnish-Soviet Commission on Economic Cooperation. The task of this commission is to prepare and supervise a long-term program of trade and production cooperation and specialization. In 1971 the commission concluded a trade agreement, effective until 1975. In the framework of Finnish-Soviet economic cooperation an important agreement was reached in 1962 to reconstruct and modernize the Saimaa Canal, which connects Finnish inland waters with the Gulf of Finland and the Baltic Sea. According to the agreement the Soviet Union agreed to lease its half of the canal to Finland. The modernization of the canal was financed by the Finns, and the canal was reopened in 1968.

Finland enjoys a most-favored-nation treatment by the Soviet Union as based upon a 1947 trade agreement and a 1960 tariff agreement and ranks fourth among the Western economic partners of the Soviet

Union, behind Great Britain, Japan, and Italy. The stable Soviet market has been an important factor for Finnish industry.

Soviet-Finnish scientific and technical cooperation has been managed by the Soviet-Finnish Commission for Scientific and Technical Cooperation. Its work focuses primarily upon exchanges of scientists between the Academy of Finland and the Academy of Sciences of the Soviet Union.

The visit of President Kekkonen to the Soviet Union in 1970 led to the renewal of the Soviet-Finnish Agreement of Friendship, Cooperation and Mutual Assistance for another twenty years. According to the published communiqué, the Soviet government again recognized Finland's status as a neutral state.

The Soviet Union and Finland, however, have held different views on some important international matters. For instance, in 1972 Finland negotiated a free trade agreement with the European Economic Community (EEC). For Finland such an agreement was not only an economic matter but also a very important political decision. Until 1972 the Soviet Union had generally expressed a negative attitude toward the supranational grouping of the EEC. Since maintaining good relations with the Soviet Union was still considered necessary for preserving Finnish neutrality, Finland decided to sign only a free trade agreement with the EEC in 1972, similar to those negotiated with other neutral European countries, such as Switzerland, Sweden, and Austria. But this agreement was still not ratified by the Finnish Parliament as of January 1, 1973.

Relations with East Germany and West Germany

Finland intended to establish economic relations with Germany after World War II but, because of disagreement among the great powers on the German question, the Finns settled for the establishment of two separate commercial missions, one in Cologne in West Germany and the other in East Berlin in the German Democratic Republic (East Germany). Because of its desire to remain outside the conflicts between the Soviet Union and the United States, Finland refused to recognize either West Germany or East Germany de jure as independent states until January 1973.

Finland has continued to enjoy economic and cultural ties with both East Germany and West Germany. In the early 1970s West Germany ranked third, behind Sweden and Great Britain, as a trade partner of Finland. The total volume of trade with West Germany represented more than half of Finland's trade with the whole EEC. Trade with East Germany was not very significant and represented only 1 percent of Finland's total trade volume. Economic relations between the two countries were improving, however. In 1971 Finland concluded an agreement on scientific, technological, and economic cooperation with East Germany.

Historically, the question of Finland's relationship with Germany has always been of great importance to Finland. The improvement of relations between West Germany and East Germany during the 1971-72 period, notably the Berlin quadripartite agreement and the Soviet-West German treaty ratified by the West German parliament in May of 1972, was considered by the Finnish government to be a significant indication of the reduction of political tension in central Europe and led to the establishment of diplomatic relations with both German states. In September 1971 the Finnish government proposed to both Germanies the opening of treaty negotiations concerning a comprehensive arrangement of relations. The sixteen months of negotiations between Finland and both Germanies brought the establishment of diplomatic relations on January 7, 1973.

Relations with the United States

The United States recognized Finland as an independent state in 1919. In that year the United States assisted Finland with deliveries of food through the Relief and Reconstruction of Europe Commission headed by Herbert Hoover. The food was supplied on credit and became known in Finland as the Hoover loan.

Since then the United States has provided Finland with other loans. All of them have been repaid. This has contributed to the development of a friendly relationship between both countries. The American public expressed great sympathy for Finland during the Winter War (1939-40) and, although the United States ambassador was recalled from Helsinki in June 1944 after Finland's decision to continue the war against the Soviet Union, the United States did not declare war.

In the post-World War II period, Finnish-American relations have been exceedingly cordial. Even though political considerations did not allow Finland to participate in the Marshall Plan after World War II, Finland received about US$200 million worth of credit from the United States to help in reconstructing its industry. President Kekkonen made official visits to the United States in 1962 and 1970. During both visits presidents John F. Kennedy and Richard M. Nixon expressed publicly their respect for Finnish neutrality. During the 1970 visit President Nixon indicated his support and appreciation for Finland's policy of active neutrality, particularly in regard to the SALT conferences.

Cultural relations between the United States and Finland have been promoted on the governmental level through exchange programs of students, scholars, and artists as well as by a number of Finnish-American organizations and through Finland's membership in the American-Scandinavian Foundation.

Relations with Sweden

The close relationship with Sweden has been particularly significant for Finland. The two countries have much in common, including their active neutrality and mutual political support in the UN and elsewhere. Economic cooperation with Sweden is important to Finland, particularly because Sweden absorbs close to 20 percent of Finland's exports, and it also employs Finland's surplus labor. Finnish-Swedish political and economic cooperation could become even more important and significant for both countries if Norway, despite its refusal by popular referendum in September 1972, ultimately joins the EEC.

MULTILATERAL RELATIONS

Finland and the Nordic Community

Nordic orientation is one of the most important features of Finnish foreign policy. The Finns, ethnically different from Scandinavians, became a part of the community of Nordic countries during 700 years of unification with the Swedish kingdom.

The candid and trusting cooperation between the Nordic countries has been a historical phenomenon with a long tradition. The origins of Nordic political cooperation—based on a desire to remain outside great power conflicts—date from World War I and joint actions in the League of Nations in the interwar period.

Post-World War II cooperation between Finland and the other members of the Nordic community was at first limited. Finland's position was complicated because its postwar foreign policy consisted of establishing the credibility of its neutrality in the eyes of the Soviet Union.

In 1955, however, Finland joined the Nordic Council, with the Soviet Union modifying its earlier position and agreeing that membership in the council did not jeopardize Finland's nonalignment policy. The Nordic Council is concerned primarily with economic and social cooperation among its members; it has no political or military policy. Contrary to the EEC system, the Nordic Council does not act through supranational organizations; it functions only as an advisory body and does not make decisions binding on the members. The charter of the Nordic Council is not based upon an international agreement bound by international law; it is only a jointly agreed upon text, approved by the parliaments of the Nordic countries. The organs of the Nordic Council are the Presidium, the Council Assembly, and various committees. The Council Assembly is composed of seventy-eight members elected from the parliaments of all five Scandinavian countries. The Finnish delegation to the Council Assembly consists of eighteen deputies. Sweden, Norway, and Denmark each send eighteen elected deputies, and Iceland sends six.

Important questions of industrial, agricultural, and social cooperation have been pursued at the government level within the framework of the Nordic Council. Finland first participated in this cooperative arrangement when it became a member of the Economic Ministerial Committee in 1956.

Political and military cooperation between Finland and the other

Scandinavian countries has developed outside the Nordic Council. The foreign ministers of Nordic countries usually meet twice a year to discuss international developments. There is also a high degree of political cohesion and cooperation among the Scandinavian countries in the UN. Finland has established smooth military consultation with the other Nordic countries on the ministerial level through regular meetings of the ministers of defense. Within the framework of the Nordic Council, Finland and the other Scandinavian states have tried to develop efficient joint assistance to underdeveloped countries. Two examples of such pragmatic Nordic cooperation are the establishment of an education center in Tanzania in 1963 and a center for training personnel for cooperatives in Kenya in the late 1960s.

As a member of the Nordic Council Finland enjoys some other advantages of Scandinavian cooperation. Finnish citizens benefit from the existence of the so-called passport union allowing travel without passports in all countries within the Nordic community. Furthermore, a free labor market agreement permits Finns to work in the other Nordic countries. In 1955 Finland became a member of the Social Security Convention, which enabled Finns living in other Nordic countries to enjoy local social benefits. The Finns also may gain citizenship in other Scandinavian countries more easily than non-Scandinavians. On the other hand, Finland does not participate as a member in another form of Nordic collaboration, the Scandinavian Airlines System (SAS).

Especially in the 1960s and 1970s, Finland actively contributed to the improvement of Scandinavian collaboration within the framework of the Nordic Council. At Finland's request the Nordic Council agreed in February 1971 to amend its charter. The amendment includes a provision that the joint expenses of the Nordic Council be divided among the countries in proportion to their gross national product (GNP). It also strengthened the status of the Presidium of the Nordic Council and established a new organ, the Council of Ministers, to which each Nordic country appoints a minister. The Council of Ministers coordinates all Nordic cooperation.

Plans were drawn for a Nordic Economic Union (NORDEC) in 1969, but certain political considerations, primarily in Finland, prevented their realization. After a period of hesitation Finland decided not to participate in the plan, apparently because it believed that the Soviet Union might consider the organization as a steppingstone to the EEC, which would be incompatible with the Finnish policy of neutrality.

Finland's Relations with Western Europe

Though Finland had to adjust its foreign policy after World War II to the changing international environment, it continued to enjoy good relations with Western European countries, particularly in the field of economic cooperation. The peace treaty in 1947 obliged Finland to avoid joining any kind of political or economic alliance that the Soviet

Union would consider a threat to its national security. Because the Marshall Plan and its implementation became a source of disagreement between the Soviet Union and the United States, Finland—because of concern for relations with the Soviet Union—did not participate. On the other hand, Finland joined other nonpolitical Western economic projects, such as the General Agreement on Tariffs and Trade (GATT) and the Organization for Economic Cooperation and Development (OECD) in 1967. An important step was taken in 1961 when Finland became an associate member of the European Free Trade Association (EFTA), enjoying the same kinds of rights as an ordinary member. Finnish membership in EFTA became feasible after the Soviet Union agreed that associate membership in EFTA was compatible with the Finnish policy of neutrality and after the conclusion of the tariff agreement with the Soviet Union, ensuring the continuity of Finnish-Soviet economic cooperation.

Finland and the United Nations

Because Finland had fought with the Axis powers during World War II, it was ineligible for charter membership in the UN in 1945. Finland applied for membership in 1947, but cold war disagreements among the great powers on UN admission policy delayed Finland's entry until 1955.

Finland had not been very enthusiastic about membership in the UN in the 1945-55 period. Finland tried to pursue the Paasikivi policy of passive and cautious neutrality and feared that joining the UN would be incompatible with its nonalignment status. A strict interpretation of the UN charter, agreed upon at the San Francisco Conference in 1945, made UN membership and neutrality incompatible. According to Article 25 of the charter, members of the UN are obliged to follow the decision of the Security Council in applying economic or military sanctions against other member states of the UN. The dispute on admission policy was finally resolved in 1955 with an agreement among the major powers, and Finland was admitted as a UN member in December of the same year, together with fifteen other nations.

There have been two main lines of Finnish policy in the UN. It avoids any political or economic confrontation in which the interests of the great powers are directly involved, and it collaborates and consults closely with the other Scandinavian countries. Consistent with its neutral position, Finland abstained from voting on the resolutions condemning Soviet intervention in Hungary in 1956 and in Czechoslovakia in 1968. Nor did it vote on any resolutions concerning the Arab-Israeli War of 1967. Finnish policy in the UN often has been characterized as a policy of playing the role of a doctor rather than a judge, meaning that Finland approaches international conflicts with a pragmatic outlook, trying to find a political solution or offering assistance and avoiding condemnatory action. Thus Finland was not in favor of the

161

resolutions of the General Assembly in the 1960s calling for sanctions against Rhodesia or South Africa. Instead, Finland increased its economic support to developing countries, especially those in Africa.

Roughly 90 percent of Finnish assistance to less developed countries has been funneled through the various agencies of the UN, through the United Nations Development Program (UNDP) and the International Development Association. In 1968 Finland became a member of the so-called million club, composed of UN members whose contribution to the UNDP was more than 1 million dollars a year. The Finnish government also provides scholarships for students from underdeveloped countries, and Finnish experts participate in the UN assistance programs for the Third World.

Finland supports and actively participates in the peace-keeping activities of the UN. Finnish armed forces were first put at the disposal of the UN during the Suez crisis (1956–57). Finnish officers served in observers units in the Lebanon crisis of 1958 and on the Indian-Pakistan border in 1961. Finland also sent a battalion of soldiers as a part of a UN peace-keeping mission on Cyprus in 1967. Furthermore, a Finnish general was named commander in chief of the UN armed forces on Cyprus in 1966, and another Finnish general became a commander of UN troops at the Suez Canal in 1970. Like the other Nordic countries, Finland has organized several standby military units available only for the purpose of participating in UN peace-keeping operations whenever they are required.

Finland and the other Nordic countries have coordinated their UN policy to a high degree through meetings and consultations of their ambassadors and representatives at the UN. Each of the Nordic countries often represents the interests of the entire Nordic community. In 1962 Finland and Norway were the first members of the UN to try to improve the unfavorable financial situation of the organization.

Finnish membership in the UN has been one of the factors enabling the extension of the Paasikivi concept of passive neutrality into a policy of active neutrality intimately connected with President Kekkonen. For example, in 1959 Finland was not willing to accept an unofficial offer to become a candidate for membership in the UN Security Council because this would not be compatible with its principle of neutrality. During the 1960s Finland's active policy in the UN helped it achieve broad international recognition of Finnish neutrality. Finland then was able to accept election as a member of the Security Council for the 1969–70 period. During this time Finland intensified its international activities, especially with regard to such important issues as disarmament and arms control. The Security Council accepted the Finnish proposal of adopting a system of a regular foreign ministers conference. The Finnish ambassador to the UN, Max Jakobson, was one of the principal candidates for the position of secretary general in the fall of 1971.

CONDUCT OF FOREIGN POLICY

The President

The Constitution of 1919 assigns to the president considerable powers with respect to foreign policy (see ch. 9). According to Article 33, "the President shall determine the relations of Finland with foreign issues." Only the questions of war or peace are matters requiring approval by Parliament. They are to be decided "by the President and with the consent of Parliament." The constitution stresses the responsibility of the Ministry of Foreign Affairs for the "management of foreign affairs," but political developments after World War II, particularly the need for a strong guarantor of Finnish Eastern policy impelled the president to assume responsibility for their direction. In fact, the president, rather than the prime minister or minister of foreign affairs, is the supreme leader in foreign affairs.

Because the president is elected by popular vote for a six-year term and may be reelected, he is considered to be a guarantor of a stable foreign policy, ensuring its continuity. The strong position of the president in foreign affairs is buttressed by other important powers given him by the constitution. He is commander in chief of the armed forces; he can exercise a veto over legislation; and he has the right to dissolve Parliament. The other factor contributing to the predominant position of the president in regard to foreign affairs has been the relative instability of the State Council. In the 1917-73 period, Finland has had more than fifty state councils, whose average life has been no more than one year. The president is not politically responsible to the State Council, and he may make a foreign policy decision even if it is in opposition to the majority of the members of the State Council (see ch. 9). The president has often used official and unofficial speeches and statements to present foreign policy developments.

The Parliament

Because of the predominant position of the president in the Finnish political system generally and in the field of foreign policy particularly, Parliament's influence upon conduct of foreign affairs is limited. Its role in foreign affairs is chiefly devoted to formulating and approving treaties.

The matters resolved by Parliament deal generally with the most serious agreements concerning the political and territorial integrity of the Finnish republic, such as the resolution of war and peace, or other serious treaties having provisions that require Parliament's approval. In some cases, however, even such important agreements have been considered in Parliament after they have been concluded, such as the armistice of the Winter War in 1940 or the armistic of the Continuation War in 1944.

The parliamentary supervision of foreign affairs and the preparation of treaties demanding the approval of Parliament are the most important tasks of its Foreign Affairs Committee. But the formulation of foreign policy is not seriously influenced by this committee, nor has it participated effectively in the conduct of foreign affairs.

The State Council

The State Council also has a permanent Foreign Affairs Committee in which important matters of foreign affairs can be considered. The members of the committee include the prime minister, who serves as chairman; the minister of foreign affairs; and three other ministers. Only during World War II did it have an important role in the formulation of foreign policy. After World War II, however, its role diminished, and it began serving as an advisory body to the president.

THE ADMINISTRATION OF FOREIGN AFFAIRS

The administration of foreign affairs is undertaken by a minister and his assistant, a state secretary. There are five major divisions of the Ministry of Foreign Affairs—administrative, political, commercial, legal, and protocol.

In the early 1970s there were no formal or informal requirements for a diplomatic career. The requirement of an academic degree was abolished by governmental reforms in 1970. Subsequently, candidates were admitted once a year without significant preconditions for a three-month course on the diplomatic service. According to their achievements in a highly competitive examination, the candidates are selected for diplomatic training, which lasts two years.

The members of the Finnish diplomatic corps are Finnish citizens, with one exception. As in many other Western countries, the rules permit the president to designate nonsalaried honorary consuls who are not required to be Finnish citizens. Honorary consuls are usually foreigners with a special interest in some aspect of Finnish economic, political, and cultural life.

The foreign service is regarded as a prestigious profession by certain segments of Finnish society, particularly by the middle class. Foreign service personnel are drawn from all segments of the society, but the most highly educated sector of the population predominates.

Finland maintains forty-four embassies and has one legation in the Republic of South Africa. A permanent mission is stationed at the UN in New York and another is in Geneva, representing the country's interests at UN special agencies in Switzerland.

DOMESTIC REACTION TO FOREIGN RELATIONS

Finland's foreign policy has not usually been a matter of broad public or parliamentary discussion. The conduct of foreign policy becomes a topic of domestic political struggle among the parties and various pressure groups only in a period of crisis, such as the 1958 and 1961 episodes of strained relations with the Soviet Union.

Even so, all parties are in agreement on the basic lines and future of Finnish foreign policy, that is, a neutral orientation, friendship with the Soviet Union, and Nordic cooperation. During periods of strain in relations with the Soviet Union in 1958 and 1961, for example, no one questioned the official Paasikivi-Kekkonen political doctrine of a friendly Eastern policy. Discussion focused instead on the issue of what should be done in order to improve Soviet-Finnish relations.

This is not to say that there are no obvious differences among the various political parties. The predominantly communist Finnish People's Democratic League has been the most outspoken advocate of closer relations with the Eastern European countries, especially with the Soviet Union. The Finnish People's Democratic League has also been a bitter opponent of any form of arrangement with the EEC. The National Coalition Party has assumed a rather pro-Western orientation, particularly in regard to economic cooperation with Western European countries. In 1972 the governing parties—the Center Party, the Social Democratic Party, the Liberal People's Party, and the Swedish People's Party—opted for a commercial arrangement with the EEC, compatible with Finland's nonaligned position.

Political parties also have taken different approaches toward specific foreign policy issues. Regarding the question of assistance to the under-developed countries, the left-oriented parties—the Finnish People's Democratic League and the Social Democratic Party—have favored some form of economic assistance connected with social reforms. Non-socialist parties have been in favor of a pragmatic kind of economic assistance provided primarily in the framework of the UN and not necessarily connected with political development.

The Finnish leaders have succeeded in creating broad support for their foreign policy program, based primarily upon the policy of neutrality and its importance for the national security of Finland.

In the last presidential election in 1968, President Kekkonen was elected with 65.1 percent of the electoral votes. Since the basic issues in presidential elections usually are concerned with foreign policy, the 1968 results seem to show that the majority of the Finnish people support the official foreign policy. In 1973, the president's term was extended by Parliament until 1978.

SECTION III. ECONOMIC

CHAPTER 12

CHARACTER AND STRUCTURE
OF THE ECONOMY

The ravages of World War II wreaked heavy destruction upon the Finnish economy. The rapid recovery of activity in the early postwar years represented enormous effort and sacrifice. Twelve percent of the national territory and productive capacity was ceded to the Soviet Union along with the equivalent of US$570 million (at 1952 prices) in war reparations paid out over an eight-year span, 1944 to 1952. Consumption had to be restricted to allow for higher rates of savings and investment. Despite these difficulties, by 1948 per capita output had regained its 1938 level.

In the twenty-year period after 1948 total output expanded at a rate of 5 percent annually. Exports increased at an annual average rate of 8 percent. Productivity rose 4 percent per year. This general performance was roughly in line with the trend for all Western European countries combined, according to the figures of the Organization for Economic Cooperation and Development (OECD). Gross fixed asset formation (total investment) remained at about one-quarter of the gross national product (GNP—see Glossary) throughout the 1960s and early 1970s.

The agriculture and mining sector's share of output and employment contracted sharply after 1948. The other sectors of the economy expanded their shares. During World War II and immediately thereafter, manufacturing grew most rapidly to meet the demand for war supplies and, later, reparations deliveries (especially metal and engineering products). Since 1948, however, public utilities, transport and communications, commerce, and other services have become the largest producers and employers (see table 4). These structural changes confirm that Finland has nearly reached the stage of a mature developed country, although agriculture and mining remain somewhat more important than in other industrialized countries.

In 1970 GNP was valued at Fmk42.84 billion (for value of the markka—see Glossary). Per capita income was Fmk9,282—fourteenth highest among all developed countries. This high standard of living was achieved despite relatively poor transport, the severe northern climate, and a lack of coal and of most other mineral resources vital to

	Net National Product (in percent)			Employment (in percent)		
	1938	1948	1971	1938	1948	1971
Agriculture and mining	35	32	14	51	43	19
Manufacturing and construction	31	39	40	26	30	37
Utilities, transport, communications, commerce, and services	34	29	46	23	27	44

Source: Adapted from Jussi Linnamo, *Finland: A Growing Economy*, Helsinki, 1967; and Kansallis-Osake-Pankki, *Finland in Figures*, Helsinki, 1971.

the development of heavy industry. Extensive forest reserves and abundant water power combined with a skilled work force, high savings and investment ratios, and a stable government committed to modernization had transformed Finland from a predominantly agricultural economy to an industrialized state.

Finland is the world's foremost producer of plywood and icebreakers, is second in paper pulp, third in vanadium ore, and tenth in roundwood cuttings. In addition, it practically dominates world trade in lanthanide ores and is one of the leading exporters of pulp, paper, plywood, sawed lumber, meteorological instruments, and other metal and engineering products. Finnish design in glass, ceramics, stainless steel cutlery, and textile manufacture is internationally acclaimed. Even with this highly successful and expanding export trade, however, over the past fifteen years, imports have exceeded exports almost every year.

CAPITAL STRUCTURE

In the early 1970s Finland had a predominantly free market economy. Private enterprise accounted for 72 percent of GNP in 1971. Ownership remained largely in private hands in commerce, agriculture, forestry, housing construction, manufacturing, and banking and insurance. Government investment had developed other sectors, including mining and quarrying, nonresidential construction, public utilities, and transport and communications.

In the late 1960s joint ventures between government-owned, private domestic, and foreign corporations were organized in certain capital-intensive, high-technology sectors, such as automobiles and chemicals. In all, government-controlled firms accounted for only about 16 percent of industrial production, and their powers of decision making were fairly independent of the government. In the private sector no single group or company dominated the economy, although there were several large cooperatives for instance in wholesale trade.

PROBLEMS OF ECONOMIC DEVELOPMENT

Certain economic objectives have provided direction for government policy and illustrate the kinds of policy instruments utilized. General objectives include high rates of economic growth, full employment, redistribution of personal income, rapid increases in real disposable income, stable prices, and a sound international reserves position.

Export Dominance and the Cyclical Instability of Growth

Economic growth has been satisfactory; however, there have been marked fluctuations in annual rates of GNP expansion. Much of the fluctuation can be explained by the strong influence of export earnings on the level of domestic activity. Income from exports was over 26 percent of GNP in 1969. Merchandise export value has shown greater instability in Finland than elsewhere in Europe. This can be accounted for largely by the high variability of foreign demand for forestry products, which represented 54 percent of total export value in 1971.

Price Behavior

A second area for official concern has been the problem of rising prices. The rate of inflation was distinctly higher than the average for the OECD countries. The pattern of price behavior was marked by short periods of stability succeeded by longer periods of rapid rises. The sequence was: 1945 to 1951—most of the time rapid inflation; 1952 to 1955—stability; 1956 to 1958—steep rises in prices; 1959 to 1962—renewed stability; 1963 to 1967—upturn of prices (5+ percent per year); 1968 to 1970—stability again; early 1970s—another round of inflation. Excess demand—stemming in the early years from payments of the war indemnity and resettlement of refugees from the ceded areas—seems to have been the most important cause of price inflation. Strikes and inflationary wage settlements, however, have played important roles on at least two occasions—1956 and 1971.

The Balance of Payments

Finland's balance of payments reflects an excess of imports over exports and a rising debt service burden. The trade balance has been in deficit for every year but one since 1958. The 1971 trade deficit of US$457 million, about 4.5 percent of GNP, was unprecedented. Even with a favorable current service balance amounting to US$115 million, the remaining deficit of US$342 million in 1971 was one of the highest ever experienced by Finland. Indeed, only twice in nine years has the current account been in surplus (see table 5). The debt service burden, included in the amortization of long-term loans, has fluctuated but is generally headed in an upward direction.

There also has been a shift in the structure of foreign debt. Average loan maturity has shortened. This development should reinforce the

Table 5. Finland, Balance of Payments, 1965–72[1]

	1965	1966	1967[2]	1968	1969	1970	1971	1972[2] Forecast
Exports f.o.b.[3]	1,419	1,495	1,523	1,626	1,975	2,294	2,344	2,754
Imports f.o.b.[3]	1,652	1,732	1,706	1,602	2,030	2,643	2,801	3,171
Trade balance	-233	-237	-183	24	-55	-349	-457	-417
Services:								
Transportation	107	111	122	115	138	170	157	
Travel	-34	-30	-26	-2	1	34	59	
Investment income	} -41	} -50	} -62	} -67	-77	-95	-117	
Transfers (net)					17	-4	16	
Other services	11	8	5	-6	-3	4	16	
Total services	43	39	39	40	59	113	115	125
Current Balance	-190	-198	-143	64	21	-240	-34	-292

Long-term borrowing	136	162	267	296	251	352	650
Amortization of long-term loans	-85	-85	-119	-207	-172	-165	-204
Long-term export credits (net)	-21	-19	-10	-40	-43	-60	-50
Other long-term capital items (net)	1	-10	4	-19	-12	-48	-21
Short-term capital	71	39	-30	47	-8	270	138
SDR allocations[4]	...	...	...	...	...	21	20
Nonmonetary transactions	-88	-111	-32	142	37	130	191
Change in reserves:							
Central Bank (including International Monetary Fund credit branches)	-63	-100	-25	158	-27	134	132
Other	-25	-11	-7	-16	64	-4	60

[1] In million US$.
[2] Figures as given in source.
[3] Free on board.
[4] Special drawing rights.

Source: Adapted from Organization for Economic Cooperation and Development, *OECD Economic Surveys: Finland*, Paris, May 1971; and Organization for Economic Cooperation and Development, *OECD Economic Surveys: Finland*, Paris, June 1972, pp. 14, 50.

trend toward higher repayments in the 1970s and consequently intensify pressure on the balance of payments.

Over the long term, Finland's ability to continue financing its current account deficits by foreign borrowing will be mainly limited by the ability to finance repayment out of proceeds from export earnings.

Regional Underdevelopment

Four major regions of different industrial development—south, central eastern, central western, and north—can be distinguished (see fig. 5). Almost 60 percent of the population, including a slightly higher percentage of the labor force, is located in the south. Yet, the rate of unemployment is far lower than the national average. The reason can be found in the varying importance of agriculture and mining relative to manufacturing and services. In the cental and northern regions, 40 to 50 percent of the work force was employed in agriculture and mining in 1960 in contrast to only 25 percent of the labor force in the south. Employment in agriculture and mining declined in all regions during the 1960s. The number of workers released from these two sectors was greater than the number of workers absorbed by the manufacturing and service sectors combined in those regions, leading to a net decline of the work force in all regions except the south. Thus, regions outside the south manifested familiar elements of regional underdevelopment—erosion of the traditional economic base with insufficiently diversified economies to absorb displaced workers, relatively high rates of unemployment, and contraction of tax revenues posing serious difficulties for local governments.

In 1966 the central government sought to combat these growing disparities by the establishment of a Regional Development Board. Two development zones were designated, covering the entire country outside Region I. The largest amount of assistance was reserved for the northern region. Three broad tactical approaches were adopted: investment incentives, including government-sponsored loans on easy terms, tax deductions, and subsidies of interest on loans and transport charges for goods delivered from development zones to other areas; promotion of labor mobility through job retraining and relocation allowance schemes; and selective development of large communities that appeared to offer the greatest potential for future expansion through greater concentration of government investments in infrastructure (communications, energy, and others).

In early 1973 at a time when new policies were still being formulated, it was not possible to draw any definitive conclusions about the efficacy of these approaches, given their relatively short period of operation. Over 11,500 people completed six-month retraining courses in 1971—approximately 0.6 percent of the labor force. This was about twice the number retrained in 1969, suggesting that progress in this

172

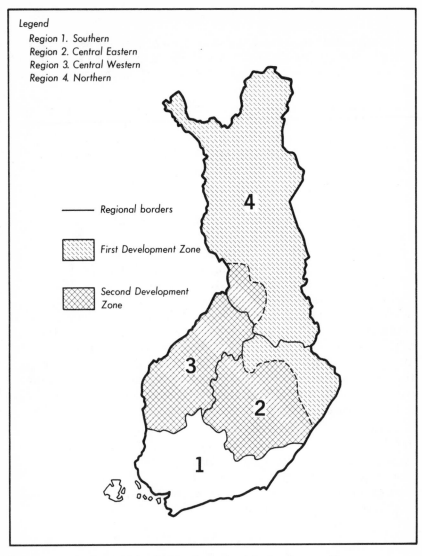

Figure 5. Finland, Major Regions and the Development Zones

Source: Adapted from Organization for Economic Cooperation and Development, *OECD Surveys: Finland*, 1971, Paris, p. 28.

area was moving ahead rapidly. On the other hand, the investment incentives, particularly the tax exemptions, seemed less trenchant in effect. According to studies carried out by the Regional Development Board, most entrepreneurs did not consider the incentives significant; and indeed, only twelve out of the 339 firms benefiting from the provisions came from outside the development zones implying, perhaps, that efforts to induce industry from the south to relocate in the north were not turning out as well as was hoped for.

Emigration

Linked closely to the regional development problem is that of emigration. Since the end of World War II, Finland has been a net supplier of labor to the rest of the world, Sweden absorbing the largest number of Finnish immigrants (see ch. 3).

Until the late 1960s the flow of emigration was regarded by many Finns as beneficial. It was thought that emigration acted as a safety valve, relieving the heavy unemployment in the north and center; that it provided a significant source of foreign exchange through remittances by emigrants from abroad; and that it permitted the training of many unskilled workers whose talents would be useful to Finland when they eventually returned home.

Findings of various studies published in the early 1970s cast some doubt on these assumptions. One investigation of the origins of Finnish immigrants in Sweden, for example, revealed that one-third of the total had come from the southern region of Finland, where no serious unemployment problem existed. Another survey indicated that among Finnish residents in Sweden only a minority had any desire to return to their homeland. Still another study of the same group indicated that rather than having been unemployed in their native country, 78 percent of the men and 68 percent of the women had been gainfully employed at the time of their departure. Official statistics showed, moreover, that remittances received from Finnish emigrants and from Finnish workers temporarily abroad altogether constituted less than US$60 million of total current receipts of over US$3 billion.

In the early 1970s the Finnish government was developing its policy for dealing with the emigration problem. Because it was found that a close negative correlation existed between the degree of industrialization in any given region and the net outflow of emigrants as a percentage of the work force, that policy was being formulated largely within the context of more balanced regional development.

Income Distribution

Decisive changes have occurred in the distribution of national income since 1938 (see table 6). When wages and other labor income (principally old-age and disability pensions) were combined, the share of total income from wages rose from 50.1 percent to 64 percent of total income. At the same time a marked decline occurred in the share of income from unincorporated enterprises. The term *unincorporated* refers to the self-employed. Most of this decline resulted from the diminishing role of agriculture and forestry, both of which contain high percentages of the self-employed. Since the number of workers in these sectors also has declined, there has been no per capita decline of the income of workers in unincorporated enterprises. Little change

Table 6. Sources of National Income in Finland, 1938 and 1970

	1938 (in percent)	1970 (in percent)
Wages	50.1	55.0
Other labor income	...	9.0
Income from unincorporated enterprises	26.2	14.0
Interest and rent	14.4	12.0
Corporate profits and surplus of government enterprises	9.3	10.0
TOTAL	100.0	100.0

Source: Adapted from Kansallis-Osake-Pankki, *Finland in Figures*, Helsinki, 1971.

has been registered in the shares of interest and rents and corporate profits.

GOVERNMENT ECONOMIC POLICY

Fiscal Policy

Fiscal policy—the management of aggregate demand by changes in government tax receipts and expenditures—has not played a significant role in demand management. Indeed, the failure to use it has probably contributed to the cyclical instability of the economy. During inflationary periods, rises in government expenditure have given an extra push to prices. During recessionary periods, government savings have tended to increase, denying the economy needed stimulation. Only in 1959 and 1963 was added spending used effectively to end a recession. In part, fiscal policy has not been used more often because of the difficulty of bringing about sudden shifts in taxation or spending policies, a problem that is common to many democratic societies. Many changes require parliamentary approval. The need for an increase or decrease in taxes may be the subject of long debate. Often the criteria applied are not primarily economic. Meanwhile, the time for optimal results has passed, and implementation of new policy no longer produces the desired effect.

Monetary Policy

Monetary policy—regulation of the supply of credit and its cost— has been employed more frequently and with better timing in general than fiscal policy. By and large, the Central Bank has been able to move quickly to tighten credit and raise interest rates when the economy showed signs of overheating and vice versa. As an autonomous institution whose policies are subject to review but not advance approval by Parliament, a bank obviously has greater freedom of action to switch policy in different directions than does the government.

As a result of the restricted domestic money and capital markets,

175

monetary authorities do not have as many options for managing the supply of money as can be found in most other Western developed countries. Varying the volume of rediscounting (the acceptance of personal loan notes from member banks in exchange for cash payment of their face value minus a small discount) is the principal technique used. Occasionally the bank changes the lending rate, imposes ceilings on bank advances, recommends changes in the rate of credit expansion, and restricts borrowing from abroad. The tendency at the beginning of the 1970s was toward greater flexibility in the use of different policy instruments. Nevertheless, the impact of monetary policy has often been difficult to assess because of the dominance of trade and capital flows (often impossible to adjust without sacrificing balance of payment objectives) in the determination of money supply. Furthermore, the direction of fiscal policy has often been contrary to that of prevailing monetary policy, which may have largely neutralized its effect.

Incomes Policy

Incomes policy—regulation of wages and prices—became a key control instrument in the late 1960s with the signing of the Stabilization Agreement of 1968. Under the agreement, workers assented to limiting wage increases to the overall rise in productivity. Farmers accepted a ceiling of 4 percent per year on the rise of support prices. The government pledged itself to avoid any tax increases during the following two years and to put a limit on its long-term borrowing. Controls on rents and prices were introduced. The agreement was renewed twice, once at the end of 1970 and again in March 1972. Despite some inflation in the early 1970s, the agreement brought measurable benefits to the competitiveness internationally of Finland's exports.

There were signs of erosion in the stability of prices toward the latter half of 1970 and in 1971, however, as the economy began to reach near capacity under pressure of strong foreign demand. The wage clauses in the 1970 agreement also were interpreted with considerably greater flexibility in the application of the productivity criterion, resulting in higher wage settlements. In the 1972 agreement the flexible component in regard to wage settlement was expanded, and the ceiling on agricultural support prices nearly doubled from 4.0 percent to 7.6 percent. Thus there were definite signs that income policy was fading under the pressures of a new wage-price spiral. The success of the 1968 agreement nonetheless presages increased reliance on wage and price controls in the future, when monetary and fiscal policy fails to curb inflation.

PUBLIC FINANCE

The System of Taxation

In 1970 current government revenue represented 36.4 percent of

GNP. This ranked Finland in the middle among developed countries. The gross tax burden is less than in lender countries, such as Sweden, Norway, the Netherlands, and Great Britain but higher than in Japan, Switzerland, Australia, and the United States.

Central government revenue is heavily dependent on indirect taxes, although the share of these taxes in total revenue has gradually declined (see table 7). Almost half of these taxes derives from an 11 percent sales tax. The other half derives mainly from excise duties on

Table 7. Central Government Revenue and Expenditure in Finland, 1972
(in million U.S. dollars)

Current Revenue		Current Expenditure	
Direct taxes on households 1,347		Purchase of goods and services ...	918
Direct taxes on corporations	151	Defense	(204)
Indirect taxes 1,857		Civil	(714)
Income from property and		Subsidies	394
entrepreneurship	172	Interest on public debt	73
Other domestic current		Current transfers 1,482	
transfers	110	To other public authorities ..	(426)
Current transfers from rest		To household and other ......(1,044)	
of the world	1	To rest of the world	(12)
Total Current Revenue 3,638		Total Current Expenditure. 2,868*	
		Net Current Savings	770

*Totals may not add because of rounding.

Source: Adapted from Organization for Economic Cooperation and Development, *OECD Economic Surveys: Finland*, Paris, March 1973.

alcohol and fuel oil. Import and stamp duties, which before World War II provided over 50 percent of all revenues, now yield less than one-tenth.

Income and inheritance taxes yield only about one-third of all tax revenue but have been steadily gaining in importance. The corporation tax is flat rate, whereas the personal income tax is progressive. The 1970 tax rate on corporate income was 47 percent, and the personal rate ranged from 13 to 51 percent depending on income.

In addition to state income taxes there is also a flat-rate local income tax, ranging from 10 to 18 percent of taxable income, depending on the commune; and 1 percent church tax and national pension and health insurance premiums, which take 1.5 percent and 1.25 percent, respectively, of taxable income.

Many types of exemptions were available. Among them was the standard deduction, which was 40 percent of distributed profits for corporations and up to Fmk3,500 (on a yearly income of Fmk20,000 or more) for individuals.

Parliament must approve both taxation schedules and current government expenditure for each fiscal year (which coincides with the calendar year). Proposed changes in tax rates may be dealt with in a matter of days, but any changes that are to last more than a year require the approval of a two-thirds majority in Parliament. The government may alter certain charges, such as the tax on tobacco and alcohol as well as prices for services rendered by government enterprises, without prior approval from Parliament.

The Budget

Each autumn the Ministry of Finance submits the budget to Parliament, accompanied by a survey of the economic situation and the outlook for the coming year. Early in the following year, while the budget is being debated, the ministry publishes a revised version of the survey, which estimates the overall fiscal impact on aggregate demand, incomes, and money supply. After approval of the final budget, the government may return several times during the year with requests for supplementary appropriations.

The role of central government expenditures in the economy actually declined slightly in the postwar era. In 1948, 30 percent of GDP was devoted to government activities whereas in 1971 the figure was 29 percent. When compared to the prewar level, however (16 percent of GDP in 1938), there can be little doubt that government spending has become much more significant in recent times.

In terms of resource allocation there have been some significant changes. In the late 1940s and early 1950s temporary expenditures associated with war—namely, reparations and compensation to evacuees from lands ceded to the Soviet Union—dominated the budget. From 1953 to 1971 the fastest growing sectors in the budget were education, social welfare transfers, and capital investments.

Public expenditure on goods and services is about equally divided between local and central governments. The central government budget usually shows a net financial saving. Tax revenues usually cover only about two-thirds of local government expenditure, the remainder being financed mainly by transfers from the central budget.

FINANCIAL INSTITUTIONS

The Finnmark (Fmk), or markka, is the official monetary unit and is a convertible currency. The banking system is controlled by the Bank of Finland (Central Bank), an autonomous public institution administered by a nine-man Board of Directors. The directors are appointed by Parliament, and their actions are subject to review by that body. In practice, the bank works in close cooperation with the government on the elaboration of monetary policy.

The Bank of Finland's chief responsibilities are: the coinage of currency and the regulation of the rate of growth in the money supply; the establishment of the official lending rate on credit extended to the other banks; the regulation of cash reserves held by the other banks; the control of capital flows involving the foreign sector; and the grant of loans to the government and even private investors in certain cases.

Other institutions in the banking system include seven commercial banks (828 branches), 330 savings banks (1,254 branches), 464 cooperative banks (1,223 branches), six mortgage credit banks, one postal bank (2,911 branches), one development bank (Industrialization Fund of Finland, Ltd.), one export credit bank (Finnish Export Credit, Ltd.), and one long-term lending bank for enterprises operating in the field of tourism (Tourism Development Fund, Ltd.). In addition, there are several nonbank institutions: The National Pensions Fund, two institutions that finance corporate research and development, and sixty-two private insurance companies.

Financial institutions in Finland do not, as a rule, offer specialized services. Nearly all provide both consumer and commercial credit as well as savings deposit services. Few institutions operate exclusively in capital markets, and their business is not very large. Commercial banks have very limited portfolio holdings, and the market in short-term government notes and bonds is small.

THE ROLE OF FOREIGN CAPITAL

Foreign capital has been useful to the economy both as a means of promoting structural change and as a source of loans to finance the government debt. The small size of the Finnish domestic capital market leads the government and private investors to draw on foreign suppliers in order to supplement internal savings.

In the 1960–67 period, capital imports (net) amounted to 6 percent of gross fixed capital formation, or 1.5 percent of GNP. Over 70 percent of this capital came in the form of financial and commercial credits and bond loans. In addition, the government of Finland has negotiated certain loans from the International Bank for Reconstruction and Development (IBRD, commonly known as the World Bank).

Foreign investment in Finnish companies has been comparatively modest (about 5 percent of capital imports in the 1960–71 period), but in the late 1960s it grew rapidly. The liberalization of trade and capital movements and Finland's accession to a number of international economic institutions, such as the European Free Trade Association, the IMF, and the OECD, have increased the attractiveness of the home market for foreign investors. In 1969 some 500 partially or totally foreign-owned firms were established in Finland. Most foreign capital has gone into manufacturing. The most important investing country was Sweden.

CHAPTER 13

AGRICULTURE AND INDUSTRY

Agriculture and industry to some extent embody Finland's past and present—coexisting, but clearly in a state of changing balance. As late as 1967 agriculture and forestry employed a larger portion of the labor force than any other sector of the economy. By then, however, saturation of internal demand for the most important agricultural products and greater efficiency of output had eliminated many jobs and created widespread underemployment in rural areas. The incomes of small homesteads in the more remote rural areas of the country had become increasingly marginal. A process of labor transfer from agriculture to industry had begun, however, which could ultimately scale down the agriculture work force to a size consistent with the needs of a fully mechanized agriculture.

In the industrial sector of the economy, the forest industry was dominant until the late 1950s, and the metal and engineering industry was a distant and modest second. The economy was then organized primarily to service the domestic market. After 1957 a policy of trade liberalization induced a fundamental restructuring of industry. Product diversification and specialization, guided by foreign patterns of demand, brought many new industries to the fore—first and foremost metallurgy and engineering, but also such newcomers as petroleum, chemicals, plastics, and automobiles.

AGRICULTURE

Until the mid-twentieth century Finland was an agrarian country. Severe winters and the generally poor soil made profitable farming difficult. Untimely frosts and droughts in the autumn and spring seasons caused crop yields to vary greatly from year to year. Nevertheless, agriculture and forestry were the largest employers of labor, and a strong agricultural research program enabled farmers to make the most of limited resources.

The small independent farmer-owner was the bulwark of agriculture. Small-scale farming became a widespread reality as early as 1922, when the first of a series of land reforms was carried out. In 1969 the average farm size was about twenty-two acres (see table 8). Ninety-nine percent of all farms were privately owned and operated. Farm families provided 90 percent of the work force. The rest was made up of wage workers.

Table 8. Number of Farms in Finland by Size, 1969

Size	Number of Farms	Percent of Total Farms
Fewer than 13 acres	108,796	36.6
13–50 acres	165,924	55.8
50–125 acres	20,625	6.9
125–250 acres	1,620	0.5
More than 250 acres	292	0.1
TOTAL	297,257	99.9*

*Total does not add to 100 because of rounding.

Source: Adapted from Finland, Central Statistical Office, *Statistical Yearbook of Finland 1970*, Helsinki, 1971.

In the 1960s, however, the importance of agriculture in the Finnish economy began to diminish. By 1970 its contribution to the gross national product (GNP—see Glossary) had declined to roughly 7 percent of total output, as compared with 11 percent in 1960.

Mechanization accelerated and resulted in the same quantity of output being produced by ever fewer and fewer workers. Tractors, for example, of which there were a mere 14,000 in 1950, by 1970 numbered more than 240,000, or about one for every twenty-two acres. Mechanization contributed to a steady exodus from the farm to the city, where the farmer's sons sought the gainful employment the land could no longer provide.

In the early 1970s arable farmlands constituted 9 percent of the total area of the country; meadows and pastureland occupied 0.5 percent. Dairy and livestock production were the mainstays of agricultural production. Dairy products—milk, eggs, butter, and cheese—contributed about 50 percent of agricultural output; meat production—principally beef and pork—added another 30 percent; the remaining 20 percent of output derived from crops. The major cultivated crops were wheat, oats, barley, and rye. Hay, fodder grains, potatoes, sugar beets, and garden produce were important also.

The cooperative movement was strong because the average farmer has limited resources to finance his production and to get his output to market. By 1971 there were more than 3,000 of these associations, totaling around 2 million members. The marketing of 98 percent of the milk production, 90 percent of the meat delivered to the slaughterhouses, and around 75 percent of egg exports was arranged through rural cooperatives.

A large part of the rural credit made available came from the cooperative banks. Savings banks, which had many branches in small towns, were another important source of financing. The government provided lesser amounts, usually for specific projects in harmony with official agricultural policy, such as farm consolidation. Research was provided for out of the regular state budget, and the results of that research reached the farmer through a broad-based extension service that also furnished technical advice on all aspects of farming.

In general, farm products were reserved for home consumption. The export market was quite important for certain commodities in surplus, however. Beef, pork, and wheat were also actively traded. Altogether, approximately one-tenth of the 1970 production was exported.

A principal aim of government agricultural policy has been the attainment of national self-sufficiency in basic foodstuffs. There are quota restrictions on imports of agricultural commodities. There is also a system of government-subsidized price supports and income supplements paid directly to the producer. These policies have met with a reasonable degree of success. The country was self-sufficient in dairy and egg production—with a surplus of 20 percent for export— and in meat; it was 80 percent self-sufficient in bread grains and vegetables, but only 33 percent in fruits and 25 percent in sugar.

Rapid productivity increases in agriculture since World War II, occasioned by greater mechanization and better organization, gave rise to huge surpluses of milk, butter, cheese, and even certain cereal grains. Beginning in the latter half of the 1960s, therefore, policy was reversed; production incentives were reduced, and the stock of productive resources devoted to surplus production was cut back.

The greatest attention was focused on the dairy herd, which was far larger than the country's consumers required to satisfy their needs. Slaughtering bonuses were offered to reduce the size of the herd. A soil bank was established to take pastureland out of production. Producer prices were lowered by imposing a supplementary tax on the sale of certain dairy products. Quotas were placed on imports of feed and fodder for cattle, and Finland signed an agreement with the European Free Trade Association (EFTA) countries to lower butter prices. All of these policies succeeded in cutting the size of the dairy herd by 40 percent in the 1966–71 five-year period. Nonetheless, thanks to superior breeding, milk production averages rose so quickly that hardly any reduction in milk output resulted.

FORESTRY

About 71 percent of the total land area is covered by 54.5 million acres of forestland, which bolsters Finland's position as one of the world's great wood-producing economies. One-third of the forestlands are publicly owned. The main tree species are pine (44 percent of the growing stock), spruce (36 percent), birch (18 percent), and aspen and elder (2 percent). Pine, spruce, and birch are valuable raw materials for the sawmilling, cellulose, and paper industries. Aspen is utilized in the manufacture of matches.

Most of the wooded area is taken up by farm forests with an average size of roughly ninety acres. In the north the average size runs somewhat larger (132 acres), whereas in the south it is somewhat smaller (sixty-seven acres). There is consensus among Finland's forestry experts that the average farm forest size needs to be increased before optimal silvicultural practices can be generalized.

As marketing prospects in agriculture have grown more unfavorable, larger numbers of farmers have turned to forest farming as a supplement to their income. In the late 1960s so-called forest money constituted more than one-third of total farm income, and in some areas it accounted for more than one-half. Nevertheless, here too, mechanization—power saws, tractors, and other machinery—was far advanced, and the work force was declining rapidly. Still, in the wintertime, when there was little work to be found on the farms, nearly 100,000 farm laborers worked as lumberjacks.

Horses continue to be of use for hauling logs to the roadside or onto ice-covered lakes in heavily snowbound forests. When the ice cover melts, the logs are floated down streams, rivers, and channels. From there, the bundled timber is towed across the larger lakes by small tugs. Finland's dense network of waterways provides natural, cheap, and rapid routes for timber transport, although a great deal of the raw wood is also hauled by truck.

The volume of timber felled grew by almost 50 percent during the 1955–70 period. In the latter year over 56 million cubic meters was cut, but this was 4 million to 5 million cubic meters more than was being replaced by natural growth. Since the middle of the 1960s, repeated overcutting of the natural stock has resulted in a small but perceptible decline in the country's forest reserves. The problem is especially acute in that the demand from the wood-processing and paper and pulp industries grows incessantly. During the 1960s Finland was converted from a net exporter into a net importer of raw timber. In 1969 the forest industry imported 6 percent of its raw material requirements, mainly from Sweden and the Soviet Union.

In the early 1960s Finnish authorities became aware that the growing stock had been in a state of stagnation for almost two decades. In response to ever-clearer signs of impending timber shortages, the government launched the first five-year silviculture improvement plan in 1965. About Fmk820 million (for value of the markka—see Glossary) was budgeted to realize several priority objectives: the expansion of the cultivated forest area from 408,000 to 730,000 acres; the enlargement of the drainage area from 618,000 to 805,000 acres; the replacement of slow-growing trees with high-yield, qualitatively superior varieties; the introduction of high-intensive cultivation techniques, particularly fertilization; and the construction of 340 miles of new roads linking major production to major consumption centers.

Despite these efforts, in 1970 the Bank of Finland announced that it considered unrealizable new projects involving an increase in timber consumption, except at the risk of seriously depleting the country's available forest reserves. Attention was called to the reforestation and fertilization programs, which were not meeting production targets. These lags have left open the question as to whether the silviculture plan can avert the growing crisis of timber reserves.

MINING

Mining and quarrying have grown more slowly than manufacturing or construction. The country's mineral resource endowment is not abundant; still the discovery of previously unknown deposits of cobalt, chromium, and uranium has injected a brighter note into the prospects for expansion. Uranium, so far, has not been exploited, but chromium entered into production in 1967, and cobalt refining started in 1968. By the late 1960s twelve mines were in operation. Annual production of raw ore surpassed 7 million tons. In 1971, 25 percent of mines and quarries were privately owned, and the remainder were public property.

In early 1973 iron was the most abundant metal by volume but was not being produced domestically in quantities sufficient to service the needs of the metal industry. The Otanmäki mine, about nineteen air miles southwest of Kajaani in the central part of the country, was the leading producer of iron ore. Annual output ranged from 600,000 to 800,000 tons. A second center near Raajärvi in northern Finland was expanding very rapidly. Estimated reserves of iron ore were on the order of 300 million to 400 million tons. Not all of this was of commercially exploitable quality, however.

By far the richest deposits were located at Outokumpu not far from the eastern border with the Soviet Union. Iron, sulfur, and copper are found in large quantities, whereas zinc, cobalt, nickel, gold, and silver are in commercial concentration. About 60 percent of the original deposit, estimated at 25 million tons of ore, had been taken out by 1972.

Finland is the leading producer of copper and nickel in Western Europe. It also produces 10 percent of the world's vanadium, 7 percent of the world's cobalt, and will soon be one of the largest chromium exporters.

MANUFACTURING

The manufacturing sector of the economy displays an extraordinary range and sophistication of products. The major product groups are metal and electrical engineering, wood and paper, food, and textile and clothing. About 84 percent of the manufacturing industry is privately owned.

Metal and Electrical Engineering

The metal and engineering industry has a history that dates back to the earliest days of Finland's modern industrialism. Before World War II it served mainly the domestic market, the needs of which it largely

185

satisfied. The heavy demand for war matériel and afterwards the onerous reparations paid to the Soviet Union placed a tremendous strain on the productive capacity of the heavy engineering sector in particular. The unrelenting pressure to drive output towards ever higher targets molded the modern Finnish metal industry into a production complex of considerable capacity. The impact of foreign markets, where tastes are varied and competition is fierce, explains why the range of Finnish metal products is so diverse and why standards remain so high (see table 9).

There are five divisions in the metal and engineering industry. Judged by the amount of value added by processing and by the number employed, their order of relative importance is: the machine division,

Table 9. Metal Production in Finland, 1969

Metal	Production (in metric tons)[1]
Pig iron, crude steel, and iron concentrate	3,188,000
Titanium concentrate	138,200
Zinc concentrate	132,436
Electrolytic copper	33,877
Chromium[2]	20,400
Lead concentrate	7,884
Electrolytic nickel	3,722
Vanadium pentoxide	2,403
Cobalt	778
Silver	19,436
Gold	587

[1]Except gold and silver, which are in kilograms.
[2]1970 production figure.

Source: Adapted from Metal Industry's Year Book 1970, Helsinki, 1970.

the transport equipment division, the metal manufacturing division, the electrical engineering division, and the basic metal division.

The machine division produces boilers, washing machines, factory machinery, locomotives, hoists, and elevators. The transport equipment division produces such items as ships, railway cars, trucks, and motorbikes. In the metal manufacturing division, forgings, nails, and sheet metal are produced. The electrical engineering division produces items such as cables, light bulbs, generators, motors, instruments, and radio and television sets. The basic metal division produces such items as pig iron, ingots, rails, pipes, and various copper devices.

Most of the domestically mined metal supplies the country's large metal and engineering industry. There it undergoes various degrees of processing. A long-term problem is high dependence upon foreign imports, because the domestic mining industry is able to meet only about one-half of the raw material requirements in the basic metal industry. The basic metal industry in turn suffices to meet only about half of the raw material requirements of the other metal and engineering industries.

All signs point toward greater need to import metal ores in the future. The capacity of the iron and steel industry, for example, has skyrocketed. Pig iron production in 1969 exceeded 1 million tons. Steel plate and special steels are also major lines. Raw materials and semimanufactured steel are delivered in large quantities to the Swedish automobile industry and to the Danish agriculture machine industry.

Copper is converted to cathode copper and profile products. A portion of the latter is further processed by the Finnish electrical industry. Another 20,000 tons (about 60 percent of primary production) are exported as is about 90 percent of the cathode nickel output.

A new zinc factory began production in 1971 and turns out approximately 70,000 tons of zinc concentrate.

The Wood and Paper Industry

The wood and paper industry led early industrial growth following independence. Growth continued in the years after World War II, but certain signs of slowdown became apparent during the 1960s. The domestic supply of timber leveled off; and the climbing price of wood began to menace the industry's heretofore competitive cost structure, based upon cheap and abundant supplies of raw wood that the forest industry traditionally depended upon to penetrate foreign markets. The industry could not afford to lose these markets because they absorb two-thirds of its output. Thus, reinvigoration of the growth stock to broaden the raw materials base is critical to the future health of the wood and paper industry. Producers can turn to higher degrees of processing to increase the value added to wood products, but the capital investment requirements are formidable. It is not clear that Finland would have much of a competitive edge in raising large capital sums, particularly when it is competing with areas such as North America where capital markets are larger and better organized. In any event, the role of the forest industry has been gradually diminishing until, in 1969, it ceded first place in value added and employment to metal and engineering.

The mechanical wood branch of the industry differs from the pulp and paper branch. The latter branch is already very capital-intensive and highly efficient. Its international competitive position is not threatened, nor is its share in total exports, which continues to grow. The pulp and paper industry includes mechanical pulp mills, semichemical pulp mills, sulfite and sulfate pulp mills, paper, paperboard and cardboard mills, fiberboard mills, wallpaper factories, cardboard box factories, bag and envelope factories, and so on.

Production has evolved more sluggishly in the mechanical wood branch. In this category fall the sawmills and planing mills, wood-wool mills, plywood mills, bobbin and spool factories, and a number of other mainly small-scale factories for mechanical woodworking. The need for modernization is more urgent here, although a number of mills and factories are thoroughly up-to-date.

The Food Industry

The rapid urbanization of Finnish society has heightened the reliance on processed foods, and the relative importance of the food industry has grown very rapidly. It is Finland's largest industry by gross value of production and third largest by value added. About 90 percent of production is reserved for home consumption. But the United States and EFTA are good customers, and sales prospects in South Africa, the Federal Republic of Germany (West Germany), Canada, and the Benelux countries are good. The principal production lines by value added are the dairies, the bakeries, the flour mills, the sausage factories, and the confectionary industry.

The Textile and Clothing Industry

The textile industry is one of the oldest in Finland. Its beginnings date back more than 200 years. The principal products are cotton, wool, and knitted goods. Linkage to international markets is becoming stronger. In 1970 about one-quarter of production went to exports.

Garment production ranges from clothes for all age groups to undergarments and accessories, overcoats, and furs. Thirty percent of production is shipped abroad, and the share of exported production is rising.

In general, the role of the textile and clothing industry has declined in the postwar period relative to other manufacturing groups, which have grown much faster.

Minor Industries

These industries cater chiefly to the home market, although a few, such as chemicals, china, and rubber, are engaged in exports. Industries whose orientation is primarily domestic include beverages, tobacco, footwear, petroleum, asphalt, leather, plastics, clay, glass, stone, and graphics. The most dynamic industries in this class are the chemicals, the plastics, and petroleum.

CONSTRUCTION

Housing accounts for 70 percent of the value of construction industry production. Owing to war destruction and the influx of the homeless from the lost territories, the country confronted a housing shortage in 1945. Notwithstanding the rapid increases in annual new construction, rapid urbanization and the growth of the population have made shortages a permanent feature during the following quarter-century and beyond.

Average annual completions of new housing were 38,000 to 39,000 during the 1955-70 period. Production in both 1970 and 1971 attained the level of nearly 50,000—a new record. The cause for this jump in output can be traced to the sharp rise in government housing loans— the sum of which doubled in the space of three years from 1969 to 1972. The government finances or subsidizes the construction of six out of every ten new dwelling units. Some 85 to 90 percent of the actual construction is done by private companies.

Up-to-date information on the shortage of housing is not readily available; however, by 1968 there were some 1.5 million dwelling units in the country, giving a living density of three persons per unit. New dwellings were being built at the rate of 7.8 units per 1,000 inhabitants. No doubt, a significant explanation for this rate of production, despite huge investments by the public authorities, is the comparatively meager return on capital invested in housing. As in many developed countries, productivity gains in construction are modest compared with industry. Furthermore, labor and material costs have escalated, taking a large bite out of profits. Consequently, it is believed that private capital withdraws from the housing market in direct proportion to the amount of new funds invested by the government. Judging from the announced targets for new completions, actual output continues to fall well short of official expectations.

The governmental role in other construction is even more prominent than in housing. Public enterprises are responsible for 70 percent of nonresidential construction, including such projects as the erection of factories, commercial and agricultural buildings, schools, hospitals, and office buildings as well as construction of streets and roads, bridges, airports, railways, harbors, and canals.

Private capital is expected to play a much greater role in the future expansion of nonresidential building, since the government took the decision in the late 1960s to deemphasize public works as a means of providing employment. Public works appropriations, which underwrite about 70 percent of land and waterway construction, have remained at roughly the same levels from 1968 to 1972 and, when the effects of inflation are discounted, have probably declined somewhat. In this period the volume of nonresidential building represented about 60 percent of total building volume.

POWER

In the 1959-70 period, volume output in electricity, gas, and waterworks grew faster than that of any other industry. The production level in 1970 was about 2½ times that of the base year 1959.

Finland has no known deposits of coal, petroleum, or natural gas and is not likely to discover any significant domestic sources of these fuels in the future. As a result imported fuels and coal constitute nearly two-thirds of Finland's energy supply. Hydroelectric power capacity has remained about the same from the mid-1960s to the early 1970s—

roughly 10.5 billion kilowatt-hours. Waste fuel, derived principally from industrial waste wood and the residual caustic sodas originating in the pulp industry, is being increasingly utilized but has not kept pace with the general trend of expanding consumption.

The prices for imported fuels rose 60 percent in 1971 at the conclusion of the new participation agreements negotiated by the major oil companies with the oil-producing companies in 1971. It is expected that the use of waste fuels, peat, and atomic energy will gain proportionately from this improvement in their competitive position. The injection of these changed internal price ratios should also lead large energy users to favor construction in the future of more capital-intensive power plants that conserve on fuel.

The maximum hydroelectric power potential from all lakes and streams is rated at 19 billion kilowatt-hours per year, of which 55 percent has already been developed. Over half of the 1972 capacity came from three major dams: the Kemi River complex in the far north, the Oulu Dam in the East, and the Vironkoski Project in the southeast. Almost all the remaining undeveloped potential is located in the north.

Although hydroelectric power is still an important source of electric power, it is not as important as it once was. In the early 1960s 85 percent of electric power was water generated; in 1971, only 45 percent. Coal- and fuel-operated thermal plants are now more important. The total electric power used in 1971 was on the order of 24 billion kilowatt-hours. Industry consumed three-quarters of this energy, while residences used the balance.

Peat is a largely underexploited source of fuel. Finland has one of the largest known reserves in the entire world, approximately 600 million tons. The cost of exploitation is cheap, but transportation overhead is high because it is a bulky commodity. Therefore, it is only competitive within a relatively short radius around the site deposits. For this reason, output has remained at negligible levels—between 100,000 and 200,000 tons a year. The rising price of competing energy fuels, however, is likely to enhance the competitiveness of peat. Two cities have already switched to peat combustion in their district heating plants, and several additional projects are under study.

Various atomic energy plants were under construction in the early 1970s. They could be supplied from the domestic uranium that was discovered in 1959 but had not been exploited. The first atomic power plant began operations in 1972.

LABOR

The labor force is of high quality. Nevertheless, a 1970 poll conducted by the Federation of Finnish Industries found that shortages of skilled labor and technical staffs are the most often-reported production bottleneck when overall demand conditions are good.

In 1968, 32 percent of the industrial labor force was employed by the metal and engineering industry, 20 percent worked in the wood and paper industry, 11 percent was employed by the food industry, 12 percent worked for the textile and clothing industry, and 25 percent was employed in other industrial activities.

Significant reorientation of official labor policy has been carried out since the late 1960s. Less reliance has been placed on public works as a stopgap solution to structural unemployment problems, and greater emphasis has been laid on the development of a comprehensive manpower policy. In part, this has implied a more systematic attempt to get the unemployed to move to centers of industrial activity. Over 70 percent of production is located in the south around Helsinki, Tampere, Turku, Lappeenranta, Lahti, Jyväskylä and the valleys of the Kymi and Kokemäki rivers. Only 5 percent of industry to date has located in the north; so the government has sought to make it easier for the northern unemployed to go south. Job retraining, vocational guidance, travel and resettlement allowances, and a program of subsidies for housing construction, of which there are critical shortages in most industrial regions—all of these policies are being brought into play. A particularly effective mechanism is the nationwide employment exchange system, which brings together persons seeking employment with potential employers. In 1969 it filled 320,000 positions.

Another important part of manpower policy is the attempt to influence future investment decisions so that the pattern of industrialization will better integrate the central and northern regions with the south. Increasingly, it is hoped that the job will move to the unemployed worker rather than the reverse. To coordinate this growing array of new labor programs, the Ministry of Labor, which replaced the old Employment Division in the Ministry of Communications and Public Works, was created in March 1970.

The Finnish wage earner benefits from a high percentage of fringe benefits as required by law (see table 10).

The quality of labor and management is high by international

Table 10. Indirect Wage Costs to the Employer in Industry, Finland, 1969

	Percent of Direct Wages
Holiday wages	7.3
Social security premiums	7.2
Work pension premiums	6.5
Sick day wages	1.2
Accident insurance	1.2
Unemployment compensation	0.5
Free-day wages	0.4
Total fixed by law	24.3

Source: Adapted from Bank of Finland, Establishing a Business in Finland, Helsinki, 1970.

standards. Finnish consultants and contractors have mainly operated in the Middle East, Africa, and Europe, but in recent years North America, South America, and the Far East have come to the forefront. Most international contracts are in fields where the Finnish experience is long standing—in pulp and paper mills, in water and waste treatment plants, and in earthmoving. Town and regional planning requests have started coming in. The Finns cannot compete for projects that require vast financial backing. But by specializing in fields where advanced technology is important, they are getting a fair share of the international bids and, perhaps, more.

The majority of the labor force is unionized. Most wage agreements are negotiated through nationwide collective bargaining between the central trade union organization and the large employers' confederations. Contracts have an average duration of from two to three years. Disputes are heard by a labor court. Strikes do occur, but they must be preceded by a two-weeks' notice given to the National Arbitrator of Labor Disputes. Work stoppages tend to increase in boom conditions and to decrease during recessions.

The major trade unions are the Central Association of Finnish Trade Unions having forty-one affiliates and a membership of nearly 600,000 workers; the Confederation of Salaried Employees with twenty-nine affiliates and roughly 200,000 members; and various unions for managerial and supervisory employees with a combined membership of 70,000.

The Central Federation of Finnish Employers (Suomen Työnantajain Keskusliitto—STK) is the largest organization of employers. It is composed of twenty-nine trade associations including approximately 2,400 employer groups. The STK maintains close working relations with the other major employer alliance—the Confederation of Commercial Employers—which includes six associations and 2,100 employer groups. About 3,000 additional employer groups are divided into various other confederations.

CHAPTER 14

TRADE, TRANSPORTATION, AND SERVICES

Since the first decades of the twentieth century the domestic trading network has been dominated by a few large, competitive marketing societies. In the early 1970s, however, the tougher competition for the consumer's preference has forced the central dominant trading organizations to completely rethink management methods and plans for the future.

Transportation is modern and suitably adapted to the needs of elements of the population found in remote locations. Air service is exceptionally developed. Nevertheless, given the existence of a good network of principal roads and relatively lower costs, most consumer goods are moved by truck.

Services and transport combined absorb huge investments of both physical capital and human energy. In the 1970s three-fifths of all capital investments and nearly 30 percent of total man-hours worked were in support of the operation of these two sectors.

COMMERCE

In 1971 commerce contributed 10 percent of the gross national product (GNP—see Glossary) and provided employment for 15 percent of the labor force, or 322,000 people. Its three subsectors, domestic trade, banking, and insurance, had a combined growth rate of 5.5 percent over the 1954-68 period, slightly higher than the economy as a whole. Productivity increases in the same period, however, were modest—2.2 percent per year.

Domestic Trade

In the early 1970s four large marketing societies had captured 70 percent of the wholesale trade and 73 percent of the retail trade (see table 11; table 12). The Finnish Cooperative Wholesale Society (Suomen Osuuskauppojen Keskuskunta—SOK) and the Central Cooperative Society (Keskusosuusliike—OTK) are the oldest of the societies. The Wholesale Company of Finnish Retailers (Kesko Oy) and the Foodstuffs Wholesalers Central Association (Tukkukauppojen Oy—TUKO) are private enterprises whose phase of greatest growth dates from the mid-1940s.

The retailing branch of domestic trade employed 160,000 workers in 1971. The wholesaling branch employed 75,000.

Table 11. Sales Volume of Wholesale Distribution Centers, Finland, 1970

Marketing Group	Number of Warehouses and Distribution Centers	Sales Volume Value*	Percent of Total Value
Finnish Cooperative Wholesale Society	18	1,805	18
Central Cooperative Society	9	1,331	13
Wholesale Company of Finnish Retailers	17	2,339	23
Foodstuffs Wholesalers and Retailers Association	92	1,621	16
Other	339	2,860	30
TOTAL	475	9,956	100

*In millions of markka; 4.2 markka equal US$1.

Source: Adapted from Hannu Kärkkäinen, "The Structural Change in Distribution in Finland," (K-O-P), *Economic Review*, No. 1, 1972.

Table 12. Sales Volume of Retail Outlets, Finland, 1970

Number of Outlets			Sales Volume Value[1]	Percent of Total
Supermarkets and Self-service Shops	Department Stores and Discount	Other Sales Points and Retail Shops		
526	207	3,487	2,956	22
562	105	2,561	1,671	13
928	57	3,259	2,735	21
1,080	...	3,435	2,300[2]	17
...	...	19,500	3,680	27
3,096	369	32,242	13,342	100

[1]In millions of markka; 4.2 markka equal US$1.
[2]Estimate.

Source: Adapted from Hannu Kärkkäinen, "The Structural Change in Distribution in Finland," (K-O-P), *Economic Review*, No. 1, 1972.

From its inception each competitive group was structured around a core enterprise, which negotiated central purchasing and imported goods from abroad on behalf of hundreds of small retail outlets. This was the situation that prevailed in what was essentially a seller's market until the late 1950s. As domestic production advanced steadily and the supply of foreign goods became more abundant following relaxation of exchange controls in 1957, the greater quantity and diversity of goods converted the seller's into a buyer's market. In a climate of fierce competition for the Finnish consumer's rising income, the structure of distribution was profoundly affected.

Whereas the central enterprises had until then directed only purchasing activities for their respective groups, by the early 1960s they had taken over market promotion as well. Since then each group has featured a single trademark, which national advertising campaigns impress upon the consumer.

In the 1960s retail and wholesale trade activities tended to merge. The process of urbanization called for major investments in additional retail outlets to service the new residential areas. Moreover, a number of already-established outlets proved to be too small or too inefficient to survive. These shops were forced to close and were replaced by new stores with larger floor areas, better layout, and stronger management. Hence, the central enterprises, equipped with vastly superior financial and managerial resources, entered directly into the retailing end of distribution.

Major changes transformed wholesaling. Rational application of technology, including electronic data processing, weekly ordering, and routed transport on fixed days, together with larger average warehouse size, enabled the central enterprises to capture 70 percent of national sales with fewer than 30 percent of the distribution centers in 1970. Because they pass on to retailers the savings that result from lower distribution costs, the four large marketing groups are forcing wholesale competitors to imitate their improved techniques.

Department store chains and discount houses made their first appearances in the 1960s. They were usually clients of a large central wholesaler but made their own decisions on investment, marketing, and pricing policy. Their price-cutting offensive, possibly because of high-volume turnover and the elimination of specialized services, had squeezed out some of the more traditional shops and forced many others to follow suit by organizing chains of their own.

The Finnish consumer has shown an unmistakable preference for the shopping center (discount house, department store, supermarket) over the specialized store (small shop, neighborhood shop). The decisive advantages of the universal store—lower prices and the convenience of one-stop shopping—appear to have carried the first round of the battle. In the early 1970s, however, the specialized stores were counterattacking. In their advertising they stressed their wider selection of goods, the custom services not offered by the chain houses, and their location near or within residential areas. The small retailers had even extended business hours to lure back the late evening shopper.

All of this has given pause to the larger competitive groups, which are no longer building the immense shopping centers so popular in the early 1960s. Taking their cue from the independent retailers, the large distributors invested in the construction of their own residential stores beginning in the mid-1960s. By the early 1970s the ranks of the independent retailers seemed destined for further reductions. Most threatened with closure were the rural shops, the basement stores of old urban areas, and the small speciality shops in different lines. It is not only the larger scale competition that is hastening the end of the independent shops. The depopulation of rural areas has eroded the sales potential of the rural store. The basement store effectively subsidizes upper level tenants because the store is taxed at higher rates.

But without doubt the death blow to the small shops was the stabilization program instituted during the latter 1960s. Price controls prevented the independent store owner from passing on to the consumer the inflationary wage hikes granted during the period just preceding stabilization. In this way general economic policy has indirectly accelerated the structural change in distribution.

Banking

At the end of 1971 there were more than 6,300 banking institutions, of which the most important in volume of credit granted were the commercial banks, the savings banks, the cooperative banks, and the postal banks, in that order (see table 13). Banking contributed less than 2 percent to the 1971 GDP and employed on the order of 60,000 workers. Deposits by the public in that year totaled Fmk72.48 billion (for value of the markka—see Glossary); total lending reached approximately Fmk22.26 billion.

Table 13. *Finland, Deposits and Loans by Banking Group, 1971*
(in percent)

Type of Bank	Deposits	Loans
Commercial	39.7	42.9
Savings	27.1	22.3
Cooperative	19.4	17.8
Post office	10.7	7.0
Other	3.1	10.0*
TOTAL	100.0	100.0

*Including mortgage societies, which provided 8 percent.

Source: Adapted from Yhdyspankki Pohjoismaiden, *Facts About Finland 1972*, Helsinki, 1972.

According to a 1969 study of bank lending, industry received the largest slice of credit (29 percent of the total), followed by private individuals (18 percent). Commerce and real estate came next in order; each absorbed about 12 percent. Agriculture and forestry received 9 percent, power plants 6 percent, and communes and churches 5 percent. The remainder (9 percent) was distributed among transportation, services, construction, and mining sectors.

Insurance

The contribution of the insurance business to the GDP is about half that of banking, or less than 1 percent. Over 1,200 companies were in operation in 1969 (including the pension and benevolent funds), employing 20,000 to 25,000 people. Three-fifths of this amount was collected by the pension and benevolent funds. The next largest insurance groups in value of annual premiums were automobile accident, life, overseas insurance, and workmen's compensation. Other forms of insurance offered included fire, burglary, water damage, fidelity guarantee, credit, sickness benefit, and funeral costs (see ch. 12).

TRANSPORT AND COMMUNICATIONS

A variety of facilities and related services made up the transport industry, the chief of which were trucking, rail, shipping, and air transport. The transport industry and related services employed 145,000 workers in 1971.

Truck and Bus Transport

Trucking has become the major means of moving goods essentially because it offers the most extensive coverage of supply and consuming areas and the lowest costs on short-haul traffic. In 1971 about 46,000 trucks and 67,000 vans traveled over a road network totaling 42,000 miles, one-third of which was paved (see ch. 3). A growing share of international freight is being carried by trucks because of excellent roll-on, roll-off ferry connections. Since the early 1950s the proportion of medium-weight trucks has decreased, and that of the heavy and light trucks has increased.

There were about 8,000 buses operating nationwide in 1971; the number of passengers carried had almost doubled between 1953 and 1969. The growing availability of the private passenger car, of which there were over 750,000 in 1971, however, has somewhat undermined the popularity of the bus as a means of transportation.

Marine Transport

The Finnish merchant marine is of primary importance for foreign trade, 90 percent of which is transported by sea. In 1971 sea cargoes weighed 31.5 million metric tons. Slightly less than half of this total (14.8 million metric tons) was transported in domestic bottoms. Moreover, the Finnish merchant fleet provides important freight services for foreigners. Indeed, Finland has consistently earned more from foreigners for marine transport than it has paid out, and merchant marine income is a significant source of foreign exchange earnings.

There are some thirty ports for foreign traffic, of which twenty have a minimum depth of twenty-seven feet. Import traffic is concentrated at Naantali, Helsinki, Kotka, and Turku; Hanko, the ports of Kotka, Hamina, Pori, Kemi, Oulu, and Rauma handle most exports. Nine efficient icebreakers patrol the shipping lanes during winter months. The ice situation is at its worst in February. Usually only four ports, located on the southwest coast—Turku, Helsinki, and Kotka—can be kept open year round. When the winter is particularly severe it is possible to maintain only one or two of these ports open for heavy ships.

Car and container ferry communications between Finland, Sweden,

197

Denmark, and the Federal Republic of Germany (West Germany) sharply increased in the 1960s and 1970s. Ferries carried about 350 trailer-containers daily between these four countries in 1971.

Regular sailings connect Finland to many parts of Europe and to ports in Asia, Africa, Australia, New Zealand, North America, and South America. About 3.8 million voyagers arrived and departed by sea in 1971. Roughly 85 percent of the inland water network is unnavigable for all but the smallest tugs and launches. The rivers, marked by frequent rapids, shallows, waterfalls, and other hazards, are used mainly for pleasure boating and timber floating. Lakes and canals, most of them in the central region, are the principal navigable waterways. Lake boats carry tourists and modest amounts of cargo. Timber is massed into huge rafts of bundled logs for towing by tugs to sawmills located on the shores. Altogether, the rivers, lakes, and canals provide 4,000 miles of navigable waterways. The network of floatable waterways is, of course, much more extensive, being on the order of 25,000 miles. In 1969 about 25,000 ships and 19,500 timber rafts passed through inland canals.

The number of vessels in the merchant fleet declined from 1,015 in 1925 to 488 in 1972. On the other hand, average ship size increased elevenfold from 261 to 2,880 metric tons per ship. The fleet as a whole had a metric tonnage of 1.39 million in 1972. Ninety percent of the vessels were motor ships; 10 percent were steamers.

Railroads

Finland is one of the few countries in Europe that is still laying rail lines. Tracks in use at the end of 1971 exceeded 3,500 miles in length. All but twenty miles were state owned. The 3.2 billion metric ton-miles registered by the railroads in 1971 represented perhaps one-sixth of gross freight volume for that year. Trains do mostly long-distance hauling. Income from freight transport is four times greater than that from passenger traffic.

Railroad shipping westbound to Europe has always presented a special problem because the five-foot track gauge does not match the gauge prevailing elsewhere in Western Europe. Containerization and improved ferry service with Sweden and West Germany are changing this situation, however. Tornio and Naantali have railroad-ferry transshipment points that handle all rail traffic to and from Western Europe. Rail transport eastward is not a problem because the track gauge in Finland is the same as that in the Soviet Union. Most of the foreign trade between the two countries is transported by rail via Leningrad.

In the late 1960s the state began electrification of some of the major trunk lines. Rail services are normally not self-sustaining financially and must be subsidized by a special allocation from the central budget.

Airlines

Finland's network of domestic air services is the second densest per capita in Europe. In June 1971 the two Finnish airlines (Finnair and Kar-air) maintained scheduled traffic with sixteen domestic airports. Over a million passengers a year were carried on domestic flights alone.

Even more remarkable has been the expansion of international air services, which at one point just after World War II had to be suspended entirely because of extensive damage suffered by the fleet and air installations. In early 1973 Finnair and ten international airlines scheduled over 150 regular flights per week between Finland and major centers in Europe and North America.

Finnish airlines flew 13.3 million miles in 1971, carried 1.4 million passengers, and logged 14.2 million metric ton-miles of freight and mail. The fleet consisted of three DC-8-62s, three DC-6s, eight Super Caravelles, four DC-9s, and nine Convair Metropolitans.

Communications

The telegraph and postal systems are entirely state owned. In 1969 there were approximately 4,000 post offices, 3,300 telegraph dispatch points, and over 800 joint offices. Domestic postal services meet high international standards. A letter usually reaches its destination a day after it is posted. Overseas letters are distributed within a day.

The telephone lines are both state owned and privately owned. Ninety-one percent of the 1.2 million telephones in use during 1970 were automatic. An automatic exchange in Helsinki makes it possible to dial international calls from most Finnish telephones. There were 252 telephones per 1,000 inhabitants for the country as a whole; for Helsinki, the figure was 600 per 1,000.

Another communications service is Telex, for which there were 3,500 lines in 1969. Direct computer contacts are also available between terminals in Finland and central units abroad via the international telephone network. Electronic data processing is a rapidly growing industry. In 1970 there were an estimated 250 units in operation, and the rate of increase is 10 to 15 percent annually. Shortages of competent personnel have not hampered the growth of the industry in Finland as has often been the case elsewhere in Europe, thanks to a rapidly growing number of courses being offered at Finnish universities and at the Electronic Data Processing Institute of the Finnish Data Association.

OTHER SERVICES

Other services contributed over one-quarter of the GDP and employed 445,000 people in 1971. Of these, 70 percent were employed in governmental services and 30 percent in nongovernmental services.

The state principally provides the following public services: general administration, judiciary and police, defense, education, and research. The municipalities furnish social welfare, educational, and general administrative services. The intermunicipal authorities are predominantly connected with the production of health, medical and educational services.

The public sector has assumed an increasingly important position in the provision of services and service employment. In 1971 government services contributed 13.7 percent of GDP and employed 310,000 persons.

Nongovernmental services include those provided by hotels, restaurants, laundries, domestics, undertakers, private educational and cultural services, own-account medical and health services, artists, legal services, and civic organizations. These services accounted for 13.3 percent of GDP and employed 135,000 workers in 1971.

THE ROLE OF GOVERNMENT

Broadly speaking, government policy has allowed free market prices to dictate the restructuring of domestic trade. With the exception of a state alcohol monopoly regulating the buying and selling of alcoholic beverages, ownership within domestic trade was 99 percent private in 1971. Responsibility for policy formulation lies within the Ministry of Commerce and Industry.

The government impact on transport and other services, on the other hand, is substantial because public agencies and enterprises produce about one-half of these services directly. The Ministry of Traffic is the coordinating agency in the field of transport. The Administration of Posts and Telegraphy has similar authority in the field of communications. A number of subsidiary departments are assigned the direction of specific branches in transport. For example, the Board of Railway Administration formulates investment plans, oversees day-to-day operation, and prepares annual budgets for the country's railroads. The National Board of Public Roads and Waterways is charged with the maintenance of the existing network of highways, canals, lakes, and rivers and with contracting for new construction. The Board of Navigation regulates the merchant marine, and the Harbor Association controls ports and installations. Finally, the two publicly owned domestic airlines as well as all foreign aircraft operating in Finnish airspace fall under the jurisdiction of the Air Section in the Ministry of Traffic.

Overall responsibility for regulation of governmental and nongovernmental services resides in the Ministry of Social Affairs. The National Medical Board establishes and enforces standards of qualification for health and medical personnel. Among the many agencies concerned with educational and cultural services, some of the most important are the Board of Vocational Education, the Matriculation Examination Board, the State Library Bureau, and the State Film Censors Office.

FOREIGN TRADE

Commodities have been the major component of both receipts and payments on the current account of the balance of payments. Export of services—21 percent of current receipts in 1971—consists mainly of freight transport and tourism. Tourism has grown particularly fast. It contributed a net surplus of Fmk250 million. Principal service imports—26 percent of total receipts in 1971—are accounted for by expenditures of Finnish tourists abroad and freight charges paid to foreigners for commodity transportation services.

Significance of Foreign Trade in the Domestic Economy

Exports are vital to the country's industries in a number of ways. In the first place, access to foreign markets allows the country to specialize in those products such as wood and paper where Finland's comparative advantage is greatest. Another important gain Finland derives from exports is the foreign exchange required to finance imports. Most of these imports are needed for production. The percentage of investment machinery imported, for example, is very high (about 50 percent). As much as two-thirds of the energy consumed annually is furnished by foreign fuels and lubricants. More self-sufficient in the 1970s than it was in the 1950s, the country nevertheless had to import 25 percent of its raw material requirements. Less than one-fifth of total imports are nonessential consumer goods.

Lastly, the need to export is a potent force for structural change in the economy. It is only by shifting into more highly processed and sophisticated products that the Finnish economy can retain its share of foreign markets. Undeniably, the domestic consumer benefits from the selection and low prices offered by foreign imports.

Structure of Exports

The two most important export groups, wood and wood products and paper products, performed the most poorly over the 1949-71 period (see table 14). Their combined share of exports declined from 88 percent in

Table 14. Commodity Composition of Finland's Exports, 1949, 1958, and 1971

(in percent)

Main Commodity Group	1949	1958	1971
Wood and wood products	48.3	31.1	17.6
Paper products	39.7	46.5	37.6
Metal products	4.3	13.7	23.5
Agricultural products	3.3	4.3	5.5
Other goods	4.4	4.4	15.8
TOTAL	100.0	100.0	100:0

Source: Adapted from Yhdyspankki Pohjoismaiden, *Facts About Finland 1972*, Helsinki, 1972.

1949 to 55.2 percent in 1971. The forest industry in Finland has been hampered by raw material shortages and mounting competition from North American producers. Its exports fared indifferently in the European Free Trade Association countries (EFTA) and actually lost ground in the European Economic Community (EEC, known as the Common Market). Because wood and paper products are dominant in total exports, their relatively poor growth more than offset the excellent performances of the fastest growing industries, such as metal products, textiles, and transport equipment.

Broadly speaking, the export of wood-based products flows west, and the export of metal and engineering products flows east. The sale of metal products to the west is gaining, however.

Regional Structure of Exports

Finland's export markets are predominantly European (see table 15). Less than one-fifth of exports go to countries outside Europe. Before

Table 15. Regional Structure of Exports, Finland, 1938, 1958, and 1971

(in percent)

Trade Area	1938	1958	1971
EFTA[1]	53.4	30.3	46.9
EEC[2]	27.5	26.9	22.4
Eastern bloc	2.8	24.9	14.3
Other countries	16.3	17.9	16.4
TOTAL	100.0	100.0	100.0

[1]European Free Trade Association.
[2]European Economic Community.

Source: Adapted from Yhdyspankki Pohjoismaiden, Facts About Finland 1972, Helsinki, 1972.

World War II the value of trade with Eastern Europe was small. Finland's defeat at the hands of the Soviet Union obliged it to sign a peace treaty in 1944, however, that called for substantial exports, mostly of heavy machinery, to the Eastern bloc countries as reparations. By 1958 nearly one-quarter of total exports were delivered to the Eastern bloc countries, no longer as reparations but as full-fledged commercial sales. In the 1960s and early 1970s the share of the Eastern European countries declined once again amid growing signs that the prewar geographic pattern was gradually reasserting itself.

A second feature regards the relationship between the size of the EFTA and the EEC export shares. After signing the 1961 agreement on associate membership with EFTA, Finland did extremely well, increasing its share of total exports to that area from 30.3 percent in 1958 to 46.9 percent in 1971. But the fastest growing export market in the world during this period was the EEC group, and there Finnish exports actually lost ground (26.9 percent of total exports in 1958, 22.4 percent in 1971).

A serious threat to Finland's future access to export markets was posed by the 1971 announcement in Brussels that three European countries had accepted membership in an enlarged EEC. Two of these— Great Britain and Denmark—were important EFTA trade partners with Finland. Free trade arrangements with both were to expire in

April 1973. They were replaced by new levies on Finnish exports to these countries, rendered mandatory by the EEC policy of a common external tariff barrier. Without a free trade agreement between Finland and the larger EEC, access to half of all Finland's export markets and 70 percent of the market for forest-based products was endangered. The text of an agreement with the EEC guaranteeing that access was approved by Parliament for formal signing in 1972. Months later the document remained on the president's desk unsigned, apparently because of Finnish concern that the agreement not be considered as haveing political implications. The Finns were reported anxious to give the Soviet Union unequivocal guarantees that agreement on closer economic ties with the EEC in no way implied eventual integration for Finland within the West European bloc.

Commodity Structure of Imports

Between 1949 and 1971 the need for foreign raw materials was substantially reduced (see table 16). The share of foreign exchange thereby

Table 16. Commodity Structure of Imports, Finland, 1949, 1958, and 1971
(in percent)

Main Commodity Group	1949	1958	1971
Raw materials	58.2	51.2	39.5
Fuels and lubricants	8.9	14.0	13.3
Investment goods	14.7	20.9	29.2
Consumer goods	18.2	13.9	18.0
TOTAL	100.0	100.0	100.0

Source: Adapted from Yhdyspankki Pohjoismaiden, *Facts About Finland 1972*, Helsinki, 1972.

liberated for other purposes was allocated to purchase fuels and lubricants and investment goods, the share of consumer goods remaining unchanged. The growth in the share of investment goods was particularly sharp in the 1960s, an indication of the role that certain kinds of highly advanced foreign equipment have in Finnish blueprints for the modernization of industry.

Regional Structure of Imports

Import sources are even more emphatically European than markets for export. Over 90 percent of 1971 imports were obtained from European suppliers (see table 17). Generally, raw material imports came from the east, and capital machinery came from the west.

The Role of Government in Foreign Trade

Exports

In the early 1970s, so as to counteract the effects of unstable export earnings on the management of internal demand, the government was

Table 17. Regional Structure of Imports, Finland, 1938, 1958, and 1971
(in percent)

Trade Area	1938	1958	1971
EFTA[1]	43.6	31.3	45.1
EEC[2]	32.9	29.8	27.1
Eastern bloc	7.8	25.7	18.2
Other countries	15.7	13.2	9.6
TOTAL	100.0	100.0	100.0

[1]European Free Trade Association.
[2]European Economic Community (known as the Common Market).
Source: Adapted from Yhdyspankki Pohjoismaiden, *Facts About Finland 1972*, Helsinki, 1972.

encouraging a move away from overdependence on wood-based exports. Large amounts of foreign capital were being imported to finance the expansion of dynamic export industries, such as metal and engineering, and the creation of new industries with high export potential, such as chemicals and plastics. Moreover, the Bank of Finland assumed a very critical attitude toward further investment in forest product industries beginning in 1970. The government's aim was to scale down the role of wood-based exports to a position roughly equal to that of other product groups so that, when demand for one group drops, the others would tend to offset any decline in foreign revenues.

The Finnish government has taken the position that trade among nations should be free and unrestricted to the maximum feasible extent. It has expressed particular misgivings that the growing trend toward regional trading blocs might proceed at the expense of small nations that choose not to accept full membership. In Finland's case this means that the right to reject any commitment in favor of political integration even while it agrees to enter on the road of greater economic integration should be respected by other countries.

In the early 1970s over 80 percent of Finland's trade was transacted under multilateral agreements with 113 countries. About 95 percent of the imports from these countries entered Finland free of any import permit; 3 percent required individual permits; and 2 percent were subject to global quotas. Quotas mainly affected agricultural products and mineral fuels.

Since 1950 Finland has been a participant in the General Agreement on Tariffs and Trade (GATT) negotiations. Until 1957 all trade was conducted on a bilateral basis. Since then considerable liberalization has taken place. In 1961 Finland became an associate member of EFTA. At the end of 1967 all import duties and quantitative restrictions on industrial goods between Finland and the EFTA countries were abolished. In negotiations between 1964 and 1966 Finland undertook notable trade concessions. It agreed to lower tariffs in two phases, the first to be

204

completed by July 1968 and the second by January 1970. At the time Finland was fulfilling these commitments, it also carried out a number of independent tariff reductions without reference to reciprocal concessions. These additional concessions had the effect of lowering the maximum permissible tariff rates to the level agreed upon in the mid-1960s. This measure was principally designed to benefit the Eastern bloc countries. In 1969 Finland joined the Organization for Economic Cooperation and Development (OECD). It observes in all respects the liberalized scheme of treatment for invisible service transactions and capital transfers recommended by that organization. The average duty on imports, including fiscal duties and import levies, was 4.5 percent in 1969.

In the early 1970s trade under bilateral agreements accounted for about 15 percent of total trade. Two-thirds of the bilateral exchange took place between Finland and the Soviet Union. Trade between these two countries was based on a treaty of 1947, a customs agreement of 1961, and trading agreements covering five-year periods. Under the customs agreements, tariffs on imports from the Soviet Union were reduced on a schedule identical to that governing imports from the EFTA area. Because there was no system of multilateral payments between bilateral countries, trade took place essentially on a barter basis. Private businesses in Finland advised the authorities about their export and import needs before a trade agreement was negotiated. Implementation depended on subsequent direct contact between Finnish firms and Soviet foreign trade authorities. Generally, the limiting factor in Finland's bilateral trade has been its ability to absorb imports from the Eastern bloc countries. Other countries with which Finland maintained bilateral trade agreements in 1969 were Bulgaria, Czechoslovakia, the German Democratic Republic (East Germany), Hungary, the People's Republic of China (PRC), Poland, and Romania. Since January 1, 1966, about 40 percent of the imports from these countries were freed from any import permit requirements as long as the country of export and the country of origin were the same. Imports from the Mongolian People's Republic (Mongolia), the Democratic People's Republic of Korea (North Korea), the Republic of Korea (South Korea), Rhodesia, the Democratic Republic of Vietnam (North Vietnam), the Republic of Vietnam (South Vietnam), and a few other countries were subject to individual import licensing.

Certain imports and exports were controlled for noneconomic reasons—for example, radioactive materials, pharmaceuticals, arms and ammunition, drugs, poisons, live animals, meat, seeds, and plants. The State Granary controlled all trade in grains, except rice, with other countries.

Export licensing was discontinued in 1962 except for scrap metal. Exporters of other products need only submit an export declaration except when there are reasons to believe that the goods will be reexported to a third country, the exportation would be in conflict with conditions laid out in bilateral agreements, or the export goods consist of raw timber, in which case an opinion of the Roundwood Export Commission is required. Exports from Finland are free of all duties.

Foreign Exchange Controls

The system of foreign exchange control has been progressively liberalized since the 1960s. At the beginning of 1970 the Bank of Finland administered the system. Foreign exchange could be purchased from the bank or from authorized exchange dealers, mainly commercial banks. Authorized banks could make payment for most commercial trade, freight, and foreign chartering transactions and certain other noncommodity transactions. Payments for imports had to be completed within six months after the arrival of the goods in the country. Extensions in certain cases could be obtained from the Bank of Finland.

Foreign exchange export earnings had to be sold to an authorized bank or to the Bank of Finland. Exporters were permitted to keep a portion of their export proceeds in foreign exchange accounts with Finnish banks or abroad. These proceeds could be used to meet incidental expenses related to exports and for the purchase of authorized imports of raw materials, machinery, and equipment. The Bank of Finland was entitled to claim these accounts at any time against payment in markka at the official rate.

Authorized exchange dealers and shipping firms were also allowed to maintain working balances in foreign exchange under supervision of the Bank of Finland. The import of Finnish and foreign currency into the country was unrestricted.

Repatriation of profits, dividends, and securities and liquidation of foreign-controlled physical assets were liberally granted even when a foreign exchange transfer was involved as long as the holders were bona fide nonresidents who had gained possession of the assets in a way approved by the Bank of Finland.

SECTION IV. NATIONAL SECURITY

CHAPTER 15

PUBLIC ORDER AND SECURITY

Responsibility for law enforcement and the maintenance of public order in early 1973 rested with the central government. The minister of interior exercised control over all police forces, including the general police who were stationed throughout the country and specialized units, such as the Security Police who dealt with matters involving national security.

The importance of internal security in Finland and the scope of government efforts required to protect and maintain it can be explained in part by the special conditions governing the country's relations with the Soviet Union, the proximity between the two nations, and their various mutual security and trade agreements. In part, too, the importance of the national security issue reflects the ideological cleavage, violence, and polarization of political sentiments that marked Finnish history during the early decades of the twentieth century.

PUBLIC ORDER AND SECURITY

Incidence of Crime

Few recent data on the incidence of crime in Finland are available. Studies made over the past decade indicate, however, that arrests for drunkenness have been at a comparatively high ratio as compared to those of other Scandinavian countries. The same appears to be true for the crime of murder. In major and minor thefts, however, Denmark and Sweden both had more than three times as many offenses in proportion to population as Finland. Strict regulations against irregular behavior under the influence of alcohol may to some extent—although not fully—explain Finland's very high rate of arrests of persons abusing alcohol (see table 18).

Police Organization

The Finnish police system dates back to the Middle Ages as a part of a structure that gradually developed in the Scandinavian countries. It maintained its basic form through the many centuries of Swedish domination and through the more than 100 years when Finland was

Table 18. Crime Rates in Finland, Denmark, and Sweden, 1962
(crimes per 100,000 population)

Offense	Finland	Denmark	Sweden
Willful murder[1]	2.3	1.3	0.7
Larceny (major and minor)[1]	774	2,501	2,841
Sex crimes, crimes involving drugs and fraud	218	281	372
Other[1][2]	1,304	142	837

[1]Figures rounded.
[2]Primarily illegal use of alcohol.

Source: Adapted from Preben Wolf, "Crime and Development," *Scandinavian Studies in Criminology*, Oslo, III, 1971, pp. 108–109.

under Russian rule. In that period the police forces were organized within the old administrative boundaries.

In the early 1970s police forces were operated and controlled entirely by the central government, through the Ministry of Interior. Within the ministry was a Police Division, supervised by a commander in chief and an inspector general. Provincial commands, in which the highest police officer was the superintendent, corresponded to the twelve administrative units into which the country was divided (see ch. 9). These commands were in turn divided into districts, of which there were roughly 240. Senior officers of urban districts were called police chiefs; those of rural districts were called sheriffs. Local authorities were required to provide one-third of the cost of maintaining police forces in their area but had no authority in police activities.

The general police were responsible for maintaining law and order in the areas to which they were assigned. Other branches of police, by contrast, had limited or specialized functions. The Mobile Police, for example, stationed throughout the country, were charged with the enforcement of traffic laws and the conduct of antismuggling operations. The Central Criminal Police, located in Helsinki, constituted a central bureau of investigation whose officers assisted the general police in investigating serious crime. Still another specialized group was the Security Police, involved with counterespionage activities.

In accordance with the principle of central direction, motor vehicles, weapons, and other equipment for the police forces were distributed centrally from depots directly under the Ministry of Interior. The depots procured, maintained, and repaired all cars, communication equipment, and weapons and ammunition that the police forces required. They were also responsible for implementing weapons control regulations imposed by the ministry.

All Finnish policemen are educated and trained centrally at the Police School, which is under the direction of the Ministry of Interior. Recruits must be between twenty and thirty years of age, at least five feet nine inches tall, and in excellent health. All those admitted must have completed high school education and the obligatory military service. Personnel of the Finnish police force are ranked in a three-step hierarchy like that of the military—officers, noncommissioned officers, and enlisted men or constables. Most officers are trained by the Police School. In the higher positions, however, people with university degrees can be admitted directly, without previous training at the school. For the highest positions in the police hierarchy a law degree is mandatory. Training in law is important also in some instances where police officers may act as prosecutors.

The General Police

The general police were mainly occupied with the local problems of law and order within the district in which they served, but they also had a responsibility to go on duty anywhere in the nation where a need emerged. The local policeman, however, was expected to live within the police district where he had his major duties.

In 1972 the government proposed a new set of regulations for the general police forces, allocating more personnel and equipment to the police districts and tightening the command of the provincial headquarters. The rapid changes in the distribution of the population, now concentrating in larger centers, required closer coordination, better communication, and tighter chains of command.

The authority and responsibility of a Finnish policeman is extensive. Even when he is off duty, if some sudden need should emerge, he is expected to use his initiative to maintain law and order.

The Mobile Police

The Mobile Police was formed in 1930. Its establishment as a separate entity within the police force reflects the degree of political unrest during that particular period. The existence of a highly mobile police force, full controlled by the government, ready at a moment's notice to assist any of the local police forces that might be unable to control a rioting mob was seen as an assurance for the maintenance of law and order.

In 1973 the main function of the Mobile Police was traffic regulation, particularly on the highways, where its helicopters, or "flying patrols," were respected by all drivers. It was also responsible for preventing illegal imports into the country, particularly the smuggling of alcohol and drugs. Among its duties in this field were checks on the production and sale of liquor. Protection of the environment, game regulations, and hunting and fishing restrictions had become important parts of its activities. A major function, however, was to act as a reserve, always ready for immediate service in any part of the country.

The Central Criminal Police

The Central Criminal Police assisted other branches of police in investigating serious crimes. It could also initiate and carry through its own investigations independently of the local police forces in a given area.

The basic function of the Central Criminal Police was to take responsibility in all cases that involved technical investigations of crimes. It was able to draw on universities, hospitals, and other scientific institutions for assistance. It kept records on crimes and convicted offenders throughout the nation. Another of its functions was to act as the national agency for Interpol and to contribute to the work on international levels for limiting crime and aiding police forces in other countries.

NATIONAL SECURITY

The problems of the nation's internal security and the activities of the fourth major branch of the Finnish police force, the Security Police, come into perspective when viewed against the country's history of subversion, revolutionary activities, and internal violence. During the last years of Russian rule, Finnish independence was promoted as an antigovernment movement which, in character if not in size, resembled the revolutionary movements in Russia. As both had the tsarist government as their common enemy, it might appear that the revolutionary goals were the same in both countries. The ideological clashes that resulted in the Finnish Civil War of 1918 proved that this was not the case.

The Finnish Communists, some of whom were driven into exile in 1918, formed a Finnish Communist Party in the Soviet Union, whereas others who were able to stay in Finland formed their own organization, the Socialist Workers Party. The latter received Vladimir Ilyich Lenin's blessing and under the skillful guidance of a Finnish Bolshevik, Otto Kuusinen, developed an effective Moscow-oriented organization. After the Socialist Workers Party had been outlawed by the government in the mid-1920s, activities were continued underground and through various cover organizations. These activities were quite intense, including the training of "red guards" in northern Sweden and Norway as well as in Finland; clandestine accumulations of weapons; and attempts to create mass movements, strikes, and disobedience campaigns. According to a prominent Finnish historian: "In Finland's geographical position the operations of the Communists were felt to be a threat to national independence."

On the nationalist side, right-wing extremists started to make themselves heard. In the early 1930s such organizations as the Lapua Movement and the right-wing elite group, the Academic Karelian Society, gained prominence and for a while also substantial political influence. The nationalist organizations pushed toward extremist positions in the early 1930s until they were also repressed by the government (see ch. 2).

The Communist Party in Finland was not allowed to appear above ground nor was it recognized as a legal political entity until the Finnish military suffered final defeat against the Soviet Union in 1944. The Soviet government did not look upon the political cleavages as things of the past. Article 8 of the peace treaty that Finland had to sign in 1947 reads:

> Finland, which in accordance with the Armistice Agreement (of 1944) has taken measures for dissolving all organizations of a Fascist type on Finnish territory, whether political, military or para-military, as well as other organizations conducting propaganda hostile to the Soviet Union or to any of the other United Nations, shall not permit in future the existence and activities of organizations of that nature which have as their aim denial to the people of their democratic rights.

This provision in the treaty not only branded the basically nationalist Finnish organizations as fascist, it also left to the discretion of the signatories to define what future organizations "have as their aim denial to the people of their democratic rights."

Animosity toward communism remained strong in Finland, so much so that the newly recognized Finnish Communist Party found it necessary to create a new sister organization, the Finnish People's Democratic League (Suomen Kansan Demokraattinen Liitto—SKDL), hoping to avoid the onus of the communist label in order to widen the socialist appeal. As required by Article 9 of the treaty, the most ardent nationalists—and anticommunists—in the higher echelons of Finnish political life were tried and sentenced in a fashion similar to that done to Nazis and collaborators in those countries that had been occupied by Germany during the war.

The Security Police

Maintaining public order and security and acting against threats of subversion and conspiracy have been a major part of the activities of the Security Police organization since its inception. Originally known as the Detective Central Police and later as the State Police, the Security Police had its headquarters in Helsinki. Requirements for recruitment were somewhat stricter than those pertaining to other police personnel.

Other functions in addition to counterespionage have been added over the years to the organization's duties. Among these are responsibility for advice on classified government documents, numerous liaison functions, and the checking on foreign citizens who work in or visit Finland.

From time to time, leftist political leaders, apparently objecting to surveillance activities of the Security Police, have called for changes in the structure and responsibilities of the force. A demand made by the Finnish Social Democratic Party (Suomen Sosialidemokraattinen Puolue—SDP), for example, drew nationwide attention in the summer of 1970. As of early 1973, however, no significant changes in structure or authority of the force were under public consideration.

The Border Police

The Border Police was a special paramilitary force whose daily activities were directed by a small staff under the jurisdiction of the Ministry of Interior. In times of grave crises or war, it would be joined with other national police forces for supreme overall defense.

Its main responsibility was surveillance of Finland's borders, territorial waters and, by implication, its air space. Further, the border police forces played an important part in search and rescue operations, particularly in the Finnish north and in certain coastal areas. A large part of its activities took place along Finland's border with the Soviet Union, partly in surveillance, partly at the regular border crossing points. The force was gradually requiring new helicopters and suitable vessles for controlling the territorial waters. In 1970 the Border Police was reported to have five helicopters and fifteen vessels for control purposes.

CHAPTER 16

THE ARMED FORCES

The position of the armed forces is determined by their usefulness as perceived by the nation. The people at large feel that the armed forces either have improved their situation or at least have prevented it from deterioration. Defense has a high place on the list of national priorities, and military personnel enjoy a favorable social standing.

The mission of the Finnish armed forces is to defend the territorial integrity and national sovereignty of the country. Treaty agreements limit the size of the total force to about 41,900 men and restrict its equipment to defensive weapons. The president is the supreme commander of all armed forces. He is assisted by a Defense Council composed of cabinet members and senior military officers. Service is required of all men between the ages of twenty and sixty years, training is rigorous and effective, and the armed forces have an international reputation for military efficiency.

MILITARY TRADITIONS AND LIMITATIONS

Military Heritage

Although Finland did not achieve full national independence until 1917, its military traditions go back more than 300 years. As a part of Sweden, Finland supplied the Swedish armies not only with drafted foot soldiers but also with an array of highly qualified officers from the Swedish-Finnish aristocracy and the upper classes of Finnish society. Finnish elements of the Swedish armies, which for more than a century played an essential role in European power politics, were among the most effective and respected units.

The victories to which they contributed confirmed their belief in the usefulness of armed forces for national purposes and increased their self-confidence as performers of military roles. The setbacks that Sweden eventually suffered in Europe were explained by the Finns, with considerable justification, as mistakes that had been made by the Swedish kings on political levels where the Finns had no influence. On the level of purely military performance the Finns had done the best that could be achieved under the existing circumstances. As soldiers they felt that their performance on various battlefields had justified their reputation for bravery.

The Swedish campaigns in which the Finns played a great role gave the Finns the additional incentive of defending their own territory against the traditional enemy, Russia. Although the Finnish military organization was under Swedish political leadership, its tasks included the defense of Finland's borders to the east as well as the more adventurous campaigns in continental Europe. On three major occasions Russian armies invaded Finland and occupied parts of the country for a number of years before eventually being driven out by Finnish and Swedish forces.

During the more than 100 years of Russian domination from 1809 to the Bolshevik Revolution, when Finland was a dependent grand duchy under Russia, it was still possible to maintain a core of Finnish military activity. Between 1819 and 1903 the Finnish Military Academy in Hanuna educated close to 1,000 officers, many of whom served with great distinction in the Imperial Russian Army. Among these graduates was Carl Gustav von Mannerheim, who later became the great hero of Finnish resistance and the struggle for independence.

It is characteristic of Finnish behavior and experience that the claim to full independence had to be settled by armed forces on the battlefields of Finland's Civil War. The Civil War confirmed the earlier Finnish experience that the achievement of national goals and national security required the use of armed force.

Partly because of the Soviet Union's weakness in the early years after the Revolution in 1917 when its new leaders were arranging their new state and partly because of the temporary mirage of collective security provided by the League of Nations, the Finns were slow in building a strong national army. In 1938 they allocated only 3.7 percent of their gross national product (GNP) to national defense. Defense improvement was barely underway when, in 1939, Josef Stalin demanded concessions of Finnish territory as part of his preparations for a future showdown with Nazi Germany. The Finns nevertheless resorted to arms to resist the Soviet claims on their sovereignty and territorial integrity. When the Soviets attacked in November 1939 they were met by Finnish forces that, in a matter of a few weeks, destroyed thousands of invading Soviet troops. Momentarily it looked as if Finland would turn back the aggressor and inflict a definite military defeat on its great and powerful neighbor. Massive Soviet replacements ended the conflict, however, and on March 12, 1940, an armistice confirmed most of the initial Soviet demands, including losses of some parts of Finnish territory. But, unlike the Baltic states, Finland was not occupied, nor did it suffer any further infringements on its national sovereignty.

In the Continuation War, which Finland fought in alliance with Germany from 1941 to 1944, the Finnish forces demonstrated their superior qualities while fighting with the world's two foremost ranking military forces, the Soviet and the German armies. During this campaign the Finns never lost their sense of purpose. Their goal was not conquest and occupation but regaining the Finnish territories that seemed essential to Finland's national security. Confined in the losing Axis coalition, they had to retreat for a second time and only escaped total Soviet invasion and occupation by entering into a separate agreement that provided for Finnish military actions against the retreating German armies. This willingness to use armed forces even against their allies of more than three years of joint struggle against the Soviet Union is an illustration of the extremely realistic Finnish attitude toward military means and their adaptability in using armed force.

Treaty Limitations

Considering the magnitude of the defeat and the blows that were dealt to other nations fighting on Germany's side during World War II, Finland did not fare too badly when the terms for a peace treaty were drawn on February 10, 1947 (see ch. 2). In terms of national security, the most important parts of the peace treaty were the restrictions it put on Finland's armed forces. Part III, Articles 13 to 22, limited a future Finnish army to 34,400 men, the navy to 4,500 men, and the air force to 3,000 men, allowing for a total force of less than 42,000 men. There were also severe restrictions on equipment and weapons. Naval vessels were not allowed to exceed a total of 10,000 tons, which could not include submarines, speedboats, or other vessels with explicit attack facilities. The air force could acquire up to sixty planes, not including bombers or fighter bombers. None of the services was allowed to deploy missiles nor to construct, procure, or even study nuclear weapons of any kind.

During the 1941–44 war Finland had brought more than half a million soldiers into the field. After the war, with less than a tenth of that number available, it could no longer plan for military resistance of the kind it had attempted during the 1939–44 period.

The problems of national defense were further complicated by the Agreement of Friendship, Cooperation and Mutual Assistance requested by Stalin in February 1948 and signed by the Finnish government in April of the same year. The most important clauses were probably Articles 1 and 2, which read:

Article 1.

In the event of Finland or the Soviet Union, across the territory of Finland, becoming the object of military aggression on the part of Germany or any state allied to the latter, Finland, loyal to her duty as an independent state, will fight to repulse the aggression. In doing so, she will direct all the forces at her disposal to the defense of the inviolability of her territory on land, on sea and in the air, acting within her boundaries in accordance with her obligations under the present treaty with the assistance, in case of need, of the Soviet Union or jointly with the latter.

In the case indicated above, the Soviet Union will render Finland the necessary assistance in regard to the granting of which the parties will agree between themselves.

Article 2.

The parties will consult each other in the event of a threat of military attack envisaged in Article I being ascertained.

The agreement was to last for ten years but was renewed in 1955 for a twenty-year period. In 1970, however, after only fifteen years, it was renewed for a third time, to be in force until 1990. If no other arrangement were made, it would automatically remain in force for another five years. These frequent renewals seemed to indicate intense Soviet interest in the treaty, a circumstance that has increased the persistent controversy as to what restraints the pledges of mutual assistance put on Finnish sovereignty and independence (see ch. 11).

ORGANIZATION AND STRUCTURE OF THE FINNISH DEFENSE FORCES

As in the United States, the president is the supreme commander of all armed forces. As an advisory body he has a council consisting of the prime minister (chairman), the ministers of defense, external affairs, internal affairs, finance, trade and industry, the chief of defense forces, and the chief of staff. The Defense Council has its own secretariat with high ranking officers in charge. On the military side there is a Defense Staff (Pääesikunta) heading all three services with a total of sixteen subdivisions. On the same level as the Defense Staff is the Defense Cabinet and the Ministry of Defense, which is responsible for administrative matters and the civilian institutions.

The armed forces comprise three services: army, navy, and air force. In 1972 the army had about 34,000 men on active duty and 630,000 in reserves; the navy had some 2,500 men in active service and 25,000 in reserves; and the air force had approximately 3,000 active duty personnel and 30,000 reservists. There was also a paramilitary force of some 4,000 border guards (see ch. 15).

In 1972 the army was composed of six infantry brigades, one armored brigade, six independent infantry battalions, six coast artillery battalions, and four antiaircraft battalions. The navy had two Soviet-built frigates, one British frigate converted to a training ship, two corvettes, two minelayers, five inshore minesweepers, thirty patrol craft, nine transports, eight icebreakers, and one cable ship. The air force had three operational groups equipped with thirty-eight MiG-21 day fighters, four MiG-21 trainers, and an older squadron of Gnat fighters, which were to be replaced with twelve Swedish Saab 35XS supersonic all-weather interceptors in 1974 and 1975. Other air force equipment included Saab 91D primary trainers, Magister jet basic trainers, MiG-15 jet advanced trainers, DC-3 transports, Il-28 target tugs, and miscellaneous helicopters.

The obligatory period of military service for all males aged twenty to sixty is eight months, which can be extended up to eleven months for those acquiring special skills. The training is intensive, with the first four months devoted mainly to promoting physical fitness and adjusting to the psychological requirements and the spirit of military service. Motivation and purpose receive great attention. Considering its relative shortness, the training period seems to be effective. Generally speaking, the units have a high rate of performance at the end of their term of service.

The most important part of the Finnish military program is probably the training of reserve officers. Training lasts almost a year; about 75 percent of the time is devoted to practical matters—military exercises and maneuvers designed to give the students high proficiency in fieldwork and leadership in actual operations. It speaks well for Finland's strong military tradition that the school for reserve officers is sought eagerly by young, able-bodied men and attracts some of the elite groups. More than three-fourths of the students have successfully passed the gymnasium, the senior secondary school, which is the equivalent of grades ten through twelve in a United States high school (see ch. 7). A major emphasis is on developing leadership. The students are encouraged to take initiative and to move and act independently.

The reserve officers school graduates about 1,500 officers a year, a number considered to be much higher than one would expect the rather modest military organization to need. Reserve officers enjoy high social standing. To have completed reserve officers training remains a solid recommendation to almost any position in civilian life.

Regular army officers are trained at the Cadet School at Santahamina, Helsinki. A candidate must have completed gymnasium and reserve officers school, have proven military qualities as a leader and organizer, and be no older than twenty-six years. As is the case with the reserve officers, there are many more applicants than the Cadet School can handle. In recent years only one of five has been admitted. The annual number of graduates is between seventy and 100 officers. The permanent staff usually comprises thirty to forty teachers, of whom more than three-fourths are active officers. As in other Finnish educational institutions for military training, there is a heavy stress on motivation, leadership, and character building, practical military subjects holding a clear predominance over theoretical approaches. A final stage in the military education hierarchy is the War College (Sotakorkeakoulu), which conducts two-year courses and trains officers for staff work at the highest levels.

The percentage of conscientious objectors usually has remained less than 0.5 percent, one of the lowest figures among Western military establishments. Of the roughly 40,000 young men eligible for military service in 1968, 8 percent became officers and 22 percent noncommissioned officers during their tours of duty. Usually each year about 20,000 reservists are given refresher training, which is forty days for soldiers, seventy-five days for noncommissioned officers, and 100 days for officers.

EXPENDITURES

Given the severe treaty restrictions on Finnish military forces, in numbers as well as equipment, the cost of national defense is lower than in most other countries of comparable size. The low profile has been further stressed because the Finnish government has chosen not to fill the quotas to which they are entitled by the 1947 peace treaty. This holds for men as well as equipment. Over the years the Soviet government has become more confident that Finnish armed forces will not be used against the Soviet Union. Consequently, the 1947 restrictions on certain types of weapons have been modified to allow the Finns to use more modern means of warfare.

It caused some surprise in the early 1960s when the Finnish air force purchased twenty-five MiG-21s, then one of the world's most advanced fighter planes. It was not generally known at that time, however, that the delivery did not include such important accessories as the equipment to overhaul the planes. Thus, the operational value of the MiG-21s has been somewhat limited because after a certain number of air hours they have to be flown back to the Soviet Union for complete service and overhaul. In order to overcome this handicap, the Finnish government in 1970 contracted to buy twelve Swedish Draken planes, which could be fully serviced, and even partly produced, in Finland.

There also has been a slow but persistent attempt to modernize the Finnish navy, which consists mainly of small gunboat-type vessels. As the Finnish metal industry gathers momentum, there has been a gradual improvement of lighter weapons for the infantry, such as a very effective Finnish assault gun and mortars. The Finns have shown great ingenuity in partly building and partly adopting effective means of military transportation.

Apart from the more sophisticated equipment, such as planes and warning devices, the logistical elements are mainly Finnish supplied. The Soviet Union also has allowed the deployment of missiles for battlefield operations.

Except in 1963 and 1964, Finland's postwar defense expenses have amounted to less than 2 percent of its GNP. Since the middle 1960s this proportion has declined gradually and in early 1973 was less than 1.5 percent of the GNP. The peak in the 1963-64 period was clearly influenced by the so-called note crisis in 1961, when the Soviet Union threatened to call the military consultations provided for in Article 2 of the Agreement of Friendship, Cooperation and Mutual Assistance (see ch. 11). There was at that time a strong popular demand for a higher allocation to defense measures, which is clearly possible within the limits of the existing treaty regulations.

MILITARY POLICY

Official Missions

The military organization that emerged after World War II had two clearly defined objectives: to assist the civil authorities in maintaining internal security and to deal with border incidents and prevent any violation of national territory. The official version of the mission of the military, often repeated in presidential addresses and more explicitly in writings by Finnish strategic analysts, defines the task of the armed forces as a maximal defense effort directed against any aggressor, regardless of who it may be or where the attack may come from. Finland will defend its territorial integrity and its national independence under all conditions and circumstances and will use its armed forces against any intruder that might try to force its way into Finnish territory or by other violent means try to infringe on Finland's national sovereignty. In a recent handbook for defense matters the tasks are spelled out in more detail: to repel violations of the nation's territory and airspace in peacetime and during wars between other states; to repel attacks against the government; and to defend the country with all the force the nation can provide.

Capabilities and Intentions

Article 13 of the 1947 peace treaty puts severe restrictions on the Finnish army, navy, and air force by limiting personnel and equipment strictly to what is necessary for internal security, local surveillance, and defense of Finland's borders. The Agreement of Friendship, Cooperation and Mutual Assistance could be interpreted as an extension of these two major tasks. It implies that Finland and the Soviet Union will deal jointly with threats to the area. Finland is further requested to use all its available forces to defend the integrity of the country. Participation in what amounts to a de facto alliance with the Soviet Union might be expected to lead to Finnish demands for more capabilities than the patrolling of borders and the maintenance of internal security, but mutual assistance does not necessarily imply equal contributions. Neither in the 1948 agreement nor in the 1955 and 1970 renewals was there any major modification of the force restrictions that were laid down in the 1947 peace treaty. Indeed, the agreement emphasizes the limited tasks that the Finnish forces are expected to perform on their own or in cooperation with Soviet forces. The objectives remain the same: internal security and guarding the borders.

Finland's recent history does not suggest that its internal security would require a major military effort. This leaves only one major military objective: defense of Finland's integrity and independence, which has been formulated since 1955 as the defense of Finnish neutrality. Soviet forces were withdrawn from Porkkala, the base near Helsinki, in 1955, and from then on Finnish authorities have sought consistently to achieve recognition of the country as a neutral nation.

BIBLIOGRAPHY

Section I. Social

Ala-Könni, Erkki. "Finnish Folk Music," *The American Scandinavian Review*, LII, No. 1, March 1964.

Alexandersson, G. *Les Pays Du Nord*. Paris, 1971.

Allardt, Erik. "The Influence of Different Systems of Social Norms on Divorce Rates in Finland," *Marriage and Family Living*, XVII, No. 4, November 1955, 325–331.

Anderson, Ingvar. *A History of Sweden*. New York: Praeger, 1968.

Annual Report of Väestöliitto 1971. Helsinki: Population Research Institute, 1971.

Anonymous. "The Last of the Lapps," *Europa Magazine*, I, No. 9, December 1971, 24–25.

Arkkitehti (Finnish Architectural Review). No. 1, 1972.

Auvinen, Riitta. *The Repercussions of Scientific and Technological Development on the Status of Women*. Helsinki: Väestöpoliittinen Tutkimuslaitos, 1969.

Bacon, Walter. *Finland*. London: Robert Hale and Co., 1970.

Barrett, David. "Literature and the National Image," in *Finland: Creation and Construction*, edited by Hillar Kallas and Sylvie Nickels. London: George Allen and Unwin, Ltd., 1968.

Beer, Eileene Harrison. "Timo Sarpaneva: Dynamic Force in Finnish Design," *The American Scandinavian Review*, LIV, No. 3, September 1966.

Beijer, G. *Rural Migrants in Urban Setting*. The Hague, 1963.

Bell, Marja-Liisa. "Eila Hiltunen," *The American Scandinavian Review*, LIX, No. 1, Spring 1971.

Berry, Erick. *The Land and People of Finland*. 2nd ed. Philadelphia: Lippincott, 1972.

The Board of Women's Work. "Women's Work in the Lutheran Church of Finland." The Lutheran Church of Finland, Helsinki. Unpublished paper.

Books Abroad, book review, 37, No. 2, Spring 1963; 42, No. 1, Winter 1968; No. 2, Spring 1968; No. 4, Autumn 1968.

Bradley, David. *Lion Among Roses: A Memoir of Finland*. New York: Holt, Rinehart and Winston, 1965.

Centre for Christian Education. *Christian Education in the Church and Schools of Finland*. Vammala, 1962.

Clarkson, Jesse D. *A History of Russia*. Edinburgh: Longmans, 1961.
Commission of Education of the Evangelical Lutheran Church of Finland. *Christian Education in Finland*. Helsinki: The Lutheran Church of Finland. Pamphlet.
"Contemporary Finnish Composers," in *The Finland Year Book 1947*, edited by Urho Toivola, with the assistance of the Press Department of the Ministry of Foreign Affairs and specialists in different branches. Helsinki: Mercatorin Kirjapaino ja Kustannus Oy, 1947.
"Cultural Relations," in *Introduction to Finland 1960*, edited by Urho Toivola, in collaboration with the Press Bureau of the Ministry of Foreign Affairs. Helsinki: Werner Söderström Osakeyhtiö.
Dauenhauer, Richard. "The Literature of Finland," *The Literary Review*, XIV, No. 1, Fall, 1970.
de Biasi, Mario. *Finlandia: Profile of a Country*. Helsinki: Tammi Publishers, 1967.
Desneiges, George. *Finland*. New York: Viking Press, 1964.
"Dramatic Art," in *The Finland Year Book 1947*, edited by Urho Toivola, with the assistance of the Press Department of the Ministry of Foreign Affairs and specialists in different branches. Helsinki: Mercatorin Kirjapaino ja Kustannus Oy, 1947.
Eidheim, Harald. "Lappish Guest Relationships Under Conditions of Cultural Change," *American Anthropologist*, LXVIII, No. 2, Pt. 1, April 1966, 426–427.
Facts About Finland. 13th revised ed. Helsinki: Otava, 1972.
"Family Counseling of the Lutheran Church of Finland," The Lutheran Church of Finland, Helsinki. Unpublished paper.
Finland. Central Statistical Bureau. *Projection of Population in the Communes to the Year 2000*. Helsinki: 1972.
Finland. Embassy of Finland. *Finland: Suomi*. Washington: 1971.
Finland. The Ministry of Education. *Higher Education and Research in Finland*. October 1972.
Finland. Ministry of Social Affairs and Health. *Social Services in Finland: 1, Social Welfare*. Helsinki: Ministry of Social Affairs and Health, 1969.
Finland. Ministry of Social Affairs and Health. *Social Services in Finland: 2, Social Allowances*. Helsinki: Ministry of Social Affairs and Health, 1969.
Finland. Ministry of Social Affairs and Health. *Social Services in Finland: 3, Social Insurance*. Helsinki: Ministry of Social Affairs and Health, 1969.
Finland. Ministry of Social Affairs and Health. *Social Services in Finland: 4, Labour Protection*. Helsinki: Ministry of Social Affairs and Health, 1970.
Finland. National Planning Office. *Distribution of Population in Finland 1967*. Publications Series A: 22. Helsinki, 1968, including 4 maps, Scale 1/400,000.

"Finland's Vigorous Publishing Industry Has a Lusty Appetite for English Translations," *Publishers Weekly*, September 17, 1973.

The Finnish Academy of Science and Letters. *Proceedings*, edited by Lauri A. Vuorela, Secretary General of the Academy. Helsinki: The Finnish Academy of Science and Letters, 1972.

"Finnish Architecture Today," *Design Quarterly*, No. 84, 1972.

"Finnish Author, Publisher Prosecuted for Blasphemy," *Publishers Weekly*, February 8, 1965.

"Finnish Church Architecture," *The American Scandinavian Review*, L, No. 2, June 1962.

Finnish Society of Arts and Crafts. *Vision*. (Text by Kai Laitinen) Helsinki.

Finnish Society for Research in Sports and Physical Education. *Physical Education and Sports in Finland*. Helsinki: WSOY, 1969.

Finnish Theological Literature Society. *Finnish Theology, Past and Present*. Helsinki, 1963.

Fisher, Clyde. "The Nomads of Arctic Lapland," *The National Geographic Magazine*, LXXVI, No. 5, November 1939, 641-656 and 665-676.

The Folklore Archives of the Finnish Literature Society. Helsinki: Suomalaisen Kirjallisuuden Seura, 1965.

Freedman, Richard. "Two Neglected Choral Works," *The Washington Post, Book World*, July 9, 1972.

Furumark, Arne, et al (eds.). *Lapponica (Essays Presented to Israel Ruong)*. Studia Ethnographica Upsaliensia, XXI, 1964.

Geographical Society of Finland. *Atlas of Finland*. Helsinki, 1925-1928.

Geographical Society of Finland. *Atlas of Finland 1960*. Helsinki, 1960.

Geographical Society of Finland. *General Handbook on the Geography of Finland*. Helsinki, 1952.

Gidal, Sonia. *My Village in Finland*. New York: Pantheon Books, 1966.

Granö, J. G. "Die Geographische Gebiete Finnlands...," *Fennia*, LII, 1931, 1-66.

Gustafsson, Matti. *Education in Finland*. Helsinki: Ministry of Education, Reference Publication 2, 1967.

Gutheim, Frederick. "Alvar Aalto Today," *Architectural Record*, April 1963.

Hall, David. "Jean Sibelius," *The American Scandinavian Review*, LIII, No. 4, December 1965.

Hall, Sam. "The Country That Came in from the Cold," *Europa Magazine*, I, No. 9, December 1971, 18-22.

Hall, Wendy. *The Finns and Their Country*. London: Max Parrish, 1967.

Hard af Segerstad, Ulf. *Modern Finnish Design*. New York: Praeger, 1969.

Heiskanen Ilkka. "Direct Redistribution and Structural Regulation as the Two Strategies of Governmental Social Science Policy: The Case of Finland." Paper presented June 1972 at the Conference on National

Social Science Councils, Paris. Helsinki: Suomen Akatemia.
Helsinki City Planning Office. *Helsinki Master Plan Proposal 1970.*
Hermanus, Pertti. "Development Trends in Scandinavian Press," *Gazette*, No. 2, 1972.
Hobson, Harold. "The Theatre," in *Finland: Creation and Construction*, edited by Hillar Kallas and Sylvie Nickels. London: George Allen and Unwin, Ltd., 1968.
Hoffman, J. G. H. *L'église vit et ne se rend pas*. Geneva: Les Editions Labor, 1946.
Hulkko, Jouko, Keijo Immonen and Kalervo Siikala (eds.). *Finland 1917–1967: An Assessment of Independence*. Helsinki: Kirjayhtymä, 1967.
Institute of Technology (Helsinki). Architectural Department brochure.
Jaatinen, S. and U. Kärkkäinen. *Vuoden 1969 Pellonvaraustoiminta*. Helsingin Yliopiston, Maantieteen Laitoksen Julkaisuja. Sarja B, No. 7, Helsinki, 1971.
Juva, Mikko. *The Church of Finland*. Pieksämäki: The Inner Mission Society of the Church of Finland, 1963.
Kallas, Hillar and Sylvie Nickels (eds.). *Finland: Creation and Construction*. New York: Praeger, 1968.
Kallio, N. *Education in Finland*. 5th ed. Helsinki: Ministry of Education, 1961.
Kansallis-Osake-Pankki. Research Staff. "Economic Development in Finland in 1971," (K-O-P) *Economic Review*, No. 1, 1972, 14–48.
Kärkkäinen, H. "The Structural Change in Distribution in Finland," (K-O-P) *Economic Review*, No. 1, 1972, 3–13.
Kauranen, Pentti and Markku Linna. *Science Policy and International Research Co-operation in Finland in the 1970's*. Helsinki: The Ministry of Education.
Kaytor, John Peter and Marilyn. "The Finnish Look," *Look*, December 4, 1966.
Kivikoski, Ella N. *Finland*. New York: Praeger, 1967.
Klinge, Matti. *University of Helsinki: A Short History*. Helsinki: University of Helsinki, 1971.
Korpivaara, Eero. "Finnish Architecture Today," *The American Scandinavian Review*, LVIII, No. 3, September 1970.
Laitinen, Kai, "Aleksis Kivi: The Man and His Work," *The American Scandinavian Review*, L, No. 4, December 1962.
Laitinen, Kai, "Commentary: Finnish Literature 1967," *Books Abroad*, XLI, No. 4, Autumn, 1967.
Laitinen, Kai. "Post-war Literaure—A Finnish View," in *Finland: Creation and Construction*, edited by Hillar Kallas and Sylvie Nickels. London: George Allen and Unwin, Ltd., 1968.
Lantmäteristyrelsen. *Suomi Finland*. Helsinki: 1950.
Laurila, Aarne. "F. E. Sillanpää: An Appreciation," *The American Scandinavian Review*, LIII, No. 3, September 1965.

224

Lehto, Markku. *Regional Variation of Social Assistance.* Helsinki: Official Statistics of Finland/Special Social Studies, 1972.

Lindgren, Jarl. *Expenditure on Children.* Helsinki: Väestöpoliittinen Tutkimuslaitos, 1965.

Lindgren, Jarl (ed.). *Yearbook of Population Research in Finland.* XII. Helsinki: Väestöntutkimuksen Vuosikirja, 1971.

Lindman, Kerstin. "Finland's Swedes: An Introduction and a Bibliography," *Scandinavian Studies,* XXXIV, No. 2, May 1962.

Linnamo, Jussi. *Finland: A Growing Economy.* Helsinki: Ministry of Foreign Affairs, Reference Publication 1, 1967.

Loercher, Diana. "Finnish Designer Stresses Relaxed, Durable Simplicity," *The Christian Science Monitor,* October 6, 1972.

Lundin, C. Leonard. *Finland in the Second World War.* Bloomington: Indiana University Press, 1957.

Luterfort, Ingrid (ed.). *Theater in the Five Scandinavian Countries.* Nordiska Teaterunionen, 1971.

Maanmittaushallituksen Kivipaino. *Suomen Taloudellinen Kartta, Jyväskylä.* Helsinki, 1941, Scale 1/100,000.

Maanmittaushallituksen Kivipaino. *Suomen Taloudellinen Kartta, Kursu.* Helsinki, 1939, Scale 1/100,000.

Maanmittaushallitus. *Suomen Tiekartta.* Helsinki, 1969, Scale 1/200,000 (13 sheets).

Majava, A. "Migrations Between Finland and Sweden," *The Second Scandinavian Demographic Symposium,* 1970.

Mäkelä, Juhani and Tutta Runeberg. *Finland Grows 1970.* Helsinki: Sales and Advertising Association of Finland, n.d.

Mäkinen, Timo and Seppo Nummi. *Musica Fennica. Helsinki: Mäkinen Kustannusosakeyhtiö Otava, 1965.*

Malmström, Vincent H. *Norden: Crossroads of Destiny and Progress.* New York: Van Nostrand-Reinhold, 1965.

Mannerheim, Carl Gustaf. (Translator: Count Eric Lewenhaupt.) *The Memoirs of Marshal Mannerheim.* London: Cassell, 1953.

Mardall, Cyril. "Architecture," in *Finland: Creation and Construction,* edited by Hillar Kallas and Sylvie Nickels. London: George Allen and Unwin, Ltd., 1968.

Mead, William R. "The Cold Farm in Finland . . . ," *Geographical Review,* XLI, 1951, 529-543.

Mead, William R. *An Economic Geography of the Scandinavian States and Finland.* London: Verry, 1958.

Mead, William R. *Farming in Finland.* London: Oxford, 1958.

Mead, William R. *Finland.* New York: Praeger, 1968.

Mead, William R. *How People Live in Finland.* London: Wardlock Educational Co., 1968.

Millward, Roy. *Scandinavian Lands.* New York: St. Martin, 1964.

National Union of Finnish Students "Finland and Its Students." NUFS, 1967.

Nordenskiöld—Samfundet i Finland. *Atlas över Skärgards—Finland.* Helsingfors, 1960.

Nordenstreng, Kaarle. "Consumption of Mass Media in Finland," *Gazette,* XV, No. 4, 1969.

Nordenstreng, K. and N.-B. Stormbom. "Long-range Planning and Research in Finnish Broadcasting," *Adult Education in Finland,* VII, No. 4, 1970.

Nordic Council. *Yearbook of Nordic Statistics.* IX, Stockholm, 1971.

Nyberg, René (ed.). *Educational Reform in Finland in the 1970s.* Helsinki: Ministry of Education, Reference Publication 4, 1970.

Ojansuu, Raila (ed.). *Comprehensive School in Finland: Goals and an Outline for a Curriculum.* Helsinki: Ministry of Education, Reference Publication 5, 1971.

Organization for Economic Cooperation and Development. *OECD Economic Surveys: Finland.* Paris, 1972.

Oy Yleisradio Ab. (Finnish Broadcasting brochure). April 1966.

Oy Yleisradio Ab. Educational Programming Department. (Mimeo, reply to Radiotelevisione Italiana questionnaire), March 10, 1972.

Oy Yleisradio Ab. "School Radio/TV Programming," Mimeo, Spring 1972.

Paavilainen, Väinö. *National Planning in Finland.* Helsinki, 1963.

Paine, Robert. "Emergence of the Village as a Social Unit in a Coast Lappish Fjord," *American Anthropologist,* LXII, No. 6, December 1960, 1004–1017.

Palomäki, M. "Post War Pioneering in Finland," *Fennia.* LXXXIV, 1959, 1–23.

Paulson, Ivar. *Les Religions arctiques et Finnoises.* Paris: Payot, 1965.

Pennanen, Eila. *An Outline of Finnish Literature.* Washington: Embassy of Finland.

Pennanen, Eila. "Themes and Heroes in Finnish Fiction," *The Times Literary Supplement,* September 10, 1971.

"The Pictorial Arts," in *The Finland Year Book 1947,* edited by Urho Toivola, with the assistance of the Press Department of the Ministry of Foreign Affairs and specialists in different branches. Helsinki: Mercatorin Kirjapaino ja Kustannus Oy, 1947.

Pietilä, Veikko. "On the Accumulation of the Mass Media Use," *Long Range Planning* (FBC), Research Report 4, 1969.

Pihanurmi, K and M. Riuttu. "Adult Education on FBC Networks," *Adult Education in Finland,* VII, No. 4, 1970.

Pihlström, Bengt (ed.). *Look at Finland.* No. 1/72. Helsinki: Sanomarprint, 1972.

Platt, R. R. (ed.). *Finland and Its Geography.* An American Geographical Society handbook. New York: American Geographical Society, 1955.

Poutvaara, M. *See Finland by Air.* Helsinki, 1959.

Poutvaara, M. *Suomi Finland.* Porvoo, 1958.

Rasmussen, Carl C. *What About Scandinavia?* Philadelphia: The Muhlenberg Press, 1948.

Rexroth, Kenneth. "The Kalevala," *Saturday Review*, August 19, 1967.

Richards, Denby, "Music in Finland," *The American Scandinavian Review*, LVI, No. 3, September 1968.

Richards, Denby. *The Music of Finland.* London: Hugh Evelyn Ltd. 1968.

Richards, James Maude. *A Guide to Finnish Architecture.* London: Hugh Evelyn Ltd., 1966.

Rintala, Marvin. *Four Finns: Political Profiles.* Berkeley: University of California Press, 1969.

Rintala, Marvin. *Three Generations: The Extreme Right Wing in Finnish Politics.* (Indiana University Publications, Russian and East European Series 22.) Bloomington: Indiana University Press, 1962.

Ruge, H. *Educational Systems in Scandinavia.* Oslo, 1962.

Salokorpi, Asko. *Modern Architecture in Finland.* New York: Praeger, 1970.

Salokorpi, Asko. "New Trends—a Finnish View," in *Finland: Creation and Construction*, edited by Hillar Kallas and Sylvie Nickels. London: George Allen and Unwin, Ltd., 1968.

Sauvageit, Aurelien. *Histoire de la Finlande.* Paris: Paul Geuthner, 1968.

Scandinavian Editors. *A Businessman's Guide to Finland.* Copenhagen, 1969.

Scandinavian Studies, book review, XXXIV, No. 2, May 1962.

Schildt, Goran. *Modern Finnish Sculpture.* New York: Praeger, 1970.

"Scientific Research in Finland," in *The Finland Year Book 1947*, edited by Urho Toivola, with the assistance of the Press Department of the Ministry of Foreign Affairs and specialists in different branches. Helsinki: Mercatorin Kirjapaino ja Kustannus Oy, 1947.

Sentzke, Geert. *Finland: Its Church and Its People.* Helsinki: Kirjapaino Oy Lause, 1963.

Seton-Watson, Hugh. *The Russian Empire 1801–1917.* Oxford: Clarendon Press, 1967.

Shirer, William L. *The Challenge of Scandinavia: Norway, Sweden, Denmark and Finland in Our Time.* Boston: Little, Brown and Co., 1955.

Sidoroff, Matti. "An Outline of the History of the Orthodox Church in Finland." The Orthodox Publications Council of the Orthodox Church of Finland (mimeo).

Smeds, H. "The Distribution of Urban and Rural Population of Southern Finland 1950," *Fennia*, LXXXI, 1957, 1–21.

Smeds, H. "Post War Land Clearance and Pioneering Activities in Finland," *Fennia*, LXXXIII, 1960, 1–31.

Smeds, H. "Recent Changes in the Agricultural Geography of Finland," *Fennia*, LXXXVII, 1962, 1–19.

Smith, Clarence J. *Finland and the Russian Revolution 1917-1922*. Athens: University of Georgia Press, 1958.

Smith, Desmond. "Kalevala: Land of Heroes," *Look at Finland*. No. 2, 1972.

Smith, Desmond. "Morning, Noon and Night: An Interview with Einojuhani Rautavaara," *Look at Finland*, No. 1, 1972.

Smith, John Boulton. *Modern Finnish Painting*. New York: Praeger, 1970.

Smith, John Boulton. "Painting and Sculpture," in *Finland, Creation and Construction*, edited by Hillar Kallas and Sylvie Nickels. London: George Allen and Unwin, Ltd., 1968.

Sømme, A. *A Geography of Norden*. Oslo, 1960.

Starck, K. "Media Credibility in Finland: A Cross-National Approach," *Journalism Quarterly*, XLVI, No. 4, 1969.

Steinby, Torsten. *In Quest of Freedom: Finland's Press 1771-1971*. Helsinki: Government Printing Center, 1971.

Stolte-Heiskanen, V. "Community Structure and Kinship Ties: Extended Family Relations in Three Finnish Communes," *International Journal of Comparative Sociology*, X, Nos. 3-4, September and December 1969, 251-262.

Stolte-Heiskanen, V. "Social Structure of Finland," (Mimeo of speech delivered at Orivesi, Finland, August 1972.).

Stone, K. H. "Finnish Fringes of Settlement," *Tijdschrift voor Economische en Sociale Geografie*, LVII, 1966, 222-232.

Stone, K. H. *Northern Finland's Post-War Colonizing and Emigration*. European Demographic Monograph IV. The Hague, 1973.

Stormbom, N.-B. "Väino Linna and His Tales of Toil and War," *The American Scandinavian Review*, LI, No. 3, September 1963.

Stormbom, N.-B. "Veijo Meri and the New Finnish Novel," *The American Scandinavian Review*, LV, No. 3, September 1967.

Suviranta, Annikki. *The Level of Housing of Young Families in Finland*. Helsinki: University of Helsinki, Institute of Social Policy, Reprint Series B, No. 22, 1967.

Sweetser, Dorrian Apple. "The Structure of Sibling Relationships," *American Journal of Sociology*, LXXVI, No. 1, July 1970, 47-58.

Tarkka, Pekka. "Finnish Literature: The Great Tradition," *Odyssey Review*, III, No. 1, March 1963.

This is Helsinki. Helsinki: Saariston Kirjapaino Oy, 1971.

Thompson, Edgar T. "The Little Races," *American Anthropologist*, LXXIV, No. 5, October 1972, 1295-1306.

Tilastollinen Päätoimisto. *Tilastotiedotus*. Helsinki. (Monthly issues beginning January 1970).

Toikka-Karvonen, Annikki. "The Kalevala Illustrations of Akseli Gallen-Kallela," *The American Scandinavian Review*, L, No. 3, September 1962.

Treib, Edward Marc. "Pietilä: Rebel in Finland," *Architectural Forum*,

December 1967.

Turunen, Aimo. "The Kalevala: Finland's National Epic," *The American Scandinavian Review*, L, No. 2, June 1962.

United States. Department of State. Bureau of Public Affairs. *Background Notes: Republic of Finland*. (Department of State Publication 8262.) Washington: GPO, February 1971.

Uotila, Timo. "Broadcasting in Finland," *Adult Education in Finland*, VII, No. 4, 1970.

Veltheim, Katri and Ilona Tainio (eds.). *Finnish Theatre Today*. Kirjapaino Oy, 1971.

Venkula-Vauraste, Lea. "The Finnish National Opera," *The American Scandinavian Review*, LVIII, No. 2, June 1970.

Viherjuuri, H. J. *Sauna: The Finnish Bath*. Brattleboro, Vermont: The Stephen Green Press, 1972.

Vilkuna, K. *Finland*. Helsinki, 1960.

von Hertzen, H. and P. D. Spreiregen. *Building a New Town, Tapiola*. Helsinki, 1971.

Vorren, Ørnulv and Ernst Manker. *Lapp Life and Customs: A Survey*. London: Oxford University Press, 1962.

Vowles, Richard B. "Twelve Northern Writers," *Books Abroad*, XLI, No. 1, Winter 1967.

Wuorinen, John H. (ed.). *Finland and World War II 1939-1944*. New York: Ronald Press Co., 1948.

Wuorinen, John H. *A History of Finland*. New York: Columbia University Press, 1965.

Zilliacus, Henrik. "The Institute of Finland in Rome," in *Introduction to Finland 1960*, edited by Urho Toivola, in collaboration with the Press Bureau of the Ministry of Foreign Affairs. Helsinki: Werner Söderström Osakeyhtiö.

Section II. Political

Aaltonen, Hilkka. *Books in English on Finland.* Turku: Turku University Publications, 1964.

Allardt, Erik. *Past and Emerging Political Cleavages.* Helsinki: University of Helsinki, 1968.

Allardt, Erik. *Patterns of Class Conflict and Working Class Consciousness in Finnish Politics.* Helsinki: University of Helsinki, Institute of Sociology, No. 30, 1964.

Allardt, Erik. *Types of Protest and Alienation.* Helsinki: University of Helsinki, Institue of Sociology, No. 75, 1970.

Allardt, Erik and Pertti Pesonen. "Citizen Participation in Political Life in Finland," *International Social Science Journal*, XII, No. 1, 1960.

Ancuar, Dag. "Finnish Foreign Policy Debate. The Saimaa Canal Case," *Cooperation and Conflict*, No. 4, 1970, 201-223.

Andren, Niels. *Government and Politics in the Nordic Countries.* Stockholm: Almquist and Wiksell, 1964.

Black, Cyril E., et al. *Neutralization and World Politics.* Princeton: Princeton University Press, 1968.

Borg, Olavi. "Basic Dimensions of Finnish Party Ideologies: A Factor Analytical Study," *Scandinavian Political Studies*, I, 1966.

Borodin, Katarina, Kjell Goldman and Christian Lange. "The Policy of Neutrality: Official Doctrines of Finland and Sweden," *Cooperation and Conflict*, III, No. 1, 1968, 18-51.

Central Union of Agricultural Producers. *Farm Structure and Regional Policy in Finnish Agriculture.* Mimeo, Helsinki, 1972.

Desneiges, George. *Finland.* London: Vista Books, 1966.

Elovainio, Mauri K. "Finland and the Study of International Relations 1960-1964," *Cooperation and Conflict*, I, No. 2, 1965, 60-67.

Eriksson, Lars. (Prof. of Political Science, University of Tampere) *The Political Structure in Finland.* Mimeo. August 1972.

Eskola, Antti. *Local Self-Government in Finland and the Finnish Municipal Law.* Helsinki: Finnish Association of Rural Municipalities (monograph, 3rd ed.), 1968.

Eskola, Antti. "Perception of the Basic Cleavages in Finnish Society," *Journal of Peace Research*, VII, No. 4, 1970.

Essays on Finnish Foreign Policy. Finnish Political Science Association, 1963 and 1969.

Euman, Rolf. "Mauno Koivisto—The Prime Minister of Finland," *The American Scandinavian Review*, LVIII, No. 1, March-May 1970, 5-9.

Finland. The Finnish Parliament. *Positions and Functions of the Parliamentary Ombudsman*. Helsinki, 1967.

Finland. Ministry of Foreign Affairs. *Constitution Act and Parliament Act of Finland*. Helsinki: The Ministry of Foreign Affairs, 1967.

Finland. Ministry of Foreign Affairs. *Finnish Features*. Helsinki: The Ministry of Foreign Affairs.

Foster, Kent. "The Silent Soviet Vote in Finnish Politics," *International Journal*, XVIII, No. 4, Summer 1963, 341–352.

Fris, Erik J. "President Kekkonen of Finland," *The American Scandinavian Review*, XLIX, No. 3, September 1961, 239–245.

Fusilier, Raymond. *Les Pays Nordiques*. Paris: Librairie Generale de Droit et de Jurisprudence, 1965.

Guiton, R. J. "Die Beziehungen zwishen Finland und der Sowjetunion im Spiegel der Finnischen Regierungkrise vom Herbst 1958," *Europa Archiv*, 1959, 380–394.

Hakovirta, Harto. "The Finnish Security Problem," *Cooperation and Conflict*, IV, No. 4, 1969, 247–266.

Hakovirta, Harto. "Western European Integration and Finnish Neutrality," *Cooperation and Conflict*, V, No. 2, 1970, 129–136.

Harpe, Werner von. *Die Sowjetunion, Finland und Skandinavien 1945–1955*. Köln-Graz: Arbeitsgemeinschaft für Osteuropaforschung, 1965.

Hiitonen, Ensio. "The Republic of Finland, Its Political and Administrative Structure," in *Finland, a Democracy of the North*, Helsinki, 1947.

Hodgson, J. H. *Communism in Finland*. Princeton: Princeton University Press, 1967.

Hodgson, J. H. "The Finnish Communist Party," *Slavic Review*, No. 1, March 1970.

Hodgson, J. H. "Postwar Finnish Foreign Policy: Institutions and Personalities," *The Western Political Quarterly*, XV, No. 1, March 1962, 80–92.

Holst, Johan Jörgen. "The Soviet Union and Nordic Security," *Cooperation and Conflict*, VI, Nos. 3/4, 1971, 138–145.

Höpker, W. "Moskaus Schlinge um Finnlands Hals," *Aussenpolitik*, February 1962, 99–105.

Hosti, Kalevi, J. "Strategy and Techniques of Influence in Soviet-Finnish Relations," *The Western Political Quarterly*, XVII, No. 1, March 1969, 62–82.

Huuska, Väinö. "The Pressure Politics of Finnish Interest Groups," in *Etujärjestöjen painostuspolitiikka Suomessa*. Porvoo: W. Söderström, 1968.

Hynynen, Pertti. "The Popular Front in Finland," *New Left Review*, LVII, September–October 1969.

Iloniemi, Jaakko. "Finland and the Second World War," *Cooperation and Conflict*, I, No. 2, 1965, 94–95.

International Commentary. "Cornerstone of Soviet-Finnish Relations," *International Affairs*, No. 6, 1972, 87–88.

Jakobson, Max. *The Diplomacy of the Winter War*. Cambridge: Harvard University Press, 1961.

Jakobson, Max. "Finland's Foreign Policy," *International Affairs*, XXXVIII, No. 2, April 1962, 196–202.

Jakobson, Max. *Finnish Neutrality*. New York: Praeger, 1969.

Julkunen, Martti. *Selected List of Books in English, French, and German on Finnish Politics in the 19th and 20th Centuries*. Turku: Institute of Political History, 1967.

Kallas, Hillar and Sylvie Nickels. *Finland: Creation and Construction*. London: George Allen and Unwin, Ltd., 1968.

Kannapin, H. E. "Finnland's Position im Ost-West Konflikt," *Osteuropa*, June 1962, 421–428.

Karjalainen, Ahti. "The Foreign Policy of Finland," *The American Scandinavian Review*, LIV, No. 1, March 1966.

Kastari, Paavo. "Constitutional Protection of Civil Rights in Finland," in *Democracy in Finland*, Finnish Political Science Association, 1960.

Kastari, Paavo. "The Parliamentary Ombudsman: His Functions, Position, and Relations to the Chancellor of Justice in Finland," *International Review of Administrative Sciences*, No. 4, 1962.

Kastari, Paavo. *La Présidense de la République en Finlande*. Neuchâtel: Editions de la Balconnière, 1963.

Kastari, Paavo. "President in the Finnish Political System," *Scandinavian Political Studies*, IV, 1969, 151–159.

Kekkonen, Urho. "New Year's Address by the President of the Republic," in *Finnish Features*. Helsinki: Ministry of Foreign Affairs, 1972.

Kekkonen, Urho. "Speech" (On the occasion of the convening of the new Parliament in February 1972.) in *Finnish Features*. Helsinki: Ministry of Foreign Affairs, 1972.

Kekkonen, Urho. (Translator: Tuomas Vilkuna.) *Neutrality: The Finnish Solution*. London: William Heinemann Ltd., 1970.

Knoellinger, C. E. *Labor in Finland*. Cambridge: Harvard University Press, 1960.

Kraemer, Solveig Bugge. "Political Integration in the Nordic Countries." Unpublished paper presented at the Scandinavian Social Science Symposium, May 1971, University of Kentucky, Lexington.

Krosby, H. Peter. *Finland, Germany, and the Soviet Union*. Madison: University of Wisconsin Press, 1968.

Krusius-Ahrenberg, Lolo. "A Dilemma of Finnish Democracy," in *Interest Groups on Four Continents*, edited by H. W. Ehrmann. Pittsburgh: University of Pittsburgh Press, 1958.

Lange, Christian. "Political Unification and the Nordic Council," *Cooperation and Conflict*, I, No. 2, 1965, 94–95.

Lemberg, Magnus. "Finland: Two Years of Left-wing Coalition,"

Scandinavian Political Studies, III, 1968, 230-236.

Lewenhaupt, Count Eric. *The Memoirs of Marshal Mannerheim*. New York: Dutton, 1954.

Lindman, Sven. "The Parliamentary System in Finland," in *Finland, a Democracy of the North*. Helsinki, 1947.

Lindman, Sven. *Problems in Finnish Legal Government*. Ekenäs, 1964.

Mäkinen, Eino. *The Finnish Parliament*. Helsinki: The Finnish Parliament, 1957.

Martin, Laurence W. (ed.) *Neutralism and Nonalignment*. New York: Praeger, 1962.

Mead, William Richard. *Finland*. New York: Praeger, 1968.

Minn, Eeva K. *Finland: Subcontractor's Monograph*, New Haven: Human Relations Area Files, 1955.

Molotov, V. M. *Soviet Foreign Policy. The Meaning of the War in Finland*. New York: Worker's Library Publishers, Inc., 1940.

Nielson, Gunnar P. "The Nordic and the Continental European Dimensions in Scandinavian Integration. NORDEK as a Case Study," *Cooperation and Conflict*, VI, Nos. 3/4, 1971, 173-181.

Nousiainen, Jaakko. *The Finnish Political System*. Cambridge: Harvard University Press, 1971.

Nyholm, Pekka. "Parliament, Government and Multi-dimensional Party Relations in Finland," in *Commentationes Scientiarium Socialium*, No. 2, 1972.

Ogley, Roderick. *The Theory and Practice of Neutrality in the Twentieth Century*. London: Routledge and Keagan Paul, 1970.

Ørvik, Nils. "Integration—for Whom Against Whom?," *Cooperation and Conflict*, II, No. 1, 1967, 54-57.

Pajunen, Aimo. "Finland's Security Policy," *Cooperation and Conflict*, III, No. 1, 1968, 75-92.

Pakarinen, Erik. "News Communication in Crisis," *Cooperation and Conflict*, II, Nos. 3/4, 1967, 224-228.

Pesonen, Pertti. *An Election in Finland: Party Activities and Voter Reactions*. New Haven: Yale University Press, 1968.

Pesonen, Pertti. *Political Parties and the Finnish Eduskunta: Voters' Perspectives, Party Nominations and Legislative Behavior*. Tampere: Institute of Political Science Report, No. 17, 1970.

Procopé, Hjalmar J. *Finland Reveals Her Secret Documents on Soviet Policy, March 1940–June 1941*. New York: Wilfred Funk, Inc., 1941.

Prokofiev, V. *Severnaya Europa i Mir*. (Northern Europe and the Peace). Moscow: Izdatelstvo Mezhdunarodnye Otnoshenya, 1966.

Puntila, L. A., et al. *Finland, 1916-1967. An Assessment of Independence*. Helsinki: Kirjayhtymä, 1967.

Rantala, Onni. "The Political Regions of Finland," *Scandinivian Political Studies*, No. 2, 1967.

Reinton, Per Olav. "Nordic Aid and the Politics of Inequality," *Cooperation and Conflict*, V, No. 2, 1970, 112-124.

Rintala, Marvin. *Four Finns*. Berkeley: University of California Press, 1969.

Rintala, Marvin. *Three Generations: The Extreme Right Wing in Finnish Politics*. (Indiana University Publications, Russian and East European Series 22.) Bloomington: Indiana University Press, 1962.

Rosset, Renaud. "Political Life in Finland," in *Finnish Features*. Helsinki: Ministry of Foreign Affairs, 1971.

Royal Institute of International Affairs. *The Scandinavian States and Finland: A Political and Economic Survey*. London, 1951.

Sankiaho, Risto and Laakso, Seppo. "Results of the 1970 Parliamentary Election and Formation of the Cabinets of Aura and Karjalainen," *Scandinavian Political Studies*, 6, 1971.

Stolte-Heiskanen, Veronica. (Prof. of Social Science, University of Helsinki) *Social Structure in Finland*. Mimeo, August 1972.

Sunquist, Ulf. "Finland and Cooperation in Development," *Cooperation and Conflict*, V, No. 2, 1970, 102–111.

Suomen Gallup Oy. (Finnish Gallup Corp.) "Political Anomie in Finland," survey taken November 1970. (Not available in English.)

Suomen Gallup Oy. "Public Attitudes on Government Allocation Priorities," *Helsingin Sanomat*, November 23, 1969 (Not available in English.)

Suomen Gallup Oy. "Public Attitudes on How to Elect the President," *Helsingin Sanomat*, November 23, 1969 (Not available in English.)

Suomen Gallup Oy. "Public Attitudes on Political Power," survey taken January 1971. (Not available in English.)

Toivola, Urho. *Introduction to Finland, 1960*. Porvoo: W. Söderström, 1960.

Törngren, Rolf. "The Neutrality of Finland," *Foreign Affairs*, XXXIX, No. 4, July 1961, 601–609.

Törnud, Klaus. "Composition of Cabinets·in Finland 1917–1968," *Scandinavian Political Studies*, IV, 1969, 58–63.

Törnud, Klaus. *The Electoral System of Finland*. London: H. Evelyn Ltd., 1968.

Törnud, Klaus. "Finland and Economic Integration in Europe," *Cooperation and Conflict*, IV, No. 1, 1969, 63–72.

Tuominen, Uuno. *J. K. Paasikivi*. Helsinki: Otava, 1970.

Ulstein, Egil. "Nordic Security," *Adelphi Papers*, No. 91, 1971.

United States. Embassy in Helsinki. *Background Information on Finland*. Helsinki, July 1968.

Uotila, Jaakko. *The Finnish Legal System*. (Translator: C. H. Lundell) Helsinki: Union of Finnish Lawyers Publishing Co., 1966.

Upton, Anthony F. *Finland in Crisis 1940–1941*. London: Faber and Faber, 1964.

Vallet, René. "La Défense de la Baltique," *Revue de Défense National*, April, 1962, 649–658.

Väyrynen, Raimo. "A Case Study of Sanctions. Finland—the Soviet

Union in 1958-59," *Cooperation and Conflict,* IV, No. 3, 1969, 205-233.

Wahlbäck, Krister. "Finnish Foreign Policy—Some Comparative Perspectives," *Cooperation and Conflict,* IV, No. 4, 1969, 282-298.

Waris, Heikki. "Finland 1918-1968," lecture at University College, London, 1970.

Wuorinen, John H. "Finland and the USSR—1945-1961," *Journal of International Affairs,* XVI, No. 1, 1962, 38-46.

Wuorinen, John H. "Finland's War of Independence 1918," *The American Scandinavian Review,* IV, Winter 1963, 389-395.

Wuorinen, John H. *A History of Finland.* New York: Columbia University Press, 1965.

XYZ. "Finland: A Survey, 1957-60," *The World Today,* XVII, 1961, 12-25.

Section III. Economic

Association of Finnish Metal and Engineering Industries. Public Relations Department. *Finnmetal.* Helsinki: Suomen Metalliteollisuusyhdistys, 1967.

Bank of Finland. *Establishing a Business in Finland.* Helsinki: Commission for Foreign Investments, 1970.

Bank of Finland. Institute for Economic Research. "Foreign Trade," *Monthly Bulletin,* XLVI, No. 3, March 1972, 9-11.

Cattani, Richard J. "Finns Avoid Fiscal Problems and a Presidential Election," *The Christian Science Monitor,* January 24, 1973. "Why Do Finns Delay Trade Pact?," *The Christian Science Monitor,* February 6, 1973.

Economic Research Department. "The Economic Situation," *UNITAS,* XLII, No. 3, 1970, 142-184.

Economic Research Department. "The Economic Situation," *UNITAS,* XLIV, No. 1, 1972, 22-72.

Economic Research Department. "The Economic Situation," *UNITAS,* XLIV, No. 2, 1972, 87-132.

Ehrnrooth Göran. "Tightness on the Credit Market," *UNITAS,* XLII, No. 1, 1970, 3-6.

Finland. Central Statistical Office. *Bulletin of Statistics,* XLVII, No. 5, 1972.

Finland. Central Statistical Office. *Statistical Yearbook of Finland 1970.* Helsinki: Central Statistical Office of Finland, 1971.

Finland. Embassy in Washington. *Finland Suomi.* Washington, 1971.

Finland. Embassy in Washington. *Graphical Survey of the Finnish Economy.* Washington, 1969.

Finland. Embassy of Finland. "Highlights of Finland's Industrial Economy," *Finn Facts Newsletter,* July 23-27, 1970.

Finland. Ministry of Finance. Economic Department. *Economic Survey 1969.* Helsinki: Ministry of Finance, 1969.

Finland. Ministry of Finance. Economic Department. *National Budget for 1970: Finland.* Helsinki: Government Printing Center, 1970.

Finland. Ministry of Finance. Economic Department. *National Budget for 1972: Finland.* Helsinki: Government Printing Center, 1972.

Finland. Ministry of Foreign Affairs. *Focus on Finland.* Tapiola: Ministry of Foreign Affairs, 1969.

Finnish Foreign Trade Association. *Trade Facts: Finland 1970-71.* Helsinki: The Finnish Foreign Trade Association, 1970.

Finnish National Travel Office. *The Finnish-American Blue White*

Book. New York: J. William Pellinen, 1969.

Hellsten, Erkki and Moisio, Seppo. "The Prospects for the Current Transactions Account in 1970-71," *Economic Review,* No. 4, 1970.

Horn, Tankmar. "Finland and European Integration," *UNITAS,* XL, No. 2, 1968, 71-78.

Hultin, Sven O. "A Change in the Structure of Finland's Energy Supply," *UNITAS,* XLIII, No. 3, 1971, 133-137.

International Monetary Fund. Statistics Bureau. *International Financial Statistics,* XXV, No. 8, August 1972.

Jakobson, Max. *Finnish Neutrality.* London: Hugh Evelyn, 1969.

Jotuni, Pertti. "How to Know How," *Finland Grows 1970.* Helsinki: Sales and Advertising Association of Finland, 1971.

Kansallis-Osake-Pankki. *Finland in Figures.* Helsinki: Saariston Kirjapaino Oy, 1971.

Kansallis-Osake-Pankki. Research Staff. "Economic Development in Finland in 1971," (K-O-P), *Economic Review,* No. 1, 1972, 14-48.

Kansallis-Osake-Pankki. Research Staff. "A Review of the Economic Development in Finland in the First Half of 1970," *Economic Review,* No. 3, 1970, 110-137.

Kansallis-Osake-Pankki. Research Staff. "A Review of the Economic Development in Finland in the Third Quarter of 1970," *Economic Review,* No. 4, 1970, 152-207.

Kärkkäinen, Hannu. "The Structural Change in Distribution in Finland," (K-O-P), *Economic Review,* No. 1, 1972, 3-13.

Kemijoki Oy. *Power from the Kemi River.* Helsinki: Kemijoki Oy, 1963.

Konttinen, Veikko. "Forest Farms," in *Finland: Creation and Construction,* edited by Hillar Kallas and Sylvie Nickels. London: George Allen and Unwin, Ltd., 1968.

Konttinen, Veikko and Herbert Lomas. "The Changing Structure of Industry," in *Finland: Creation and Construction,* edited by Hillar Kallas and Sylvie Nickels. London: George Allen and Unwin, Ltd., 1968.

Laatto, Erkki. "Growth Center Policy on Finland," *UNITAS,* XLI, No. 3, 1969, 133-139.

Laurila, Eino H. "On the Development of the Public Sector Since the War," *UNITAS,* XLI, No. 2, 1969, 71-80.

Lehto, Sakari T. *Recent Developments in Finnish Industry.* Washington: Embassy of Finland, Press Section, 1971.

Linden, Caj. "Sweden Finds Finland," *UNITAS,* XLII, No. 4, 1970, 193-199.

Linnamo, Jussi. *Finland: A Growing Economy.* Helsinki: Ministry of Foreign Affairs, 1967.

Mäki, Martti. "The Finnish Metals Industry on the World Market," *Look at Finland,* No. 2, 1970, 58-60.

Mead, W. R. *Finland.* London: Ernest Benn, Ltd., 1968.

Mead, W. R. "The Waterways of Finland," in *Finland: Creation and*

Construction, edited by Hillar Kallas and Sylvie Nickels. London: George Allen and Unwin, Ltd., 1968.

Metal Industry's Year Book 1970. Helsinki: Association of Finnish Metal and Engineering Industries, Helsinki, 1970.

Nenneman, Richard. "Finland Sets Plans for Economic Growth," *The Christian Science Monitor*, April 27, 1972.

Nordic Council. *Yearbook of Nordic Statistics 1968*. Stockholm: Nordic Council, 1969.

Organization for Economic Cooperation and Development. *OECD Economic Surveys: Finland*. Paris, June 1969.

Organization for Economic Cooperation and Development. *OECD Economic Surveys: Finland*. Paris, June 1972.

Organization for Economic Cooperation and Development. *OECD Economic Surveys: Finland*. Paris, March 1973.

Organization for Economic Cooperation and Development. *OECD Economic Surveys: Finland*. Paris, May 1970.

Organization for Economic Cooperation and Development. *OECD Economic Surveys: Finland*. Paris, May 1971.

Organization for Economic Cooperation and Development. Statistical and National Accounts Branch. "The OECD Member Countries," *The OECD Observer*. Paris, 1972.

Oulujoki, Osakeyhtiö. *River Oulu: Source of Power*. Helsinki: Oulujoki Power Co., 1959.

Pekonon, Kari. "Finland's International Transactions in 1969," *Economic Review*, No. 3, 1970, 99–109.

Pohjoismaiden, Yhdyspankki. Research Staff. *Facts About Finland 1972*. Helsinki: Keskuskirjapaino, 1972.

Rajamäki, Reijo. "Big Decisions in Economic Life," *Finland Grows 1970*, 1971, 41–45.

SKK Oy. *Focus on Finland*. Helsinki: SKK Oy, 1966.

Smith, Desmond. "Green Gold," *Look at Finland*, No. 1, 1972, 46–50.

Smith, Desmond. "Milk Production," *Look at Finland*, No. 2, 1972, 46–50.

Tiivola, Mika. "The Balance of Payments in Focus," *UNITAS*, XLIII, No. 1, 1971, 3–7.

Tiivola, Mika. "Finland's Cyclical Policy—A Mixture of Old and New," *UNITAS*, XLII, No. 4, 1970, 187–192.

Tiivola, Mika. "The Prerequisites for New Investment in the Forest Industry," *UNITAS*, XXXIX, No. 4, 1970, 187–192.

Tiivola, Mika. "A Year of Paradox," *UNITAS*, XLIV, No. 1, 1972. 1–7.

Toppari, Veikko. "Forest Industry Growth and Forest Resources," *UNITAS*, XLII, No. 3, 1970, 129–134.

Torikka, Jalmari. "International Building," *Finland Grows 1970*, 1971.

Törnud, Klaus. "Finland and Economic Integration in Europe," *Cooperation and Conflict*, IV, No. 1, 1969, 63–72.

Tuomas-Kettunen, F. "The Foodstuffs Industry on the Brink of the

Seventies," *UNITAS*, XLI, No. 4, 1969, 185-190.

United States. Department of State. Bureau of Public Affairs. *Background Notes: Republic of Finland.* (Department of State Publication 8262.) Washington: GPO, February 1971.

Vanhala, Matti. "Finland's Foreign Assets and Liabilities," *UNITAS*, XLIV, No. 1, 1972, 8-21.

Vartiovaara, Klaus. "Productive Imports—Some Observations on Their Importance and Structure," *UNITAS*, XLI, No. 2, 1969, 81-87.

Vesikallio, Heikki. "Structural Rationalization of Privately-Owned Forests," *UNITAS*, XLIII, No. 4, 1971, 198-205.

Viita, Pentti and Herbert Lomas. "Foreign Trade," in *Finland: Creation and Construction*, edited by Hillar Kallas and Sylvie Nickels. London: George Allen and Unwin, Ltd., 1968.

Wuorinen, John H. *A History of Finland.* New York: Columbia University Press, 1965.

Section IV. National Security

Allardt, Erik. *Patterns of Class Conflict and Working Class Consciousness in Finnish Politics*. Helsinki: University of Helsinki, Institute of Sociology, No. 30, 1964.

Allardt, Erik. "Social Sources of Finnish Communism: Traditional and Emerging Radicalism," *International Journal of Comparative Sociology*, V, No. 1, 1964, 49-72. Also in publication of the Institute of Sociology, University of Helsinki, 22, 1964.

Anderson, Albin, T. "Origins of the Winter War: A Study of Russo-Finnish Diplomacy," *World Politics*, January 1954, 169-189.

Anderson, Albin T. "The Soviets and Northern Europe," *World Politics*, July 1952, 230-242.

Atkeson, Edward B. "Finnish Organization for National Defense," *Military Review*, 1965, 72-76.

Birnbaum, I. "The Communist Course in Finland," *Problems of Communism*, September-October 1959, 42-47; January-February 1960, 489-497.

Bonsdorff, Göran von. "Pattern for Peaceful Coexistence," *New Times*, XXXV, 1956, 8-11.

Christie, Nils. "Changes in Penal Values," *Scandinavian Studies in Criminology*, II, edited by Nils Christie. Scandinavian University Books, Universitetsforlaget, 1968.

Cramer, James. *The World's Police*. London: Cassel, 1964.

Crankshaw, E. "Finland and Russia," *National and English Review*, February 1953, 87-91.

Finland. Central Statistical Office. *Suomen Tilastollinen Vuosikirja*. Section XXVI, Justice and Crime.

Finland. General Staff. *Finlands Forsvar i et nötskal*. Helsinki, 1972, 3.

Finland. Ministry of Defense. *Vägmärken för vårt Försvar*. Helsinki, 1967.

Finland. *Regeringens berättelser för 1970, 1971 Rd. and Utsikterna för åren 1973-1976*, Helsinki: Government Printing Center.

Finlands Författningssamling, No. 84, 1966, 248; No. 119, 1969, 182-183; No. 19, 1969, 186-190.

The Finnish Air Force, London: Shores, 1969.

Försvaret it ett nötskal, Helsingfors, 1971.

Fox, Annette Baker. "Finland: Fighting Neutral." Pages 43-77 in her *The Power of Small States: Diplomacy in World War II*. Chicago: University of Chicago Press, 1959.

Halsti, Wolf. *Me, Venäjä ja muut* (We, Russia and the Others). Helsinki: Otava, 1969.

Hodgson, John H. *Communism in Finland*. Princeton: Princeton University Press, 1967.

Hodgson, John H. "Finland's Position on the Russian Empire 1905-10," *Journal of Central European Affairs*, July 1960, 158-173.

Hodgson, John H. "The Finnish Communist Party and Neutrality," *Government and Opposition*, 1967, 269-287.

Holm, Thor W. and Erkki J. Immonen. *Bibliography of Finnish Sociology 1945-1959*, with an introduction by Erik Allardt. Helsinki: The Academic Bookstore, 1966.

Horn, W. "Finnland, Russland and Deutschland," *Aussenpolitik*, 1954.

Hyvärinen, Risto. "The Defense Forces in the Service of Neutrality," in *Introduction to Finland 1963*, 1963, 57-66.

Hyvärinen, Risto. "Neutrality and Arms Limitation," *Cooperation and Conflict*, I, 1965, 65-73.

Hyvärinen, Risto. "Die Wehrmacht im Dienste der Neutralitat," in *Finnland, Geschichte und Gegenwart 1964*. Helsinki, 1964.

The International Institute for Strategic Studies. *The Ministry Balance 1972-73*. London: IISS, 1972.

Jakobson, Max. *The Diplomacy of the Winter War*. Cambridge: Harvard University Press, 1961.

Jakobson, Max. "Finland's Foreign Policy," *International Affairs*, April 1962, 196-202.

Jakobson, Max. *Finnish Neutrality*. London: Hugh Evelyn, 1968.

Jutikkala, Eino. *Atlas of Finnish History*. Helsinki, 1959.

Jutikkala, Eino. *A History of Finland*. New York: Praeger, 1962.

Keesing's Contemporary Archives, April 17-24, 1948.

Krosby, Hans Peter. "The Communist Power Bid in Finland in 1948," *Political Science Quarterly*, 1960, 229-243.

Krosby, Hans Peter. *Finland, Germany and the Soviet Union 1940-1941: The Petsamo Dispute*. Madison: University of Wisconsin Press, 1968.

Kuusisto, Allan A. "The Paasikivi Line in Finland's Foreign Policy," *The Western Political Quarterly*, March 1959, 37-49.

Lange, C. and Goldman, K. "A Nordic Defense Alliance 1949-1965-197?," *Cooperation and Conflict*, I, 1966, 46-63.

Lundin, C. Leonard. *Finland in the Second World War*. Bloomington: Indiana University Press, 1957.

Mannerheim, Carl Gustaf. *The Memoirs of Marshal Mannerheim*. London: Cassel, 1953.

Mourin, Maxime. "Finland and Coexistence," *Military Review*, 58-66.

Mourin, Maxime. "La Finlande et les problems de la coexistence," *Revue de Défense Nationale*, 1961, 1931-1947.

Niemeyer, Gerhart. *Communist in Coalition Governments*. Washington, 1963.

Nousiainen, Jaakko. "The Parties and Foreign Policy," *Finnish Foreign Policy*, 1963, 177–195.

Numminen, Jaakko. "Finland's Foreign Policy as an Autonomous Grand Duchy and the Winning of Independence," *Finnish Foreign Policy* (Finnish Political Science Association). Helsinki, 1963.

Ørvik, Nils. "Scandinavia, NATO and Northern Security," *International Organization*, No. 3, 1966, 380–396.

Ørvik, Nils. "Scandinavian Security in Transition. The Two-Dimensional Threat," *Orbis*, Fall 1972, 720–742.

Ørvik, Nils. *Sicherheit auf Finnisch. Finland und die Sowjetunion*, Stuttgart: Seewald Verlag, 1972.

Pajunen, A. "Finland's Säkerhetspolitik," *Strategisk Bulletin*, IV, 1967.

Renwall, Pentti. "The Foreign Policy Attitudes of the Finns During the Swedish Rule," *Finnish Foreign Policy*, 1963, 3–22.

Rintala, Marvin. *Three Generations: The Extreme Right Wing in Finnish Politics.* (Indiana University Publications, Russian and East European Series 22.) Bloomington: Indiana University Press, 1962.

Schwartz, Andrew J. *America and the Russo-Finnish War.* Washington: Public Affairs Press, 1960.

Smith, C. Jay, Jr. *Finland and the Russian Revolution 1917–1922.* Atlanta: University of Georgia Press, 1958.

Tanner, Väinö. *Winter War. Finland Against Russia 1939–1940.* Stanford: Stanford University Press. 1957.

Tigerstedt, Örnulf. *Statspolisen slår till.* Helsingfors: Söderström, 1943.

Tissot, Louis. "La Défense des pays Nordiques," *Forces Aériennes Francaises*, 1949, 483–499.

Toivola, Urho. *Introduction to Finland 1960.* Porvoo: W. Soderstom, 1960.

Törngren, Rolf. "The Neutrality of Finland," *Foreign Affairs*, IXL, No. 4, July 1961, 601–609.

Touminen, A. "The Northern Countries and Communism," *The Norseman*, XII, 1954, 217–229.

United Nations. Treaty of Peace with Finland, signed at Paris on 10 February 1947, *United Nations Treaty Series*, XLVIII, 1950.

Vallet, René. "La Défense de la Baltique," *Revue de Défense Nationale*, April 1962, 649–658.

Wahlbäck, K. *Från Mannerheim till Kekkonen.* Malmö, 1967.

Wilson, Edmund. *To the Finland Station.* New York: Doubleday, 1940.

Wolf, Preben. "A Contribution to the Typology of Crime in Denmark," *Scandinavian Studies in Criminology*, I, 1965, 201–226.

Wolf, Preben. "Crime and Development. An International Comparison of Crime Rates," *Scandinavian Studies in Criminology*, III, 1971, 107–120.

Wuorinen, J. H. "Finland and the USSR 1945–1961," *Journal of International Affairs*, No. 1, 1962, 38–46.

Wuorinen, J. H. "The Finnish Treaty," *The Annals of the American*

Academy of Political and Social Science, May 1948, 87–96.

Wuorinen, J. H. (ed.) *Finland and World War II: 1939–1944*. New York: Ronald Press, 1949.

GLOSSARY

Eduskunta—The Finnish unicameral Parliament.

EEC—European Economic Community, also known as the Common Market. An economic unit formed to remove trade barriers among its members.

GATT—General Agreement on Tariffs and Trade. A Western economic organization.

GDP—Gross domestic product. The value of the total output of domestically produced goods and services.

GNP—Gross national product. The money value of the total output of goods and services.

Keskustapuolue (Center Party). Largely a rural party and traditionally the most powerful group in Parliament.

KOK—Kansallinen Kokoonus (National Coalition Party). The most important conservative party.

LKP—Liberaalinen Kansanpuolue (Liberal People's Party). Represents the middle class throughout the country.

markka—Finnmark (Fmk), the name of the monetary unit. Official exchange rates per US$1 were: 1965, 3.22; 1966, 3.22; 1967, 4.21; 1968, 4.19; 1969, 4.20; 1970, 4.18; 1971, 4.15; 1972, 4.18, and February 1973, 3.90.

MTK—Maataloustuottajain Keskusliitto (Central Union of Agricultural Producers). An interest group representing 420,000 farmers in 1972.

OECD—Organization for Economic Cooperation and Development. A Western economic association.

SAJ—Suomen Ammattijärjestö (Finnish Trade Unions Association). A conservative splinter group formed in 1960 from the SAK (*q.v.*).

SAK—Suomen Ammattiliitojen Keskusjarjestö (Finnish Central League of Trade Unions). The only major trade federation and the largest interest group in the country.

SDP—Suomen Sosialidemokraattinen Puolue (Finnish Social Democratic Party). A socialist party widely supported by working class, urban lower middle class, professional people, and youth.

SFP—Svensk Folkpartiet [in Swedish] (Swedish People's Party). Promotes Swedish ethnic interests.

SKDL—Suomen Kansan Demokraattinen Liitto (Finnish People's Democratic League). Provides parliamentary representation for the Finnish Communist Party and includes noncommunist leftists in its membership.

SKL—Suomen Kristillinen Liitto (Christian League of Finland). Aims to infuse Finnish politics with Christian ideals.

SKP—Suomen Kommunistinen Puolue (Finnish Communist Party). Represented in Parliament since 1945 by the SKDL (*q.v.*).

SMP—Suomen Maaseudun Puolue (Finnish Rural Party). Represents small farmers, small business operators, and urban workers against big business as well as big government.

STK—Suomen Työnantajan Keskusliitto (Central Federation of Finnish Employers). An interest group representing the major public and private industrial employers.

TPSL—Työväen Ja Pienviljelijain Sosialidemokraattinen Litto (Social Democratic League of Workers and Small Farmers). A short-lived (1959-69) splinter group of extreme left-wing socialists, also called Simonists.

TVK—Toimihenkilo-ja Virkamiesjärjestöjen Keskusliitto (Central Federation of Officials and Civil Servants). An interest group representing over one-fourth of the salaried white-collar population.

INDEX

249

251

schools): 81, 82, 84, 85, 86, 87, 150; gymnasium, 85
Security Police: 207, 208, 210, 211
Sederholm, Jakob Johannes: 118
seits: 111
Seitseman Veljesta: 99
Senate (see also executive): 14, 15, 16, 122
service occupations: 199-200
Seven Brothers: 99-100, 104
shipping: 197-198, 206
Sibelius Academy: 80, 108
Sibelius, Jean: 28, 106, 108, 111
Sibelius Festival: 109
Sillanpää, Frans Eemil: 101
Simberg, Hugo: 110
Simonen, Aarre: 140
Simonists: 90, 140, 142
Snellman, Johan: 16, 53, 100
social allowances: 64-65
social classes (see also burghers; clergy; elite; nobles; peasants): 5, 10, 12, 142, 151; education of, 83; stratification of, 53-54, 121-122
Social Democratic League of Workers and Small Farmers (Työväen ja Pienviljelijäin Sosialidemokraattinen Litto—TPSL) (see also Simonists): 140
social security: 140, 191
Social Security Convention: ix, 160
social services: 54, 62-67, 130
Social Welfare Board: 65
Socialist League of Students: 142
Socialist Workers Party: 210
Socialist Workers Republic: 22
socialists and socialism: 4, 19, 20, 21, 22, 139, 140, 142, 144, 145, 146
Society of Finnish Artists: 110
Solzhenitsyn, Alexander: 94
Song of Hiawatha: 99
Sorsa, Kalevi: 140
South Africa, Republic of: 154, 162, 164, 188
South America: 192, 198
Southwest Africa: 75
Soviet-Finnish Commission for Scientific and Technical Cooperation: 157
Soviet Union (see also Russia): 1, 3, 25, 26, 35, 93, 118-119, 150, 178; and censorship, 94; and commerce, 27, 198, 202, 203, 205; domination, v, 5, 13; foreign relations, 153, 154, 155-157, 159, 160, 165, 211; and forests, 184; and Karelia, 23, 24, 116; and military, 214, 215, 218, 219; and security, 207, 210, 211, 212; and trade, ix, 27; and World War II, 4, 6, 30-33, 46, 61, 78, 167, 186
sports and recreation: 57, 68-69

Stabilization Agreement: 176
Stahlberg, Kaarlo Juho: 24, 25, 138
Stalin, Josef: 29, 155, 214, 215
State Alcohol Corporation: 28
State Council (see also executive): 4, 12, 119, 121, 125, 126, 127-129, 134, 156; and elections, 137, 138; and foreign relations, 163, 164; and legislature, 131, 132; and political groups, 139, 142, 144, 150
State Film Censors Office: 200
State Granary: 205
State Library Bureau: 200
steamships (see also shipping): 19
steel: 19
Stockholm: 82
stores and shops: 195, 196
Strategic Arms Limitation Talks (SALT): 154, 158
Strengell, Gustaf: 113, 115
strikes: 6, 21, 93, 127, 139, 149, 150, 169, 192, 210
students (see also education): 81, 83, 142; exchange, 158; and grants, 87
Suez crisis: 162
suffrage. See electoral system
Sunday School Association: 79
Suomenlinna: 114
Supreme Administrative Court: 123, 133
Supreme Court: 132-133, 134
Svinhufvud, Pehr Evind: 21, 22, 23, 29
Swede-Finns: 49, 50-51, 52, 53; poets, 102
Sweden: 2, 35, 36, 38, 42, 59, 150, 153, 157; art and culture, 3, 50-51, 94, 103, 104, 106, 112, 117, 145; church, 76; and commerce, 197, 198; and crime, 207; and crusades, 10; domination, v, 44, 50, 97, 207; and economy, 177, 179; and emigration, 7, 43, 174; and foreign relations, 158-159; and forests, 184; and government, 121; and industry, 187; language, 16, 17, 49, 50, 52, 81, 82, 85, 89, 91, 92, 99, 117, 134, 136, 143, 145; and military, 213, 214, 218; "red guards", 210; and World War II, 30
Swedish Law of 1734: 15
Swekomen: 16
Switzerland: 157, 164, 177
Taivalkoski: 40
talkoo: 62
Tammi: 103
Tampere: xiv, 5, 22, 40, 104, 115; growth, 57; labor force, 191
Tampere University: 86, 93; technical university, 118
Tampere Workers' Theater: 104
Tanner, Väinö: 23, 26, 140, 156
Tanzania: 75, 160

PUBLISHED AREA HANDBOOKS

550–65	Afghanistan		550–50	Khmer Republic (Cambodia)
550–98	Albania		550–81	Korea, North
550–44	Algeria		550–41	Korea, Republic of
550–59	Angola		550–58	Laos
550–73	Argentina		550–24	Lebanon
550–66	Bolivia		550–38	Liberia
550–20	Brazil		550–85	Libya
550–168	Bulgaria		550–163	Malagasy Republic
550–61	Burma		550–45	Malaysia
550–83	Burundi		550–161	Mauritania
550–166	Cameroon		550–79	Mexico
550–96	Ceylon		550–76	Mongolia
550–159	Chad		550–49	Morocco
550–77	Chile		550–64	Mozambique
550–60	China, People's Rep. of		550–35	Nepal, Bhutan and Sikkim
550–63	China, Rep. of		550–88	Nicaragua
550–26	Colombia		550–157	Nigeria
550–67	Congo, Democratic Rep. of (Zaire)		550–94	Oceania
550–91	Congo, People's Rep. of		550–48	Pakistan
550–90	Costa Rica		550–46	Panama
550–152	Cuba		550–156	Paraguay
550–22	Cyprus		550–92	Peripheral States of the Arabian Peninsula
550–158	Czechoslovakia		550–42	Peru
550–54	Dominican Republic		550–72	Philippines
550–155	East Germany		550–162	Poland
550–52	Ecuador		550–160	Romania
550–150	El Salvador		550–84	Rwanda
550–28	Ethiopia		550–51	Saudi Arabia
550–167	Finland		550–70	Senegal
550–29	Germany		550–86	Somalia
550–153	Ghana		550–93	South Africa, Republic of
550–87	Greece		550–95	Soviet Union
550–78	Guatemala		550–27	Sudan, Democratic Republic of
550–82	Guyana		550–47	Syria
550–164	Haiti		550–62	Tanzania
550–151	Honduras		550–53	Thailand
550–165	Hungary		550–89	Tunisia
550–21	India		550–80	Turkey
550–154	Indian Ocean Territories		550–74	Uganda
550–39	Indonesia		550–43	United Arab Republic
550–68	Iran		550–97	Uruguay
550–31	Iraq		550–71	Venezuela
550–25	Israel		550–57	Vietnam, North
550–69	Ivory Coast		550–55	Vietnam, South
550–30	Japan		550–99	Yugoslavia
550–34	Jordan		550–75	Zambia
550–56	Kenya			

☆ U.S. GOVERNMENT PRINTING OFFICE: 1974—O 541–140 (PO 24)